The Harvest:

The Harvest:

How a Bulgarian Farm Boy
Grew Wealthy in La Jolla, California

Dr. Luben S. Walchef

oP
Aventine Press

Published by Aventine Press
1023 4th Ave #204
Chula Vista, CA 91914, USA

www.aventinepress.com

ISBN: 1-59330-231-2
Printed in the United States of America

To my grandfather Valcho, who taught me how to learn.

Acknowledgments

My goal in writing this book was to produce something that might, in even the slightest way, ever be of service to anyone. As such, I decided to as much as possible keep its focus on those aspects of my life and experience that are most universal in nature; in other words, for the construction of the book I thought more in terms of themes and struggles common to all people than I did on my specific personal relationships. It is my hope that in doing so I have told my story in such a way that anyone can easily relate to it.

The downside of this approach, however, is that it meant leaving from the book a great deal about the relationships that do, in fact, mean so very much to me. I am grateful to so many people who have done so much to color, inform and brighten my life--and want, here, to at least hint at how much they have and do mean to me.

First and foremost, I want to thank my three children: my eldest son Luben; my youngest boy Boyan; and their younger sister, Lisa. No man has ever had three finer children. I know that it has not always been easy for them, having a father who worked as hard as I. But their love and strength never failed them or I, and it gives me no end of pleasure to look upon them now, and see three smart, capable, emotionally mature adults, each of whom I am inordinately proud. They say that, in the end, a parent learns as much from their children as their children do from them. That has indeed been my experience.

And I also want to thank their children, my grandchildren. In many ways I think the grand prize in life is to become a grandparent. Lisa's sons Shawn, Thomas and Eric; Luben's boys Scott and Kevin; Boyan's Zach and Tyler--each of these young men brings me inestimable joy. (Why there's no granddaughter in the whole group is a mystery none of us understands.) Of course, I more often see some of these guys than I do others: Shawn, for instance, lives with me, while Kevin attends school in Washington. If I had my way, the whole Walchef clan would live together under one roof.

In Bulgaria, such a plan might have a chance.

Here in America ... well, let's just say I'm not exactly holding my breath.

I would also like to thank my secretary (read: business manager), Irene Fast, who has been with me for so long I shudder to think where I'd be today without her. No man succeeds without good people backing him up; Irene is as good as they get.

I also want to express my gratitude to LaVerne and Ruth Fast (no relation to Irene; I suppose I was just destined to hang out with a Fast crowd), who have long tended to my financial concerns as if they were their own. I could always sleep at night, knowing my accounts were being tended to by these financial wizards.

I'm also deeply indebted to the two hardest working, kindest gentlemen I've ever met: Alphonso Rivera and Hilario Ortega. Neither has ever failed me; I don't even think the word is in either of their vocabularies.

I am similarly indebted to my faithful and conscientious housekeeper, Lydia Gomez. I can only hope I did half the job taking care of her when she was a patient of mine as she has since done taking care of me.

Speaking of loyal associates, Laura Galloway, the tireless administrator at Villa Troy Senior's Residence, deserves special appreciation--as do all the indefatigable VT personnel. I simply don't know what I (not to mention the seniors under their gentle care) would do without all of their hard work and careful attention to detail.

I would also be lost without the wonderful team at Country Choice, my restaurant in Spring Valley. Thanks to each and every one of you.

I'd also like to make special mention of my niece, Jennifer Pilsner, daughter of my departed wife's sister, Teddy. From letters, to phone calls, to the splendid family reunion she recently organized, Jennifer makes sure the Kellys of Cincinnati and the Walchefs of San Diego keep in touch. For that you have my deepest gratitude, Jennifer.

As for the rest--Annie, Simeon, my dear Elizabeth, whom I felt at my side the whole time I was working on this book--I'll see you all inside!

I hope you enjoy my story.

Luben Walchef
September 2004

Table Of Contents

Foreword

In 2001, my grandfather Dr. Luben S. Walchef, first proposed the idea of writing the stories of his life into a book he could share with his family and friends. While some people encouraged the idea, others felt it was too ambitious a task for someone who had never before written a book. He was eighty-two years of age when he started collecting materials for this work. At that time he was still highly involved in managing real estate properties, operating a breakfast and lunch restaurant, and running an assisted care facility for the elderly. It did not seem that he needed another challenge in his life.

Nevertheless, he started the arduous writing process by devoting a small amount of time each day to the project. Every day he would record into a dictating machine a story significant in his life. And as the amount of time he spent on his book increased, I noticed him opening up more as a person. The stories he once told at the dinner table now had a depth and a richness that he had never before expressed. Night and day I would see him reading books on how to write memoirs, on how to share one's story with others. The more he concentrated on his book, the more I learned about him and about our family. After he would dictate a story onto tape, he would give the tape to his trusted secretary, Irene, or to me, and we would type it out for him to read.

The real impetus for his book came in the summer of 2002 when my grandfather, at the age of eighty-four, traveled to Europe to pick me up from my semester abroad in Alicante, Spain. His vision was to take me across Europe to each city that had been significant in his life so that we could gather the necessary information to complete his memoir. We did just that and more. Every morning he was awake before I was, planning a schedule to conquer each city. I was often skeptical that we could jump from the red tour bus in Paris to the clay courts at Roland Garros and then to the National Opera House in the one day's allotted time, but his persistence and planning always prevailed. For me the trip became more than just a historical exercise or a tourist vacation. I was honored at a young age to have the opportunity to spend an entire month with my grandfather, learning about his life and discussing love, religion, education, politics, free will, and the meaning of work. He became not only my personal tour guide but my professor, my role model, my inspiration, and, more importantly, my best friend.

I have always respected my grandfather, but when I first saw the small farming village where he was born and raised, I gained an even higher level of respect for him. I now had a visual reference to all the stories he had told me throughout my life. To see his mud-brick house with its grape-vines and sunflowers lining the walkway and to see his village with its cobblestone roads untouched by time was indeed a humbling experience. My grandfather's constant emphasis on education and hard work now made contextual sense.

When we returned from Europe, my grandfather worked feverishly to record all that he wanted to say. Together we attended writers' conferences and seminars, attempting to find someone who could help mold my grandfather's stories into a readable book. And by a stroke of unbelievable luck we found a writer/editor by the name of John Shore, who was more than willing to help us with this seemingly insurmountable task.   From the moment he first walked into my grandfather's home, he was eager to dedicate his full effort to my grandfather's project. Every Monday for the next four months John would meet with my grandfather and me and go over the stories he had transformed into a powerful and compelling narrative of my grandfather's life. Always meticulous in getting the facts of that life correct, he made my grandfather's dream a reality.

The story begins in a small, impoverished Bulgarian village where young Luben Walchef was eager to acquire more information about the world. Ambitious to become a medical doctor, he traveled to war-torn Germany in 1941, not knowing a word of German. Having tried to study amidst heavy bombing in Berlin, he transferred to the University of Heidelberg, where he finished his medical studies during the American occupation. Hard work, education, and some help from friends along the way brought him to America, the land of endless opportunity. He raised a family in Cincinnati and then moved them to California in 1965. Never thinking about retirement, he invested in real estate and developed numerous properties in San Diego. And now his grandson has been rewarded with the opportunity to learn from a lifetime of curiosity, determination, failure, and success that have made my grandfather such a fascinating man.

Relating to another's experience is a fundamental enjoyment we have in this life. Stories are passed down from generation to generation, and in them we learn to triumph over obstacles and failures. We laugh, we smile, and we cry. What I have learned through this three-year process is that in each family parents and grandparents have valuable experience and hold precious information that we, their offspring, can cultivate and harvest in our own lives. If we take time to listen and to ask questions, the stories we hear at the dinner table and at family reunions, which hold a special place in our elders' hearts, can become a family treasure, an inheritance with timeless value. My hope is that readers of this memoir will gain inspiration from the stories of my grandfather's successes as well as the failures.

I am grateful for the man who paved my own cobblestone road and who provided me with a life of privilege and the ability to appreciate it. And I am blessed to have had the opportunity to have worked side by side with him in making this account of the story of his life.

Shawn P. Walchef
La Jolla, California

September 2004

September 29, 2017

Nicole:

I appreciate all the insight you have taught me about the event industry. When I took your class at the Event Management Program at USD I never thought I would be interviewing you on our Behind The Smoke smoke podcast about your book, Permission. I am grateful for your friendship and look forward to your thoughts on my authentic intention I emailed you while reading your book. With admiration

P. Wal

Chapter One

Born to Work

I was born to be a farmer, like my father and grandfather and so many Walchef men before me. In that sense my fate was determined before I drew my first breath on July 10, 1919, in an old house in the middle of Pordim, a village located between the Danube River and the Balkan Mountains in northern Bulgaria. My introduction into the house made for a baker's dozen living there: I joined my parents; my grandparents; my great-grandfather; my uncle, aunt, and their son; my two sisters (both still babies themselves); and, finally, our hired hand and his son. Quite a group! An extended family of this size living together under one roof was not at all uncommon at that time, and at that place.

As far as I know, Pordim has been home to generation after generation of my ancestors. My paternal great-grandfather, Theodore, was mayor of the town during and after its final years under the Ottoman Empire; he did his part to end the Turkish rule of Bulgaria by hiding revolutionaries in his attic during the revolt of 1876. Though vaguely, I remember him as a distinguished-looking man; I recall him always wearing a neatly pressed white linen suit. A vigorous and healthy man throughout his life, Theodore lived to be 115 years old. (Our family history has it that when he was over 100 years old, he grew a new set of teeth.)

I don't know or remember much about Theodore's wife, Ivanka, beyond that before she died her inability to eat or hold down food caused her to become very thin and weak. At that time there were no doctors in our village; now, as a doctor myself, it's my guess that my great-grandmother died of stomach cancer.

The one great thing I *do* know about Ivanka, though, is that as a younger, healthier woman she gave birth to her and Theodore's only son: my beloved grandfather, Valcho.

It was Valcho who gave me the gift of learning. Although as a boy he had dropped out of elementary school after only four years in order to work on his father's farm, he always took care to show me how much he cared about what I was learning in school. One night after supper he asked me to go and fetch the book from which my class daily read stories; once I'd returned with it he hoisted me and my book up to his lap.

"Read for me the story you learned today, Luben," he said. Proud and excited, I began the narration. When I had reached as far into the story as we'd gotten in class that day, I stopped and moved to close the book--but Valcho put his large, calloused hand onto the page.

"Wait," he said. "Let's read some more."

"No, Grandpa," I said. "We can't. That's where we stopped in class today. We don't read any more until tomorrow."

"But Luben," he said gently, "Surely it's okay if we just peek ahead in the book a little?"

"I don't think it is," I said. "We read so far, and then we stop. We don't look ahead. If we did, the teacher might get mad."

"Well," said my grandpa conspiratorially, "I will tell you what, then. You and I will *secretly* peek ahead in the book. And we will keep this between ourselves; no one but us will know. Tomorrow, you will pretend as if you did not know anything beyond where your class stopped today."

"But ..." I began to protest.

"Shush, Luben," he said, gently flipping over the next page of my book. "Look. There is nothing on the other side of this page waiting to bite us. Besides, I want to know what happens next in this story. Don't you?"

There was no denying that I did. Still ...

"If anything bad comes of our little intrigue," said Valcho, "I will take all responsibility." He began tickling me. "I will say that I tortured you, and beat you terribly, until finally you allowed me to find out *what happened next in the story in your schoolbook!*"

Squirming madly I squealed, "All right! All right, Grandpa! We can look! We can look!"

And so we settled down, and began to look and read. And we did not stop until we had completed the next day's lesson.

And do you know what terrible result came of this audacious transgression? Nothing. Nothing at all! The only thing that happened was that in class the next day, I was the first to raise my hand whenever our teacher asked us anything about that day's lesson. Because I was already familiar with the material!

The evening before, when we were done reading and my grandfather lifted me off his lap and back onto the floor, I noticed that he had a strangely satisfied look on his face.

"Why are you smiling?" I asked.

"No reason, Luben," he said. "But you did a very good job of reading tonight."

Walking home from the school the following day, I understood what my grandfather had been smiling about the night before. He knew that he had just opened a door for me that would never close again; he knew he had just shown me, in real, practical terms, that knowledge was out there, waiting for me to acquire it whenever, and however, I wanted.

He knew I had just learned that knowledge isn't something that's given to you: It's something you take.

When I was six or seven years old, my father, grandfather and uncle bought about an acre of land on the outskirts of town, a couple of miles from our home. They divided the lot into half for my father, and half for my uncle. On his side of the land, my father began to build a new house for his family. I've never forgotten helping him make the mud bricks we used to build that house. My father fashioned the frames for the bricks out of wood; my job was to mix earth and straw, shovel it into the frames, and then stamp it down with my bare feet. After that, the sun, our building partner, did his job. The resultant building blocks were crude, to be sure: but that two-story house, built some eighty years ago, is still serving as a fine home today.

Once our new Pordim residence was completed, I, my parents, my sisters, and my newly widowed grandfather Valcho excitedly moved from our old home into our new. (My uncle remained in the old house along with his stepson, who had a very good business operating a general store in the center of town.)

When I think back on the home in which I was raised, most often I remember being down in what I thought was its finest room: the cellar. Here we kept barrels of wine and sheep's-milk cheese; here we stored our winter vegetables--and our grapes, which we hung in bunches from the ceiling. But what we *mostly* kept in our cellar, as far as I was concerned, was a huge bottle, open at the top and equipped with a faucet at its bottom. With each fall's garden harvest my father would place in the bottle cabbages lopped into four equal pieces. He would then fill the bottle with water and salt, and I would place clean pieces of wood atop the cabbage to keep it fully submerged. Two or three times a day thereafter my father would drain the water from the bottom of the bottle, filling it back up from the top with fresh water and salt. In two or three weeks' time, we had our crate of sauerkraut! It was not the shredded sort one sees in today's market: throughout our process the cabbage remained in large one-quarter pieces. Oh, how I loved the deliciously sour, slightly salty sauerkraut juice! Unable to wait until I made it up the stairs, I used to drink mine right there in the basement. When it was available, I also had the juice with dinner. I of course didn't then know (or much care, of course), but that cabbage juice was very healthy, being packed with Vitamin C and beneficial nutrients. As I say, though, all I knew was that I thought it was the best tasting drink in the world.

Outside the front of the house was our fruit and vegetable garden, surrounded by wire that helped squelch our chickens' insatiable need to participate in the affairs of our garden. Also in the yard was a walnut tree, which before long grew large enough to allow my father to keep a small bed in its shade during the summer, where after lunch he never failed to rest for a half hour before returning to his labors. In summer we also began harvesting our corn, the cobs piled in a huge heap. Evenings after dinner my sisters and their girlfriends from the neighborhood sat on the mound and removed the husks from the corn, singing and laughing and having a good time with the few boys who worked alongside them.

In a far corner of the lot, next to the street, was a large barn for our three horses. In one inside corner of that barn was a bedroom my father kept for our hired farm hand. Between them the horses generated enough heat to keep this bedroom warm (enough), even in winter.

On the west side of the yard was a corral for the twenty-five or so sheep it was my responsibility to tend and milk. (If you have ever had fresh, warm sheep's milk, then you'll know that caring for sheep has at least one upside.) These gentle animals supplied us with the milk my father needed to make cheese and butter, and that my mother Christina daily used to make wonderful, flavorful yogurt. The method she used for this was time-honored and simple: she boiled the milk in pot; let it cool down to the temperature her little finger told her was right; stirred in a small amount of the previous day 's yogurt; and then covered the pot with a wool blanket and placed it in the corner near the stove. After a few hours, the milk would coagulate, thicken, and become creamy, delicious yogurt. (What makes the milk coagulate is an organism called *bacillus bulgaricus*--named after the country in which yogurt originated!)

We sold almost everything that we planted on our farm--with the singular exception of my father's wine grapes. Those he proudly kept for himself and us. Every spring he would prune his little vineyard; and every fall would harvest its fruit. Once our horses had carried the fruit from field to home, we would load the grapes into a giant container, into which my father, having rolled up his pants and washed his feet, would climb. At that point, the stomping would commence. This age-old method of making wine, so often associated with village life in Italy, never fails to make me think of Bulgaria! Once the seeds and skins had been separated from the juice via a long sloping shoot, the dark liquid was poured in barrels, where it would ferment into wine. I had my own small barrel of "wine," about 50 liters' worth, which a powder I bought at the local pharmacy kept from becoming alcoholic by inhibiting fermentation. Just as my father always made sure to have enough wine to last him until the next harvest, so I always had my barrel of grape juice--which I could somehow never manage to make last an entire year.

Along with his dinner my father would have one or maybe two of the only glasses of wine he allowed himself per day; my grandfather would have his single half-glass; and my sisters, mother and I would enjoy the sweet "wine" from my barrel.

The rising sun on most Saturday mornings found me failing in my attempts to sleep in the back of the horse buggy filled with watermelons my father and I used to take along the bumpy dirt road to the nearby city of Poem. Our goal was to reach the city's open market in time to sell our melons for the money to buy shoes and clothing. Arriving at the market early enough was half the challenge; the other was finding buyers during that economically difficult time. It was not unusual for that day's setting sun to find us still in possession of half the melons with which we'd arrived; we could then count upon the appearance of a wholesale dealer, who would offer to buy from us all we had left. He knew we'd strike such a "deal" in order to save ourselves from having to haul the heavy melons all the way back home again.

Ours was a medium-size farm comprising three sections. One for growing the grass and hay we needed for our horses and sheep, one (the largest by far) to grow our crops, and the third, next to a river, where we kept a vegetable garden for our personal use. If during the fall I went to water this garden, and I arrived to find the tomatoes heavy and red on the plants, I was free to pick one, and wash it in the stream, and eat it right there. Alone by the river I would smile broadly at the bursting deliciousness of it, the red juice running down my chin.

As delicious as fruit and vegetables were right off the plant, they could sail to even tastier heights once my mother had used them to work her magic in the kitchen. Like so many mothers throughout time, mine was a resourceful, outstanding cook. My mouth still waters when I think of her using eggs, milk and sugar to prepare the traditional Easter bread for us children.

My mother was of medium height, perhaps one or two inches taller than my father, with big brown eyes and beautiful long hair. A highly intelligent but illiterate peasant born into a farmer's family in Slavianovo (a village near to and slightly bigger than Pordim), she had always dreamed of going to school and securing an education. But at that time and place education was not an option for women, who were expected to stay home, get married, have children, and take care of not just their families, but also the families of their husbands. And that is exactly what my mother did. To say that she worked hard is certainly an understatement. Besides cooking for us all, she left home every day to work in the fields with my father; when I was an infant she took me with her, so that she could periodically stop her work and nurse me, before returning to the fields and leaving me, tied to our buggy with a rope, playing and slumbering in the shade of a large tree. After dark, she returned back to the house to cook dinner--following which she cleaned the kitchen, and then prepared bread, which baked overnight in order to be ready for the next day's breakfast.

As devoted as my mother was to attending to the material needs of her family, she also never neglected her own spiritual well-being. A deeply religious woman, she attended church every Sunday, always looking splendid in a national costume, and always wearing about her neck the gold necklace given to her by her father when she married mine. I often accompanied her to church--though, looking back, I find that I wish I had done so more often.

My father, a very hardworking man, had only had four years of elementary school behind him when he started working full-time on his father's farm. As a child I, too, was expected to wake up at three in the morning to start working the farm. In the cruelly hot summer months, I was in the fields every single day from sun up until dark. There was so very much work to be done on the farm, and all of it was physically demanding. We would bundle wheat, for instance, and then load it on our wagon and haul it to the mill for processing, where it became seeds we used to make flour for our bread. Or we had to remove corn from its stalks--a particularly unpleasant task, because the shells of the corn, dried by the sun, were as sharp as knives. And those are just two of the seemingly endless things that had to be done in order to keep our farm operating.

I hated doing so much hard work--but I had no choice. And I was also of course aware of my obligation to my family generally and in particular to my father, who, for as many hours in a day as was possible, always worked as hard as any man could. How, then, could I do any less?

My father was a good, fair man. I am sure that he loved me, but in truth I did not feel his love as much as I did that of my mother and grandfather. At times he was very strict with me. I will never forget an incident that occurred when I was around fourteen years old. One night after work I went out to meet some friends on the main thoroughfare that ran through the middle of our village, a wide walkway with a Russian museum on its east side, and a Romanian museum on its west. Both were set in park-like surroundings defined by sundry paths gently wending by beautiful and unusual trees, exotic scented flowers, and benches that seemed to invite convivial contemplation. Many people in Pordim, young and old, took their evening pleasures on the grounds of these museums, resting on the benches, chatting with their neighbors, and simply enjoying the fresh air. It was a truly beautiful place.

And so it was not entirely unnatural that one evening I spent too long there, relaxing and enjoying being with my friends after a hard day's work in the fields. It was customary for everyone in my house to sit down together for dinner at around eight o'clock; by the time I arrived home that night, everyone had been full for a while.

"You're late for dinner, Luben!" said my father crossly. "You weren't on time, so you won't get any dinner. Now go stand in the corner over there, and think about what you have done."

So that's what I did: I went and stood in the corner of the kitchen, my back toward my family.

Eventually my father went to feed the horses; it was then that my good mother brought me leftovers from the dinner I'd missed, so that I wouldn't have to go to bed hungry.

While at the time my father's reaction to my being late for dinner that night seemed harsh, it taught me a lesson about the importance of familial obligation. Even at the time I was (soon enough) grateful to him for the discipline he gave me.

Rounding out our family were two medium-sized dogs, Heidi and Brownie. Both were loving, gentle companions--the very best of friends to me.

Our property was enclosed all around by a wall about five feet tall, made of the same adobe we used for the house. The wall had a gate in it that was kept locked (the key for which, I suppose I can now reveal, was kept hidden under a roof shingle). On the street next to a corner of our yard there was (and still is) a water faucet utilized by everyone in the neighborhood. I remember in the winter going to get water for our family, only to find the faucet and everything around it frozen solid. This was hardly a surprise: it was so cold during the heavy snowfall season of December to March that a person could barely stay outdoors at all unless dressed very warmly, indeed. I used to help my father shovel snow in order to clear the pathway to our house; with distressing regularly I feared that I might never again feel my hands, ears or nose.

As cruel as winter was, it did offer one wonderful consolation: skiing on the big hill not too far from our house. My father made me a pair of wooden skis about three feet long, which I attached to my feet with ropes. Getting up the hill was almost as difficult as skiing down it was fun. Even when pitching face first in the snow on my way down the hill, the cold weather didn't bother me. At those times, my woolen pullover, hat and mittens seemed like all the protection I needed from elements that seemed, after all, to want nothing more than to resound with my joyous laughter.

I wasn't very long in this world before I began thinking there *had* to be more to life than getting up at four in the morning and working like a plow mule (if not *as* a plow mule) in order to wrench from the earth just enough sustenance to begin doing it all over again the next day.

And so I began to feel the pull of a world outside Pordim, a dazzling universe filled with smart, rich, well dressed, well fed people living carefree, cosmopolitan lives my young imagination could only fail to inform with specifics.

Something was out there; of that I was certain. And though I didn't know what exactly it was, or how it worked, or what it comprised, I did know that I wanted to be part of it. I hadn't taken five steps down the road of my life before I was yearning to be on a different path altogether.

But how to find--let alone begin traveling--down that new path? From where I stood, out in the fields or inside the chickens' pen or on our little second-story balcony to see as far as I could--all roads circled right back to Pordim.

And then one day I knew. I attended an elementary school that was a good distance from my home. One morning, when I was only in first or second grade, I was tromping along the dry edge of the muddy road toward the school when I heard a noise coming from behind me. I turned, and there was my math teacher, making his straight if somewhat erratic way toward me on a bicycle. I stepped further back onto the rough to allow him to pass; a good, friendly man, he waved to me as he did so. I waved back--and then stayed where I was--up off the road a bit, amongst the brittle grass and with the vast country sky spread above me to every horizon--and watched him pedaling away.

And that's when I understood: getting an education is what made everything else possible.

My math teacher owned a bicycle.

I wanted a bicycle.

That was inducement enough to emulate my teacher; I *really* wanted a bicycle. But the more I thought about it, the more I realized that what my math teacher had--and what, indeed, all the teachers at my school possessed--was something of which a bicycle, or nice clothing, or the beautiful writing pen that belonged to my grammar teacher, was but a reflection.

What they had was an education. They all spoke well, and were respected, and knew things about the world they couldn't have learned in Pordim.

And that's when I knew: As hard as we worked on our farm, we'd never be able to grow what I needed most. We'd never grow money (though one time, very young and deeply impressed by the earth's fecundity, I planted a coin, and tried). We'd never grow opportunity. We'd never grow experience of the world beyond our village.

But what I, alone, could plant, cultivate, harvest and enjoy in ways I knew I couldn't yet begin to imagine, was my knowledge.

I saw it, then: The world lie inside books.

And even in Pordim, we had books.

We had, in fact, a superb library!

Which I, that very day after school, began to visit, every chance I got.

As everyone knows, there lives beneath the bridge between inspiration and sustained, focused action the ugly and extremely persistent ogre of inertia. It's one thing, of course, to want an education; it's quite another to dedicate, say, eighteen years (not to mention the rest of one's life) to actually *getting* one. Luckily, God saw fit to bless me with a weapon that trumps inertia, every time: curiosity. There is absolutely nothing in this world like good old-fashioned curiosity to keep the engine of an education zooming right along.

It's simple: To learn, you've got to want to know.

To want to know, you've got to be curious.

After survival and love, curiosity is the greatest, purest motivating power in the world.

As a child I was, of course, hardly consumed by such grand, thematic truths. All I knew was that observing something was never enough for me: Over and over again I had to understand whatever had captured my attention; I had to grasp its structure, means, ways, secrets. This insatiable desire to comprehend what laid beneath the surface of things is how, step by step, question by question and answer by answer, I ultimately found my way out of Pordim.

Chapter Two

Learning to Learn

When I was a boy (and this is still true today), elementary schooling in Bulgaria was obligatory and free for seven years. At that time those seven years were divided into four at a "primary school," followed by three at a *progynasium,* roughly equivalent to a Junior High School in America. After that, high school was essentially a privilege for which the parents were expected to pay.

Our primary and "junior" high school buildings were very near one another--and both were a good distance from our farm. I didn't mind the long walk when the streets were dry--it was, after all, time when I wasn't working on our farm--but in the rain or snow the dirt road became a veritable morass of mud that made the trip seem interminable.

Still, as I say, I never missed a day if I could help it. I was a good student, always sitting in the front row to be able to better hear the teacher and read the notes on the blackboard. I was good, but I wasn't perfect: One day in class I was talking to the child seated beside me when our teacher suddenly struck me hard with a ruler on my head. I definitely achieved a higher level of in-class perfection after that.

My elementary and junior high school years passed quickly enough; after that, I was ready and more than willing to attend high school. The problem was that Pordim didn't have a high school. The closest was in the (ever alluring) large and ancient city of Pleven. (If I may interject a note of history here: It was to Pleven that all the world's eyes turned in December of 1877. Here, in the last major battle of the Russian-Turkish War of 1877-78, the Russians spent five long months winning the Siege of Pleven, which finally liberated Bulgaria from 500 years under the Ottoman yoke.) But tuition at the high school in Pleven was prohibitively expensive--not to mention the fact that, as accomplished a walker as I was, I couldn't walk *that* commute every day. And there was virtually no chance of my living in Pleven; this was during the terrible worldwide Depression, and money was scarce, especially--as always--for farmers.

It didn't take me long, however, to come up with a solution to my problem: as it happened, there was a two-year high school, named "Re-alka" (yet another reminder, I know, of how very different Bulgarian is from English) located in Slavianovo, a village about ten miles away from Pordim. My mother was born in Slavianovo; her family lived there still.

I could live with my mother's family in Slavianovo, and attend two years of high school!

I felt confident that I could count on my mother and grandfather's support for this plan; I was just as sure, however, that my father would object to it. He had frowned upon the seven years I'd already spent in school; it was a certainty that he would not allow me to leave him with that much more work to do on the farm.

"No," he said when I (finally) asked him. Instantly his voice turned cold and hard. "Absolutely not. I won't allow it. Your place is with your family here on the farm. You're the only son; this farm must be yours one day. The idea of your leaving is nonsense. I won't hear of it again. You're educated enough."

How my heart darkened--and broke. My father's will was unbend-ing. Just like that, my path out of Pordim was blocked by a massive, impenetrable wall there was no way around, over, or under.

I was born a farmer; and now, it seemed, I would die one, too.

Desperate, I begged my mother and grandfather to plea my case be-fore my father. One night I overheard my mother saying softly to her husband, "Please let the boy go to school. You hear how he cries himself to sleep every night. He wants it so very badly." My grandfather also did his best to change my father's mind--but to no avail. I was the only son. To my father, that settled it.

I turned outside my family for help. At night, when I went to see my friends and relatives in town, I beseeched them all to ask my father to al-low me to attend high school in Slavianovo. From my many visits to the library I had come to know quite well its director, a man named Dasho Radoeff: I asked him to talk to my father--and was thrilled to see him one evening coming up the walk toward my house. He and my father spoke privately for long enough that, in spite of myself, I dared to hope. Finally--miraculously!--my father relented. I didn't know what exactly had changed his mind. I didn't ask, either.

In the summer of 1933 my father and I climbed aboard our horse buggy and began the long, slow ride to Slavianovo. Behind us in the wagon were big canvas sacks filled with enough food to see me through a school year: bread flour, navy beans, potatoes, onions. It was a trip filled with both melancholy and (inside, for me, at least) not a little joy. This was, I knew, the beginning of a new life for me.

My new life, however, turned out to be very much like my old one, in that my mother's family also lived on a farm. I spent countless hours in the mornings before school and the evenings afterward working their farm as hard as I'd ever worked ours. I fit well into this new configuration of my family. My mother's father had a big house--and a family to match it. My grandparents lived there, along with my aunt and uncle and their two children, the youngest of whom was only a few month's old. So crowded, in fact, was their home that when my father and I first arrived we found there was no bedroom for me, save outside on a covered balcony. There was enough room there for a bed; if the space had had walls, it would have made for a perfectly decent room.

With his father-in-law's permission, my father, by now an experienced builder, turned that balcony into a new room in the house. Before he left to go back to Pordim, my grandfather and he shook hands and embraced; and my grandfather again made clear that he did not want to be paid for my room and board while I was at school.

My maternal grandfather's name was Liko. He was a giant of a man: well built, strong and tall--with, I noted, a wart over his right eyebrow, in the exact same place I had my own. As physically powerful as he was, his wife was frail; having suffered from a stroke many years before, she remained bedridden in her own room, where she was lovingly cared for by the family.

The high school in Slavianovo--a big building with a few classrooms, a large gym, and a great hallway--was about two miles away from the house, along a dirt road that in spring was dusty and in winter was mud. I didn't care; I was so glad to be continuing my education that I was happy to haul my books and backpack along that road twice a day. At night, I helped with the farm--or cooked dinner, or babysat the children. Between such chores I made sure to study; I very much respected and liked my teachers, and wanted to prove a good and helpful student. And I daresay I succeeded in that.

And it wasn't as if I never had any fun: With my new friends I would sometimes run through the prairies and fields to a nearby river to swim and fish, or to idly lie about, wondering aloud about one thing or another.

All in all it was a very good year: before I knew it, I had finished the eighth year of my education. I was already looking forward to my ninth.

On the very last day of my eighth-grade year, though, bad news struck. We were in class, itching to get *out* of class and on with our summer, when the director of the school, looking very grim and sad, came into our room and asked for our attention.

As we all knew, he said, we were in the midst of a depression. And as our school was not a private one, but was instead dependant upon government funds for its operation ... and I felt my heart seize in my chest.

Our school was being closed, he said. It would not reopen in the fall. There was no money to keep it operating. He was terribly sorry. He knew what a disappointment it was for us all. He had done everything he could. It was over.

It was over.

That was it.

It was over.

I knew I couldn't transfer to the high school in Pleven: If anything, my father was poorer than he'd been the year before.

And just like that, another wall came crashing down between me and the life I so desperately wanted to make for myself.

Chapter Three

Planting Ideas

For the next three years I became, again, a poor young man laboring on his family's farm. If possible I worked even harder than I ever had, out of pure fury at the work--and, more, out of genuine gratitude to my father for doing what he could to turn my dream of acquiring an education into a reality. He had tried. My mother's family had tried. We had all tried.

And with the denial of that dream, I set my mind and body to becoming nothing less than the very best farmer I could be.

Excellence, after all, is excellence.

In the ancient, primitive way, I tore at the ground with a plow pulled by horses. I tore at it with a hoe. I dug into it until my dirty fingers bled.

I harvested the corn.

I sowed the wheat.

I fed the chickens; I milked the sheep; I swept the barn.

This was my life. Now it was impossible for it to be anything else.

Except, not quite. Because I still had the Pordim library, which now more than ever saw me perusing its shelves, eagerly searching for another book I could read whenever I got the chance--whether at night before I went to bed, or during stolen moments in the fields. I read everything: particularly French and Russian literature, which I found fascinating. I was also extremely interested in autobiographies of famous people: I wanted to know how they lived, how they worked, how they turned their lives into something of lasting importance. I'm not sure I've ever read so much as I did during this period of my life. Maybe it wasn't possible for me to get a proper, formal education. But I could do what I could do. I could read what I could read.

After a full year back on our farm, no longer able to stand the cessation of my formal education, I decided to enroll at a college of agriculture. I did this not because I desired to know one single thing more about farming and agriculture than I already did, but because I was sure that going to *any* school was better than going to none. And *this* school, at least, was so nearby I could almost hit it with a rock thrown from our front gate.

The humble American College of Agriculture in Pordim was founded in 1929 and built via funds raised for that very purpose by one of our town's true heroes, Dr. Edward Haskell. Born into a large family of well-educated Swiss missionaries then living in Plovdiv, Bulgaria, Haskell spent his childhood traveling with his family throughout Europe: By the time the Haskell family immigrated to the United States, young Edward spoke six languages. He received his undergraduate degree from Ohio's Oberlin College, and went on to do postgraduate work at Columbia, Harvard, and the University of Chicago.

A scientist of wide and varying interests (he taught everything from anthropology to sociology), in 1948 Haskell became the driving force behind the formation of the Council for Unified Research and Education (CURE). This non-profit organization, which through the mid-1980s counted among its members many of America's leading scientists and educators, was dedicated to the idea that all knowledge could and should be synthesized into a single discipline expressed through a common language: that only a "unified science" would allow specialists from different fields to communicate in a way their exclusive terms and processes traditionally prohibited. The high water mark for CURE came in 1972, with the publication of its seminal book, *FULL CIRCLE: The Moral Force of Unified Science.*

Dr. Haskell's entire career was based upon his conviction that only after the sciences had become an integrated whole could people, through the utilization of a language common to all scholastic disciplines, achieve an education that could be called truly comprehensive.

Now *here* was a man who believed in the value of education!

When I was a boy my friends and I had no idea we had such a world-class intellectual in our midst. All we knew was that we loved Dr. Haskell--who, we also knew, was single-handedly responsible for building the college that rose from the ground so quickly we could barely tear ourselves away from watching its construction. So while we knew that Dr. Haskell was an educated man of some very real consequence, what we *mostly* knew about him was that he always had a kind, friendly word for any of us children; we knew that he took every opportunity to personally encourage us, or to stop and joke with us a while. (One of my fondest memories is of a particular fall afternoon when Dr. Haskell, dressed in a tweed three-piece suit, merrily walked by a group of my friends and I as we played outside. When he came near a bench he stopped, and, smiling and waving to us all along, pushed out his bottom in slightly cartoonish preparation to sit upon what we were all aghast to see was a very large nail protruding from a board left lying on the bench. We screamed and flapped our arms in alarm, trying to warn our beloved friend of his impending impalement; but he, all the while maintaining a blissful, happy countenance, seemed to understand our hysterical gesticulations and screams as nothing more than spirited overtures of good cheer. As we cringed and peeked through our fingers, the good doctor lowered his seat closer and closer to the deadly point; then, at the very moment he was surely upon it--for his suit jacket hid from us the actual point of contact--he stopped. Maintaining his half-seated position, he cocked his head and looked up to the sky, an expression of puzzlement now upon his face. Us children, with eyes and mouths agape, froze, and stared. Decidedly curious now, Dr. Haskell moved his rear slightly up from the nail; he then, with great hesitancy, lowered it to its former position. We gasped as he explored. But again he stopped the instant his rump, so to speak, got the point. This time he looked even more perplexed: Whatever could it be, he seemed to wonder, that was interfering with the natural order of a universe in which he had always been able to sit wherever he darn well pleased? Finally, having apparently determined that such an impertinence must be handled with firm resolution--and manifestly confident in the power of his bottom to overcome any and all challenges--he seemed, in a short and abrupt movement, to sit upon the very tip of the nail. We jumped; he, looking utterly surprised, veritably leapt from the wall. "Oh!" he exclaimed, vigorously rubbing his backside--and then he turned, arms akimbo, and crossly regarded the object of his undoing, tapping his foot with maximum intolerance. Next he turned our way, and, with one eyebrow raised in suspicion, began staring at us, one by one, as if to see who among us would crack under his withering, accusatory gaze, and admit to somehow orchestrating this offense. A certain twinkle in his eye, however, revealed to us that we'd all been had: and as we howled and jumped with delight at Dr. Haskell's performance, he let out an indignant "Harumph!" before bending and gingerly picking up the board, which he kept at arm's length while determinedly marching off, shaking his head and muttering angrily at the vast complex of conspiracies forever thwarting the efforts of an righteous, civilized man who asked nothing more of the world than that it simply behaved itself.)

While Dr. Haskell was a gifted entertainer, he was an even better audience member. Whenever we children performed any kind of little show at our elementary school, we would always find him seated in the front row, laughing and clapping as if he were at a lavish Broadway musical of which we were the dazzling stars. After one Christmas show at our school, my schoolmates and I were delighted beyond words to find waiting for us on each side of the auditorium's exit door two men, each carrying a big sack filled with a Christmas present for every one of us. Although he never took credit for being Pordim's Santa that year, we later learned that Dr. Haskell, with the blessing and gratitude of our parents, had provided for the children of our village gifts that the Depression would have otherwise denied.

Dr. Haskell's generosity toward the people of Pordim went far beyond Christmas gifts. Motivated by his love of the Bulgarian people and his desire to see their lives improved, he began, around 1928, to raise the money necessary to build and staff at an undetermined location somewhere in Bulgaria a small, local college to be named The American College of Agriculture. Once he had managed to raise the (then) considerable sum of $2,500, Dr. Haskell published notice of his intention in the Bulgarian newspaper, *Zornica*. Thirty-two villages and eight cities from across Bulgaria applied for the chance to be the home of Dr. Haskell's planned educational facility. Our mayor, Ivan Boginov, made a bid for Pordim, too.

Incredibly, we won! Great excitement spread throughout our town when we learned that Dr. Haskell had written Mayor Boginov to inform him that Pordim had been selected as the location for the new school.

And in the course of four short months in 1929, it happened: A small college rose from the ground not 500 feet from our home. And in that way was life in and around our village improved: The school offered the people of Pordim the means of learning the latest agricultural innovations and techniques, the result of which was more and better crops from gardens and farms throughout the vicinity.

In 1934 a celebration at the school was held in honor of Dr. Haskell and his wife Elizabeth, who were planning to move back to America. In attendance (in our little village!) was the King of Bulgaria, Boris the Third, who awarded a silver cross to the Haskells for their service to the community. That evening mayor Boginov also made Dr. and Mrs. Haskell honorary citizens of Pordim.

Last but not least, the street which ran right past our home and farm was renamed Dr. Haskell Avenue. On a very early morning years later I would walk down that same road, a suitcase in my hand, parting from my family in quest of the very best education I could get. And my heart would be buoyed by the thought that no matter how anxious I was about leaving the comfort of my home, and no matter how unsure I was about my ability to handle whatever challenges surely awaited me, at least I was, both literally and figuratively, following in the footsteps of the great Dr. Edward Haskell, formerly of Pordim, Bulgaria.

Before that day, however, I decided to at least take advantage of the American College of Agriculture, which had, after all, always been such an everyday part of my life. Although my father chafed at the prospect of yet again losing so much of his farm labor to the sirens' song of education, ultimately he acquiesced to my going: It was around this time, I believe, that it began to occur to him that Fate had played him a dastardly trick by introducing into his family a son who *should* have been born to, say, a Harvard professor.

"Go--learn, read your books," said my father, waving his hand at me. "I would have better luck stopping a train."

And so I began my third incarnation as a student/farmhand: In the early mornings I bent my back to my farm chores; during the days I thought, spoke and learned as a student; after school I worked the farm; I studied whenever and however I could; I fell face down onto my bed, asleep before I hit--and then, while it was still pitch black outside, I awoke, and began the process all over again.

It was, in fact, Dr. Haskell who had once taught me a lesson about the proper balancing of study and farm work. One day, when I was boy of maybe eleven, I was shepherding our sheep in the area around his school. That's what I was *supposed* to be doing, anyway--instead, though, I had my nose buried in a book. The sheep, free to roam pretty much wherever they might, were naturally drawn to the luscious-looking flower garden just inside the gates of the school. By the time I looked up, it was too late: The flowers at the entrance way to the American College of Agriculture were being decimated by my herd of stupid, stray sheep.

I dashed over to the errant grazers. "Stop!" I yelled. "Stop! No! Stop eating the flowers!"

Unfortunately, sheep don't speak Bulgarian.

As I ran back and forth, trying to get the sheep in order, I became aware of a presence behind me. I turned and saw Dr. Haskell standing there, his arms crossed atop a large book he was holding against his chest.

"Hello there, Luben," he said.

"Hello, Dr. Haskell," I said. I immediately disregarded the possibility that he didn't see my sheep eating his garden.

"Nice day we're having today, isn't it?" said the doctor.

Maybe he *didn't* see the twenty-five sheep making a meal of his flowers?

Frozen in place, I nodded wildly at him. "Yes!" I said. "It's very nice!"

"What's that you're reading there, Luben?" he said, as calm as a grandfather clock.

"Oh," I said, gesturing with the book in a way that almost sent it flying from my hands. "It's a library book. I got it from the library. It's about Genghis Khan. The things he did. He was quite the fellow!" One of the sheep nearest me let out a lout bleat. If by some miracle Dr. Haskell wasn't *seeing* the sheep, he was surely now *hearing* them.

"Genghis Khan, 'eh?" said Dr. Haskell congenially. "He's a very interesting person--and he lived in a *very* interesting time."

Maybe he thought the bleating sound had come from *me*?

"Yes, sir," I said. "Very interesting."

"You like to read a lot, don't you, Luben?"

"Yes, sir. I do, sir."

"That's a very admirable quality, Luben. Reading is the very cornerstone of a good life. A man who doesn't read doesn't learn, and a man who doesn't learn can't be happy."

"Yes, sir," I said, keeping my eyes riveted to his face. "That sure makes sense."

Maybe the twenty-five sheep behind me had disappeared and *weren't*, even as we spoke, destroying the grounds of his college?

"And yet, one must keep a balance in one's life, mustn't one, Luben? There are other things in life besides studying, aren't there?" I nodded with mechanical zeal. "It's possible for one to spend so much time reading one forgets to tend to other, more immediate affairs in one's life, isn't it?"

"Yes it is, sir."

"Have you ever had the experience, Luben, of, say, reading, when you should be paying attention to something else--and then, because of your inattention to it, having whatever it is you were supposed to be doing go very much awry?

"Yes sir" I said, unblinkingly. "I think something like that has happened to me before."

"It's a very uncomfortable feeling, isn't it?"

I nodded sincerely. "It is, sir. Very uncomfortable."

"Well, one day we shall all be perfect. Until then, we must do what we can to keep our responsibilities in balance, 'eh, Luben?"

I nodded.

"Have a pleasant day, my young scholar," said Dr. Haskell. With that he turned and continued walking along the path toward the steps of his college. About two-thirds of the way there he gently, and quietly, stepped around a single sheep standing directly in his path, contentedly chewing away.

Ten years later, when I was a student at that same school, I would sometimes walk by the monument to Dr. Haskell built on its front grounds (across the path from the long-restored flower garden), and say, "Trying to keep it balanced, Dr. Haskell."

What most pleased and surprised me about attending Dr. Haskell's school was how much I enjoyed the agricultural sciences. I had always done well in math, and found that what I was learning at the American College had much of the same rigorous logicality to it. Moreover, it was solidly *useful* information: I wasn't long attending my new classes before I realized that I was learning what my family and I needed to become truly excellent farmers. So enthusiastically did I throw myself into my studies, in fact, that in one year I completed the college's three-year program. (Which, I should hasten to add, is less impressive than it sounds: I was given one full year's credit for the work I'd already done in high school.)

I learned more than I'd ever known, for instance, about how to properly grow fruit trees. Eager to implement my new knowledge, I persuaded my father to let me plant fruit trees on a two-acre parcel of land we owned near the railroad station in our village. Why should we haul watermelons so far to market to essentially give them away at each day's end, when we could instead offer for sale a wide variety of fresh, delicious fruit, which was less common than watermelons--and *certainly* weighed less? So that spring, out by the tracks (and near to a river), I planted about twenty fruit trees: cherries, pears, peaches, apricots, apples and plums. Utilizing some of the growing techniques I'd learned in school, it wasn't long until the saplings began looking like the trees I knew I could help them become.

It was amazing, I noticed, how very much the buds growing on those little trees resembled nothing so much as unfolding money!

Chapter Four

School Times Two

It was during the spring of my third year back on the farm that a former schoolmate from the high school in Slavianovo came running up to me as I was out tilling a field.

"Luben, Luben!" he cried, waving a paper in his hand. "Look! There is a petition to reopen our old high school!"

Immediately I quelled the hope that was instantly in my chest.

"What do you mean?" I said, as calmly as I could.

"It's come down from the governing school council!" he went on excitedly. "If we get the signatures of one hundred fifty students, they'll reopen the high school in Slavianovo *this fall!*"

I ran to tell my father--who didn't even try to dissuade me from signing the petition. I believe he was impressed at the restraint I showed by not signing it one hundred fifty times myself.

Because there were many young people throughout the area chafing to get back to school, in almost no time the necessary signatures (and then some) had been secured. When my friends and I received the result, we literally jumped for joy.

They were reopening the high school in Slavianovo!

I can't possibly convey the excitement and relief I felt at learning that my formal education would, after all, continue. Suffice it to say that for the first time in the history of Bulgaria, a long row of soybean seeds were tamped into the earth via dancing.

When I told my father it was possible for me to resume my studies in Slavianovo, he didn't even wait for me to ask his permission; he only scowled and turned away, saying, "Yes, go. Heaven forbid you should stay on the farm that has nurtured you all of your life." But as he busied himself in order to ignore me I saw something that I don't think I was supposed to. I saw that, however slightly, he was smiling.

Before too very long my father and I had again loaded our horse-drawn buggy with all the food and supplies I would need for another year of study and work in Slavianovo, and we were off. My old room at my mother's family farm awaited me; when we arrived there were hugs and congratulations all around, my grandfather Liko embraced me with such robustness my feet left the ground. And even though I'd spent my whole life seeing things grow, I could not believe that the infants I'd once held while trying to study were now walking, talking, pint-size people.

Because I had three years of independent studying under my belt (and was, for that matter, three years older than most of my classmates), I found the ninth grade material being taught back at the Slavianovo high school quite easy.

Very easy.

Almost absurdly easy.

And the thought, once it occurred to me, wouldn't let me go: Why couldn't I take the ninth and tenth grades *at the same time?*

It was audacious, presumptuous and ... well, *young* of me to even consider it, but my thinking was this: Once I had finished the ninth grade, I was done at the Slavianovo high school, since it was a two-year school that only *went* to the ninth grade. The only way for me to finish grades ten, eleven and twelve was to do so in Pleven, the nearest city to offer those grades.

Living and studying in Pleven was going to be very expensive.

It would be 30% *less* expensive, however, if I tested out of the tenth grade: if, while attending the ninth grade, I simultaneously studied hard enough to pass the rigorous, week-long examination held at the beginning of each school year for those who have somehow arrived at an opinion of themselves high enough to imagine that they already know what mere mortals must study for an entire school year to learn.

Still: If I tested out of the tenth grade, my father would only have to pay for me to attend school in Pleven for two years--for grades eleven and twelve--instead of three.

It seemed like an idea worth looking into, anyway.

In researching the matter, I learned two extremely interesting facts. The first was that before I could even take the test, all costs associated with a year's worth of school had to be paid up front (besides room and board: everyone was on their own as far as that was concerned); in other words, before taking the test I had to pay for the entire school year-- whether or not I ended up actually having to *attend* that year or not. And if I failed the test, and so wanted/had to attend tenth grade, I'd have to pay the full tuition *again*--the same as if I'd never taken the test at all.

So that was the gamble: the chance of saving one year's room and board, versus the chance of having to pay that room and board *and* the cost of two tuitions.

Yikes.

Besides that, I learned that in all of Bulgaria, the number of people who had successfully passed the examination into the tenth grade after finishing grades one through eight within Bulgaria was exactly zero.

It had never been done!

So there were my options: I could ruin my family financially, or I could make history.

I decided not to rush my decision.

Two days later, I was done thinking about it: I wanted to go for it. The material they were teaching in ninth grade was so simple I believed paying attention to it at all was actually making me stupider.

I could pass the tenth grade test. I knew I could. For three years straight I'd been reading books--and *real* books, too: history, philosophy, science, literature.

Heck, I thought, I could probably pass the *eleventh* grade test, too!

This bit of internal bravado dissipated quickly enough, though. No need to get carried away, I thought. First things first.

Although I always consulted with my father before making any plans- -especially those having to do with anything as momentous as the means and ways of my education--I decided to at least for a while keep this particular plan to myself. As much and as hard as I could, I would study to pass the tenth-grade equivalency exam; at the end of ninth grade, with the summer before the tenth upon me, I would, if I thought I was truly ready to make a go of it, tell him of my idea. I was sure he was already expecting me to ask him to pay for me to finish three years of high school in Pleven. How much better would it be if when that time came, I could with confidence tell him that I believed I had a plan to save him the cost of one year's room and board for me?

I couldn't see any benefit in talking to him about it beforehand. For all I knew, I couldn't do it anyway. I knew I was pretty smart; I *sure* knew how hard I studied. But it seemed reasonable for me to have a doubt or two about whether or not I was *the smartest person in the history of Bulgaria.*

Either way, I determined to at least take a stab at being the hardest working.

The first thing I would need, I knew, was a better understanding of what material was actually covered in the tenth grade. I puzzled over how to obtain that information--when suddenly it dawned on me that the older brother of an acquaintance of mine at school went to the tenth grade in Pleven!

Perfect!

The next day at school I approached this acquaintance of mine, whose name was Stoyan. I told him of my plan, and asked him whether he thought his brother might be willing to help me.

"What do you want again?" replied Stoyan. "I don't understand what you mean."

"I'm saying that I want your brother Asparouh to provide me with whatever he can that would help me learn whatever he's learning in the tenth grade at his high school in Pleven."

"But why? What do you care about what they're learning in Pleven?"

I explained again why I cared.

Stoyan scratched the back of his neck and looked confused. "But you can't study what they're studying in Pleven. You already go to school here."

"Yes," I said, quickly rolling my eyes. "You're right, Stoyan. I do go to school here. But *next* year I want to go to your brother's high school in Pleven, see? Except that when I do, I don't want to actually *attend* to the tenth grade, like Asparouh does. I want to *skip* that grade. But in order to do that, I have to pass a test on all the same things Asparouh is learning. And Asparouh can help me do that by, for instance, bringing me his homework lessons to look at."

"You want Asparouh to bring you his homework?"

"Right, Stoyan. You've got it."

"You want to do my brother's homework."

"Not exactly. I want to *study* your brother's homework."

"In order to *do* it, you mean? You want to do his homework?"

"I don't want to *do* his homework. He would have already *done* his homework. It wouldn't make any sense for me to do his homework. I just want to *look* at his homework. I want to be *able* to do his homework, you corn cob." (I didn't really say, "you corn cob." I almost did, though.)

"But why would you want to do homework that isn't even yours? We get our own homework every day!"

Boy. I couldn't help but think that if Stoyan's brother was handling tenth grade, maybe there really *was* hope for me.

Through Stoyan's brother, and other friends or acquaintances of mine who either had siblings in high school at Pleven or went to the school themselves, I managed to get my hands on a good percentage of the actual tenth grade curriculum material. I even got my hands on the textbooks used for several subjects. When the school year ended, many friends were happy to let me have all the notes and books they'd used throughout the year.

What had begun as a slight possibility was beginning to seem distinctly possible. I spent the nights of my entire ninth grade year studying what they were learning in tenth grade in Pleven. I now had in my possession the lion's share of learning materials from that class--and three months of summer to study before the test itself, which took place in late August.

Now possessed of the necessary confidence, I decided to tell my father of my plan. I broached him on the subject one evening after supper as he worked in a field baling hay onto our wooden cart to take to back the barn.

As I told him what I had done and planned to do yet, he stopped working and stood patiently listening. When I was done, he surprised me by placing his hand upon my shoulder. "I want you to know that I'm very proud of you, Luben," he said. "Take the test. See if you can skip the tenth grade. If anyone can do it, it's you. I'll help however I can. Do the chores you are able, of course--but I'll try to leave you as much free time to study as possible. It doesn't matter that no one has ever accomplished what you are trying to. I'm sure no one has ever *wanted* it as much as you, either. You're a smart young man, Luben, and a very hard worker. What you set your mind to do, you do. You will do this. I have confidence in you."

I have no idea what changed my father's feelings about my education aspirations. Something about my resolve, I suppose--or my age: At that point, he may have simply given up trying to keep on the farm someone who was clearly leaving it. He had wanted a plow horse; he had gotten, instead, a racehorse (who, he knew, was hardly beyond pulling a plow). And it was as if at that moment he wanted me to know that he understood the value of a racehorse: They go more places; they see more things; they make a *lot* more money.

"Go," he seemed to be saying. "Race."

And with that I was out of the gate, and on my way.

Not that I went very *far*. I went to my room, actually, and began to study.

Now I had studied before. I'd been studying my whole life, in a way. But the studying I'd done before was nothing compared to the studying I now began. As far as I was concerned--and as far as my father was concerned, and my mother, and my grandfather, and my sisters--I had three months to make sure I knew, exactly, every single thing known by any A student just walking into the Pleven sunshine after finishing the very last day of his tenth-grade education.

"Now, let me make sure I have this absolutely right, Luben," my father said to me the day after our talk in the barn. "If you don't pass this test for the tenth grade, I lose one year's worth of tuition money to that school, right? Flat-out, lost. Gone. *Phoosh:* No more. Same as if it had fallen from my pocket on the way to market. Correct?"

"That's, correct, father." I said.

Hoisting a sack of feed onto to his shoulder and turning toward the chicken pen, he stopped at my side. In his sun-darkened skin I could see the crinkles around his eyes.

"I suppose you've got some studying to do, then, don't you, son?" he said.

I allowed as how I did.

"Then go, boy," he said. "I've got this."

Three months later, my father and I, having made the twenty-five mile trek from Pordim to Pleven in our ever-trusty, ever-bumpy horse buggy, were exploring the neighborhood closest the very same high school where, if all went well, I would soon be starting the *eleventh* grade. The test that would allow that to happen lasted every school day for a week; my father (bless him!) had amazed me by suggesting that besides the week of the test, I should stay an *additional* week in whatever room we found near the school, so that I would have that extra, uninterrupted time to prepare. A week, with nothing to do but study! I wasn't even sure I was *capable* of studying without a shovel in my hand! I thrilled to think of all that dedicated time--but knew the sacrifice that extra week of room and board would mean for my family.

"No, Father, I couldn't," I said. "It's very generous of you. But I don't need the extra week. I'm prepared. Being here the week of the test is all I need."

"It's okay, Luben," he said. "What you learned in the agricultural college has done our farm a great deal of good. You were right: we're making more with the fruit you grew than we ever did selling watermelons alone. And you've seen: the fruit trees are very full this year. We'll make the money. You've come too far for us to now do anything less than we can."

I wasn't going to argue with him (much). In truth, I *was* worried about the test; I, if anyone, understood the difference a week's study time would make.

Many families living near the high school rented rooms to students; it didn't take my father and I long to find one for me in a house located a block from the school. I remember almost nothing about the people from whom we let my new quarters; all I knew was that the room was quiet and clean, and came with a bed and a big, broad desk, atop of which sat waiting for me an ordinary reading lamp that, the first time I saw it, seemed so beautiful it almost made me cry.

A week later I was back in that same room, after my father and I had unloaded my suitcase, my bundles of books and my food--and after he had climbed back aboard the buggy, waved one last time, flicked the reins, and begun his long trip back home.

Then, in the quiet created when I softly shut the room's door behind me, it was just me, my dusty clothes, my things, and that desk and light, beckoning me.

A call I wasted exactly *no* time answering.

This high school--this one in Pleven whose tenth grade I was daring to try circumventing--was known to be one of the toughest high schools in all of Bulgaria. Nobody there, I knew, would care about my dreams.

They wouldn't care about my determination.

They wouldn't care how hard I'd worked to get here.

They wouldn't care how much I wanted it.

They wouldn't care what my taking the test had cost my family.

All they would care about was my grade on the examination--period. They would care about whether or not I had succeeded where no person had ever succeeded before.

And they wouldn't care *that* much about it, either: they had, after all, every last reason to be confident I would fail.

They would, I knew, fully expect to send me packing back to the poor country farm I'd come from.

"A farmer never loses the dirt under his nails," went the saying.

Well. True enough.

But there's another thing that's true about farmers: God never put a more stubborn people on earth.

For a week, day in and day out, I sat at my nice clean desk in my nice clean room, and I studied.

I didn't shuck corn, or bale hay, or feed chickens, or slaughter pigs, or plow land, or mend fences, or milk sheep, or repair roofs, or weed gardens, or do anything but study, study, and study.

I was in heaven, really.

And seven days later, it was time to find out how far away that heaven was from hell.

The first day's examination began in the gray morning light of a cold, near-empty classroom. I and a few other would-be eleventh graders were handed fat test packets we were told to keep face down on our desks until the instructor gave us the signal to begin. There would be a half-hour lunch break at noon: We were expected to eat whatever we'd brought with us right there in the room. After that, we were to continue until we had completed the test--or as much of it as we could. At exactly three o'clock we were to put down our pencils.

Each day's test results would be posted for viewing upon arrival the following morning. If you got a "C" or below on any test, the good news for you is that you wouldn't have to take any more tests, because you were finished.

"Begin," said the test administrator.

The first day's test was on mathematics.

I got an A.

The second day's test was on French.

I got an A.

The third day it was physics.

I got a B.

The fourth day was divided into two tests: geography in the morning, and history in the afternoon.

B. A.

The fifth and final test was on grammar and usage of the Russian language. This one was to be scored by the instructor in class that Friday afternoon, while we waited.

By the time the teacher, a heavy-set, white-haired elderly gentlemen, took his red pencil in hand and bent grimly over my test, he and I were alone.

Suddenly the classroom felt almost unbearably warm to me.

Russian was, by far, my worst subject. I didn't know anyone who spoke it, and the textbook I had tried to use throughout the summer to study it was mostly *in* Russian, considerably curtailing its value as a learning aid.

At one point during the previous school year I had managed to track down a fellow in our town who, some years before, had taken tenth-grade Russian at the high school in Pleven. I told him my situation, and asked if he could give me any advice on learning Russian--and whether or not he had kept any of his old tenth-grade Russian class notes or study materials. I was disappointed to hear that he had not, but heartened to hear that he believed he *did* still remember a Russian love letter his class had been instructed to memorize.

"Every day, that same stupid letter," he moaned. "I don't think I'll *ever* forget that thing."

I told him I would gladly pay him with fruit and eggs if he would agree to meet with me daily for a half-hour or so over the course of a week to teach that Russian letter to me.

The problem was that he only remembered how to *say* the letter; he didn't remember much of what its words actually meant. But it was a start.

Once I had memorized the block of odd sounds, I checked out a Russian dictionary from the library, and tried to match the "words" I was saying with their proper definitions.

This proved an inefficient way to proceed: If you don't speak the language, how can you tell where one word ends and the next begins? If you don't know English, for instance, and all you have is sounds to go on, how do you know "He sang a happy song?" isn't "Hes angah appys ong?"

The letter, from what I could gather, was from a man who lived across the sea (or was visiting across the sea, or grew up across the sea, or had once been across the sea, or something), and who couldn't return to his lover because his family obligations, or his family job, or the duties of his family, or something having to do with his family, kept him from flying to her, or flying around her, or flying and crashing into her, or some confounded thing or the other.

Well, I knew I could say the whole letter, anyway. The rest I could only hope I'd correctly surmised from my all-Russian textbook and the library's ancient Bulgarian-Russian dictionary.

From the looks of the number of red marks the teacher was putting on my test, I'd have done better taking a test on Chinese.

Finally done, the instructor dropped his pencil, leaned back in his chair, and rubbed his eyes beneath his spectacles. He then lowered his gaze, and regarded me.

"So you're the Luben Walchef we've all heard so much about."

"I'm Luben Walchef, yes sir," I said. "Though I can't think of how you could have heard anything about me. I'm from Pordim."

"And that's what makes you so interesting, son--that you're from Pordim."

"Sir?"

"What does your family do in Pordim, Luben?"

"We're farmers, sir."

"How many brothers and sisters do you have?"

"Just two sisters, sir."

"You're the only son."

"Yes, sir."

"Must make you awfully valuable on the farm."

I smiled slightly. "I suppose I do tend to come in handy, yes sir."

One side of his mouth smiled a little, too. Gazing out one of the classroom windows, he said, "Pordim's a small town, isn't it, my boy? There's not even a high school there, isn't that right?"

"That is right, sir. I went to high school for two years in Slavianovo, where my mother's family lives."

"How did you come to go to school there, young man?" he said, crossing his hands atop his desk and leaning forward a little, as if studying me. "Do all the boys go to school in Slavianovo once they've finished elementary school in Pordim?"

"No sir. I was the only one of my classmates to do that, sir."

"Why did you do it, then?"

"Because I wanted to continue my education, sir."

"And your family? How did they feel about you leaving the farm to go to high school ten miles away?"

"It was a hardship for them, to be sure. For my father, especially. It meant a lot more work for him."

"But he allowed you to go anyway."

"Yes sir."

"Why do you think that is, Luben?"

I thought for a moment, and then said, "I think he knew how much it meant to me. I have never stopped studying, sir, my whole life. There is something about acquiring knowledge through reading and understanding that is, to me, like ... food. I can't think of any other way to say it. It's like I need it to live. I know not everyone is like that. My father is not like that. He is a good, hard-working man who has learned all he needs to know about life from living and working as a farmer. And it's not that I believe learning through reading and study will make me any wiser, necessarily--I understand the difference between knowledge and wisdom. My father is not perhaps the most learned man in the world, but he is as wise as any man. But he is different than me in that I have a true need to understand things--broader things, larger things. He is happy to throw a rock; I need to know why that rock fell to the ground exactly where it did, instead of three feet further away, or three feet closer. Why didn't it just keep going, and sail away? I am forced to wonder. If my father hurts his shoulder, he rests it: eventually it gets better, and he's fine. That's not enough for me. I want to know what, exactly, *happened* to his shoulder: What happened to the muscles in there, how they are arranged, how they interact with tendons--how come more damage wasn't done, or less?

Fifteen minutes later, I'm nose deep in an anatomy book I've borrowed from the library--and then the sheep aren't being fed! So, it's difficult for him.

"But, finally, he did let me go to high school in Slavianovo, sir." I laughed. "When he at first refused, I got half of Pordim rallying to let me go. I'm not sure that, in the end, he felt he had a choice."

The professor laughed. "And how does he feel about you coming to school in Pleven?"

I told the professor about my father's change of heart--about how the high school in Slavianovo had closed down after my first year there, and how I'd gone to the agricultural college, and how, after three years of self-education, ninth grade had been so easy for me I'd decided to try skipping the tenth grade. I told him that despite what failing the test would mean to him and the rest of my family, my father fully supported my desire to take it, and did what he could to help me succeed.

"And that," said the teacher, "brings us to the matter at hand, doesn't it?" I slipped my top lip between my teeth, and nodded. "Luben," he continued, "I'm afraid your Russian test scores are not what they might have been." I felt the blood freeze in my veins. The teacher laid his spectacles on his desk, rubbed his eyes, and then leveled his gaze at me. "It's clear you're a dedicated scholar who will go far in life," he said. "Of that I have no doubt. But what am I to do with this score? It's clear you have no real grasp of Russian."

"If I may, sir," I said, trying to keep my voice steady. "I'm good with languages. I tried to learn Russian on my own, and clearly failed. I could not locate the necessary study materials. But in school, in French, I excelled. I'm almost fluent in the language. Once I was properly being taught Russian, I know I could catch up to where I should be. I learn very quickly, sir--and I'm used to studying ahead on my own."

He was watching me; he seemed to be considering my case.

"You are good with the French language?" he asked, in French.

"Well," I answered in French, "I wouldn't say I was particularly good. I would say, with just a fair degree of confidence, that I am adequate. I believe that if I were stranded in Paris for any length of time, I could at least order food in a restaurant, or rent a room. Find a bus. Simple little things like that."

We went on talking for a bit, in French.

He then switched back to Bulgarian. "What a pity you had to test in Russian, and not French."

Nearly desperate, I blurted out, "I do know how to say something in Russian."

He raised his eyebrows. "Oh?" he said. "Let's hear that."

I said the Russian letter. When I was finished, the teacher smiled, clasped his hands behind his head, leaned back in his chair, and said, "That's something *I* teach! Where did you learn that?"

I told him the story of my meetings with his ex-student, of the food I exchanged for lessons.

"I see," he said. "Very interesting. Could I bother you to go through that one more time, please?"

I repeated the passage.

After I'd fallen silent, he said, "That's really quite extraordinary. You say you learned that from a boy who learned it in my class? Well, now. That is an interesting addition to your case. Do you know what the letter means?"

I told him I thought it was about a man who misses his love but must remain oversees in order to tend to some concerns of his family.

He remained silent.

"Either that," I said, "or it's about a fly who yearns to be a family man but is instead stuck being a woman under water."

The professor's lips formed a little "O," and his eyes widened with surprise--and then he leaned back his head and let loose a roar of pure joy.

I held my breath.

He laughed so hard he went silent and began, with one hand, to softly slap his desktop.

"Oh, oh," he panted a few moments later. "My goodness, but that was funny. You're a very funny fellow, Mr. Walchef."

I kept quiet, and felt myself blush.

He looked back down at my test. He began rapidly tapping it with his red pencil. Then he stopped, and looked up at me.

"You're an impressive young man, Luben. I like you. It's clear you're a very hard worker. I myself come from a farm family in Russia; I know how hard it is to keep up with one's studies when the cows need feeding and the corn is high." He rose from his seat and walked around his desk to mine. Standing before me, he put out his hand. "You don't know Russian, that's for sure," he said as I grasped his hand. "I look very forward to teaching it to you when I see you in my tenth-grade class in a few weeks. Congratulations, Mr. Walchef. You've passed all your exams."

The next morning my father, who still had six or seven miles to go in the buggy before he reached Pleven, was, I suppose, not a little surprised to see his son far ahead on the road, bounding toward him, wildly waving a piece of paper.

I knew when he saw me, though, because at that moment he let go of the reins, stood in the rickety, moving wagon, and threw his arms open to the sky.

Chapter Five

Pleven

Three weeks later I started the tenth grade at the high school in Pleven. Being at such a large school made me feel as if my new life had truly begun. It seemed to me as if I were attending Harvard or Yale: There was such a great number of students, teachers and staff bustling to and fro--and everyone, it seemed, was constantly reading, or working on a math problem, or busily filling in the notes from the lecture they had just heard. I found the entire atmosphere exhilarating. And daunting, frankly. It was one thing to be a standout scholar at Slavianovo High; it was quite another to be one here, where the standards and level of expectation was so much higher.

At the school in Slavianovo, I'd been a big fish in a small pond.

Here, I was just another fish in a body of water so large I sometimes thought I might drown in it.

That said, though, I did all right. I was, after all, accustomed to studying late at night, after I was exhausted from doing all my farming chores. Here--no matter how many classes I took, or how many extracurricular activities I participated in--I still seemed to have all the time I could possibly use to study. And I certainly *did* use the bulk of my "free" time to study: If there was one thing I had learned in my life up to that point, it was that work, every time, trumps all.

Always, but *always* bet on sheer, uncompromised effort.

Log in the hours, and mountains start moving. That's been my experience, anyway.

And it certainly worked back then: Night after night I hunkered down over my books--and for my effort was rewarded with straight A's.

The truth, though, is that I could have finished the tenth grade with straight F's, and it still would have been the greatest experience of my life up till then. Because this was my first time being exposed to so many adults whose entire lives were dedicated to education. In Pordim and Slavianovo I had known a few grownups whom it was easy enough to imagine were at least a *little* like me when they were young--Dr. Haskell and our town librarian, to name but two. But here in Pleven I was being taught, every day, by a variety of adults, any one of whom I could only hope to one day, in any way, resemble myself.

These teachers of mine were inspiring role models: adults who all their lives had been as smart as I, and who had worked as hard as I ever had at becoming as educated as they were. And they were now being as generous and sincerely dedicated as they could be to passing their knowledge along to us students.

For the first time, I was in an environment dominated by people who clearly believed that acquiring, processing, and using knowledge didn't represent a means of any kind whatsoever: It was purely (and finally!) an end, all to itself.

In a strange and thrilling way, I felt that even though I was further from Pordim than I'd ever been in my life, I was, in some very real ways, home.

One of the teachers who had the strongest positive influence on me at that time was my French teacher, a kind, cultured and highly intelligent woman named Victoria Tzeckova. Educated in Paris, she was married to a renowned obstetrician-gynecologist, a man who was also the director of our school. For reasons I could never fathom but for which I will be eternally grateful, the Tzeckovas took a particular interest in me and my well-being. In class, Mrs. Tzeckova always took time to make sure I had thoroughly grasped her patient answers to my questions; if I needed more help, her office door was always open for what amounted to extensive private lessons. In a million different ways, Mrs. Tzeckova made it clear that my education--and not just mine, of course, but that of all her students--was the most important thing in the world to her.

The Tzeckova's care for me extended outside the classroom, too. On numerous occasions throughout my tenth grade year they invited me to their house for supper, or along with them on a trip they were taking to a museum, or out to the opera. Their home was very near the school; I considered it an honor and privilege to often help them with one project or another: planting their garden, fixing their storm door. It was, to me, the furthest thing from work: I was pleased beyond words that they thought enough of me to allow me to participate so fully in their lives.

And afterward, sitting on their front porch sipping lemonade, or in their parlor over tea, we would discuss literature, or politics, or the latest cultural trends.

And I would sip my tea or lemonade, and wonder how I had ever arrived at such a place, and come to be in the company of such people.

If my tenth grade experience in Pleven was rich, my eleventh was a veritable gold mine. One of its most exciting occurrences came at the beginning of the year, when Mrs. Tzeckova named me president of our school's Red Cross association.

"I'm extremely flattered," I said. "But why me?"

"Because you're so good at science generally," she said, "and especially at anatomy. And your background, I think, gives you a certain immunity to squeamishness relatively uncommon in boys your age: Anyone who has helped birth calves shouldn't have any trouble patching a hurt knee or icing a sprained ankle. And you're a few years older than your classmates, Luben. They look up to you. You'll be surprised at how much the Red Cross president has to do. It's a very real responsibility. I can't think of anyone who could do the job better than you."

And there it was: I was the new Red Cross president of my high school. (And Mrs. Tzeckova was right: That position *did* keep me busy. In many ways it entailed acting as the intermediary between the larger Red Cross organization and many of the schools and civic bodies throughout our region of Pleven. And she was also right about my suitability for the work: It turned out I *did* have a natural affinity for emergency preparedness and first aid administration--of all things in this world, I never found blood particularly harrowing.)

Besides my work with the Red Cross, something else happened in my life at this time that set me down the road toward becoming the doctor I eventually did. It started as I was sitting in Mrs. Tzeckova's living room one fall afternoon after school.

"Luben," she said, handing me a cup of sweetened black tea, "I invited you over here today because I wanted to talk to you about something.

As I'm guessing you know, the father of one of your classmates, Peter Zaharov, recently died in a terrible accident."

I did know. Although I was not personally acquainted with Peter, I had heard the news that about a month earlier his father, a well-respected physician, had slipped early one cold morning in the ice right outside his home, severely banging his head on the cement steps leading up to the doorway of the building that, besides his home, also served as his clinic. Suffering from severe brain hemorrhage, he had been rushed to a hospital in Sofia for surgery. Sadly, he had not survived.

"It's an awful thing," I said. "I was very saddened when I heard of it. How is the family doing?"

"Well, that's what I wanted to talk to you about, Luben. Poor Mrs. Zaharov is now, of course, left alone with her two sons. One is Peter, who like yourself is in the eleventh grade; the other, Boyan, is a few years older than he, and works as a junior accountant in the local Council of Ministers office. Mrs. Zaharov is having a difficult go of it, Luben. A terrible thing about life is that it doesn't stop for the grieving. Adding to her burdens just now is her son Peter. Do you know him, Luben?"

I said that I did not.

"Well, that's not surprising, for Peter's a very quiet boy who tends to keep to himself. There's nothing wrong with him at all; he's just a little shy. The problem is that ever since the passing of his poor father, Peter's been slipping in his schoolwork. It's become a cause of real concern for his mother, as you can imagine. The anchor of the family has gone; Mrs. Zaharov fears her youngest boy may now be floating away. And the older boy is too busy with his work to be of much help--he travels between here and Sophia quite a bit."

"Is there anything I can do to help?"

"Well, Luben, poor Mrs. Zaharov came to me the other day, and asked if I could recommend a student to her as a tutor for Peter. I am wondering if you could find it in your heart--and in your schedule, frankly, for I know how very busy you are--to be that tutor, Luben. Peter especially needs help in science and math--but I think, really, he could use a little help and encouragement in all of his subjects. You're such a good student, Luben: I know Peter would greatly benefit from an association with you."

I said that of course I would be glad to work into my schedule time to help Peter with his schoolwork.

"Very good," said Mrs. Tzeckova. "I knew I could count on you, Luben. Now here is their address," she said, writing on a piece of paper. "Is tomorrow after school---say, at four o'clock--a good time to tell Mrs. Zaharov to expect you?"

The next day, at four, I found myself standing on the very steps where Dr. Zaharov had met his terrible fate. One stupid slip on the ice--and a whole life, vanished! The thought of it put me in a sad and contemplative frame of mind as I knocked on the door of the white home, which certainly seemed large enough to accommodate living quarters for a family and a separate medical clinic.

The woman who opened the door was pale and thin, her large gray eyes ringed with sorrow. She wore a simple, full-length black dress and a black shawl about her shoulders. She looked up at me from behind her fine reddish-brown hair, which, her hand moving at almost languid speed, she moved behind one ear.

"You must be Luben," she said. Though her eyes lit up a bit with her quick smile, she seemed almost painfully shy.

"I am," I said. "I'm very glad to meet you, Mrs. Zaharov."

She moved to one side of the doorway, and invited me in.

In a large parlor nicely furnished with a large green velvet couch, a few easy chairs, a chaise lounge, and an intricately carved coffee table, Mrs. Zaharov and I spent the next hour or so discussing the sort of assistance she hoped I would be to her son.

"To be perfectly candid, I'm a little concerned about Peter," she began. "Ever since the accident, he just … he just seems so detached from everything. This is understandable, of course: I constantly find myself simply standing in front of a window staring vacantly into the street, or sitting in a chair, meaning only to stay there for a moment or two, and having I can't tell how much time go by before I realize I've been there so long it could be the following week for all I know." She stopped, and looked at me with a self-conscious smile that too soon became embarrassed sadness. Momentarily closing her eyes and then looking down toward the floor, she said, "All of us are shocked by what happened--and likely to remain so for some time." She lifted her eyes to meet mine. "I fear what's happening with Peter's schoolwork, Luben. Peter has always been a fair, if not spectacular, student. School always came easily enough for him to get passing grades with not a lot of effort, so in truth he never applied himself as he might have. But now that he seems to have given up on it altogether, I worry that before too long I'll have to decide to either hold him back a grade--which I don't want to do because Lord knows the boy does not need another setback in his life--or, much worse, pull him out of school altogether until we can figure out how best to proceed. The kind of marks he's getting now will seriously compromise his future--of that there can be no doubt.

"And then it occurred to me that perhaps a tutor would help: some-one to get his wheels back in motion, as it were--someone to at least help him catch up to where he should be--particularly in math and science, where he's always struggled a bit. So I asked Peter if he would be amena-ble to the idea of my finding someone to help him with his schoolwork, and was very grateful indeed to hear that he was not, at least, against it. So I asked Victoria--Mrs. Tzeckova--for a recommendation."

Mrs. Zaharov looked at me with a kind of hopeful resignation.

"And here you are," she said.

I smiled and nodded. There I was.

The next evening I had dinner at the Zaharov household in order for Peter and I to get acquainted. The eldest son was away overnight in Sophia: Present in the house that night were only Mrs. Zaharov, Peter, myself, and the two kindly middle-aged female housekeepers--sisters, I was told--who prepared the meal and brought it to the table.

Although upon seeing Peter I recognized him, I was not able to place him in any specific social or academic context; I couldn't remember ex-actly where I'd seen him, or with whom. Perhaps I had only passed him in a school hallway or a class; perhaps we tended to associate with people who tended not to associate with one another. He was a slight boy, a head shorter than I, thin and pale like his mother, but with dark eyes and unkempt, limp black hair. The skin on his face was as white and smooth as milk. His lips were the bright reddish hue you sometimes see in people with that almost luminous white skin, and he had dark circles beneath his eyes. He seemed, naturally enough, withdrawn, and sad.

Upon his mother introducing us we shook hands. Peter's was soft, cool, and almost alarmingly weak.

"I recognize you from school," I said, keeping his hand in mine. "I'm glad to finally make your acquaintance, Peter."

He looked up at me with his mournful brown eyes, shrugged and said, "Oh--yeah, me, too." We released hands.

"I met Luben through Mrs. Tzeckova," said Mrs. Zaharov "She speaks very highly of him."

Looking away, Peter nodded. He didn't seem inclined to pay much attention to either me or his mother. And possibly not to anything else in the world, either.

Naturally enough, in the course of the meal the three of us skidded into some long, awkward pauses in our conversation. Because it is not in my nature to spend too very long pretending, or to not at least in some way acknowledge a truth which is obvious to everyone present, fairly early into our meal I made bold to say, "Peter, I want to tell you how deeply saddened I was to hear about your father. It's an unthinkable tragedy. You have the truly heartfelt sympathy of me and every one of the students at our school. If there's ever anything any one of us can ever do for you, please do not hesitate to ask. We all want to help--yet know there's nothing we can really do." I shook my head, suddenly out of words. "I'm just ... I'm just so terribly sorry for your loss, my friend."

I glanced at Peter's mother, who, her soupspoon frozen halfway to her mouth, was looking at me with an expression the precise emotion of which was not readily apparent. Fear, maybe. Shock. Wonderment. Gratitude.

Peter fixed me with his bottomless eyes.

"Are we friends?" he said.

"Peter!" said his mother. It was a chastisement, but one softly issued. The boy instantly looked sorry for what he said--almost confused, in fact, that he'd said it at all. It was clear the question had burst forth from the deep tension and grief within him.

"No--you're right, I said. "We're not friends, Peter. But I would like very much to be friends with you. I don't have many friends--and I could certainly use another." I looked at his mother, who was smiling sadly at me. With my eyes on hers I said, "I could at least help you with your homework," and then looked back at him. "I understand you've fallen behind a bit. I feel as if I'm always behind on my homework." I shrugged. "Maybe together we can manage not to get kicked out of school."

Over the next month I developed a real affection for Peter. At first he seemed almost unaware that three times a week I was with him in his bedroom or the family den, presenting him with a math problem he'd had in class that day, or endeavoring to draw him out concerning the intricacies of a science project his class was studying. He didn't seem to in any way resent my being there; it didn't seem to affect him one way or the other. From all I could tell, as far as he was concerned I might just as well have been the coalman come to shovel coal, or a soft-spoken lunatic who had snuck into his house to wash up and shower, and then sought to engage in a little intellectual stimulation before heading back out to the streets again. Peter was lost inside what I assumed was his profound sorrow over the sudden loss of his father--and there wasn't much, if anything, that I, a strange boy his own age, could do to make him feel better.

But, of course, I persisted in trying anyway. Peter was a gentle, kind soul whom I genuinely desired to help. And he was, in fact, doing very poorly in school; I confidentially spoke with each of his teachers, and each shared with me their concern about the downward spiraling of his grades.

Although Peter and I seemed to get along well--insofar as we interacted in anything one could call a "normal" way--I knew that I wasn't helping him in the way his dear mother had hoped I would.

One afternoon, when he and I were sitting together on the settee in the parlor in which I'd first met his mother, I closed his math book after what had come to pass as one of our "lessons," and rather suddenly blurted out: "Peter, please listen to me." He immediately fixed me with his bottomless eyes. "I'm concerned about you, my friend. If you don't in some way begin to take an interest in your schoolwork, it's inevitable that you're going to flunk out of the eleventh grade. This is, of course, none of my business. But I want to tell you something, Peter. I like you. And I like your mother. And so I feel that it really *is* some of my business how you do in school--especially given that your mother has asked me to help you with that very thing."

Peter fixed me with his gaze. "I don't care about school," he said in a soft, matter-of-fact tone.

"I know you don't, Peter," I said, in his own gentle tone. "And I don't blame you. If I lost my father the way you lost yours, I wouldn't care about school either. I wouldn't care about anything. Nobody can fault you for that. Nobody ever will. But listen to me, Peter. Your mother is suffering. It's an insult for me to even say it, but she lost her husband--the man she thought she'd spend the rest of her life loving and being loved by."

He quickly rose and turned away from me; he began busying himself by moving about some decorative items atop a bureau.

"I'm sorry, Peter. Forgive me. I shouldn't have said anything."

He stopped moving his hands; indeed, his whole body froze. I waited and watched his back as he held perfectly still. As quietly as possible, I began to gather my things from the coffee table.

I heard him say, "No. Go on," and saw that he had turned to face me again.

I let go of my things, sighed, and with my shoulders hunched slightly forward in position of nervousness began slowly running my hands along my legs from the middle of my thighs toward my knees.

"It's just that ... you're in a terrible time, Peter. You've lost your father. Your brother has lost his father. Your mother has lost her husband. The whole town has lost a dear physician. These things aren't supposed to happen." I paused, and looked down at the hands in my lap. Then I looked up at him again. "But there it is. It's happened. And I think of you as a friend, Peter, and please believe that it is only as a friend that I say this. But now, more than ever, you must succeed. Your mother's life has crumbled. You are the only son--the only *man*--left in the home. Only you know your own pain, Peter. The rest of us can only watch it, and wonder at it. No one would blame you for sinking."

And here I began to convey an emotion I can only describe as angry.

"But don't," I nearly hissed. "This is what I'm saying, Peter: Don't sink. Don't let this absurd accident that snatched away your father ruin so much of what he built in this world. Then death *keeps* winning. Screw that. *Screw* that! Like it, don't like it, rail against it, recoil from it--it doesn't matter what you or anyone else thinks of it, or how you or anyone else looks at, the fact is that you're now the man of this household, Peter. Your mother needs you like she's probably never needed anyone in her life. You have *got* to be strong for her. You've got to be strong for your brother. You've got to be strong for your teachers. In a sense, you've got to be strong for *all* of us now, Peter."

"I can't," he whispered.

"That's right," I said. "You can't. You can't go on as if nothing happened; you can't do more now that you have so much less. Nobody would argue with that. But Peter, my friend, listen. There is one extremely simple, small, completely doable thing that there is no doubt in the world you *can* do."

He looked at me as if nearly desperate to find out what that thing was.

"You can do well in school," I said. "That's all. You can do well in school. And, to be perfectly honest, you don't even have to do *well* in school--you only have to start doing better."

He turned his head and body quickly away from me, back to the bureau. "I don't care about school," he said.

"Because you're spoiled," I said. Peter turned back to me, hurt and anger playing on his face. "You are. And it's not your fault. You don't have any reason to think of education as anything but a social nicety, almost--just a thing you have because it looks pretty, or makes you feel good, or is just ... something people of your class have."

"But ..."

"No. What I'm saying is true. Your education cost you nothing: There was never any doubt that you would finish high school and go on to university. Why should you value what you never earned? You cannot; no human can. To you, an education is just another plate full of food on the table: you may eat a little of it; you may pick at it and move onto something else; you may take some and just move it around on your plate until your housekeeper removes that plate and brings you dessert. It doesn't *matter* to you. And maybe before, when you're good father was alive, it didn't really need to. Because in the back of your mind, you always knew what was true: that he would take care of you for as long as that was necessary.

But the terrible truth of your life, Peter, is that it just changed. You have been forced into a different game altogether. And even though it pains me to be so direct about saying it, you're still imagining you're in the old game. You're still imagining--and let me say it's understandable that you are: Grief puts blinders on everyone--that someone, somehow, is going to take care of you.

"But they won't, Peter. Your father is *gone*. His *money* is gone, Peter. Your mother and your brother and you will of course get along for awhile on whatever you have saved and whatnot, but if you flunk out of school,

Peter, or are even held back a grade, that's going to create for you a reality I guarantee you'll like a whole lot less than you're liking the one you're in right now.

"Listen to me, Peter. I come from a small farm out in the middle of nowhere. You do *not* want to be poor. You do *not* want to be dependent for your sustenance upon whatever the ground pushes up for you to chew on, or upon a kicking, squealing animal you have to kill, drain, gut and cut up into pieces. Look how clean you are! To you hot water is nothing; to me it is still a freakish luxury--I can barely stand to part with water I've used that's still a little warm! Look at your clothes! You have different pairs of shoes for different occasions! You don't wear the same shoes to church that you wear out in the fields that you wear at night to keep your feet warm! For church you have one pair; for school you have another. And you have slippers! Slippers! Little soft shoes with no other purpose than to wear around the house! And look at this house, Peter! Just look at it! It's magnificent! If it rains, you don't find out where the leaks in your roof are. You don't stuff cracks in your house with mud to keep the cold wind out. You don't have to leave your warm bed to go out in the snow if you want to pee in the middle of the night. *We lost a whole wall of our house one time when a pair of fighting bulls ran into it!*"

I was yelling now. I could feel the redness in my face. It felt like the top of my head had floated away somewhere. Peter was looking at me with ... well, with the expression a person might make if they knew they had just stepped in something revolting, and were already at the end of the time they could legitimately pretend to ignore it.

"Oh, God, Peter," I said, "I'm so sorry. I'm so terribly sorry. Here I am, raving at you about the nightmares of bad weather." I suddenly found I couldn't stop my emotions from getting the better of me: I began to cry.

"No," said Peter. He moved quickly to sit beside me. "Don't cry, Luben. What you are saying is true."

"I can't stand what's happened to you," I said. "I can't stand what's happened to your father. If I lost my father the way you lost yours, I ... ." I shrugged futilely. "I don't know what I'd do."

After a time of Peter and I sitting quietly in the dimming haze of the late afternoon, I said softly, "I worry about you, Peter. If you drop out of school, I fear for the future of your family. Without a high school education you'll get some job--someone, knowing your history, will work out some position for you--but it won't be enough to keep your mother and you living the way you're used to. You'll have to move from this house. You'll be trapped in some employment unsuitable for a person of your intelligence, and instead of growing old in the home in which she knew your father and raised you and Boyan, your mother will be forced to live ... somewhere else. Somewhere less comforting to her. Away from ..." I looked about me. "This.

"It's going to happen, Peter. Your teachers care for you, and of course the idea of increasing the suffering of you or your family appalls them, but what can they do? You're not doing the work. They can't let you pass the eleventh grade; they know it means you'll get buried in the twelfth. They're in an awful position.

"You've got to do better in school, Peter. That's all. You don't have to be strong, and you don't have to be anyone's hero, and you don't have to perform any miracles. You simply have to do better in school. You do your homework, every night, and nothing more in your life will fall apart. If you don't, what's *left* in your life will begin to unravel. It doesn't matter how you, or I, or your mother, or Boyan, or your teachers feel about that: That is what will happen. Things will get worse. It can't *not* happen.

"If you do your homework, things will at least remain the way they are. And for your family, right now, that's a wonderful thing. If you cause that to happen, you will be a hero--to your mother, to your brother, to your teachers, to me. Everyone knows how you're hurting. You pull out of this nosedive you've gone into at school, and ... and I believe they'll hold a parade for you right through downtown."

Peter smiled wanly. "I'm afraid it's too late for me, Luben," he said. "I'm quite sure I've fallen too far behind in school to catch up now."

"No," I said with a sharpness that caused him to jerk back a bit. I looked him dead in the eye. "No. You're mistaken about that. I studied for and passed the tenth grade exam *while* I was in the ninth grade. If you're too sad to go on, I cannot help you. But you tell me you *want* to catch up with your schoolwork, and I *guarantee* you: You'll get caught up. This is nothing. You're ... what: six weeks behind? That's *nothing*, Peter. I know more about how to study, and how to catch up to school-work, than I know about ... repairing cow-damaged walls."

Peter seemed to collapse into his laughter--and this is where I learned the literal meaning of the phrase "laugh until you cry." I put my arm around Peter's shoulders, and he fell against me, heaving great, choking sobs. It made me feel that perhaps he had not cried since the terrible accident.

While he was lost in his pain against my chest, my eyes met the teary eyes of his mother, who was standing with one hand pressed tightly against her mouth just inside the doorway between the parlor and the entrance hall. Apparently she had been there for a while. Though I could see that she was teetering on the near desperate edge of grief, I saw that she was also, almost imperceptibly, nodding.

A few days later Mrs. Zaharov offered me room and board in her home in exchange for my continued tutoring of Peter. That very night I moved my few belongings into her guest bedroom: Her kind offer represented substantial savings for my father and I over the room I had been renting.

A few days after that it was clear enough that Peter would, after all, pull out of his slump at school. The change in him was apparent very soon after our time together in the parlor. Once I took up residence in his house, he and I would study for hour after hour in his room or mine, every night after supper.

Sometimes, if Peter was tired of studying but about to reapply himself to his books anyway, he would mutter, "Don't want any cows stumbling through the dining room," or "Saw a bull leaning against the side of the house yesterday. Better study up."

Whatever motivated him, Peter proved to be a quick learner, and a good student. The very many people who knew and cared about the Zaharov family were deeply gratified to learn that not only was Peter catching up in his studies, he was excelling. It was impossible to know his story, and not in some way feel encouraged yourself.

The building in which the Zaharov family lived had two floors. The first comprised the family's living quarters and the two-room office from which Dr. Zaharov ran his medical practice; the floor above held about a dozen beds and served as a kind of hospital for those patients the doctor wanted to keep under his watch for a day or two before being releasing them. This floor was now, of course, empty. I went up into this area a few times, and tried to imagine the doctor tending to the patients who once lie on the beds now perfectly made up, and perfectly empty.

The second floor of the Zaharov house still strikes me as being as lonely and haunting as any place I've ever been. Before Dr. Zaharov's death, life in his second-story clinic was constantly and vigorously trying to reassert itself, to gain the upper hand on whatever was seeking to thwart its progress. And now that death had forever snatched away the leader of that righteous effort, the place seemed eternally suspended in a complete expression of the silent, knowing moment that exists between hope and loss, between life and its opposite.

And on the floor below it, life forged ahead.

Early one evening I noticed the door leading to Dr. Zaharov's office was slightly ajar. It never was: As far as I knew, it had remained closed since the terrible accident. I approached it. Everywhere the house was silent; I believed Mrs. Zaharov to be just then back in the kitchen with her housekeepers. The office door was dark and heavy, its wood polished to a dull gleam; its brass knob was ornate, and stoic-seeming. I took the knob and began to pull the door closed; I assumed it had been inadvertently opened by the wind, or something of that nature. The door was just about shut again when I heard Mrs. Zaharov's voice from inside the room.

"Hello?" she said.

I slowly pushed the door open just enough to see around it. "It's me, Luben," I said. I saw a man's classic study: full, wall-to-wall, ceiling-high bookcases; a thick, Turkish rug nearly the size of the floor; two polished leather easy chairs with a reading lamp between them; a dark maroon leather couch; a large wooden desk piled high with books.

Mrs. Zaharov was sitting upon one of the easy chairs, her hands clasped together on her lap. The chair seemed imposing large around her. I saw she was not reading, or sewing, or doing anything at all but quietly sitting. The room's only illumination came through a window near the desk that looked out onto the street; the pair of crème-colored inner curtains that covered it infused the room with a soft, pale cast.

"Come in, Luben, please," she said. As I moved into the doctor's study, she said, "Do you know, I haven't been in here since he died?"

With my eyes on hers I nodded slightly. I felt awkward; I'd come in, I knew, at a profoundly personal moment. I looked away from her, and began to take in the room. The closest to anything I'd ever seen like it was my beloved library in Pordim.

"It's a ..." I looked around, and lost my words. "It's ... awe-inspiring."

"It is, isn't it?" she said. "That's just the right word for it. Thank you." She moved her gaze slowly across the room. "I've not spent very much time in here at all. This is where he studied, and came to think about things. It was just ... his."

Silence filled the room.

"It's the books," I said.

"I'm sorry?"

I immediately regretted I'd said anything, that I'd intruded upon the reverent silence--much less upon Mrs. Zaharov's communion with the soul of her husband. I needed to gracefully exit the room--and had instead blurted out a random, inane comment.

"It was nothing," I said. "Please forgive me."

"No, Luben" she said warmly. "Tell me what you said."

"I only meant to say that what's so ... striking about the room is the number of books it contains. I've never dreamed of so many books in a single room."

Again the room became silent. I stole a glance at Mrs. Zaharov--hoping, I suppose, to see some evidence that my insipid chattering was forgotten. She was looking about the high shelves of the room. "It really is remarkable," she said softly. "He so loved his books. He read for hours, every night. Besides the practice of medicine, it was his greatest passion."

So deeply did I share this passion for books and reading that answering her or referring to that passion at all--particularly in this circumstance, in this room--seemed too much. I remained silent.

"Luben," said Mrs. Zaharov, "Please come sit here beside me." I crossed the room and took a seat in the other leather easy chair. "Luben," she said, "I want you to listen to me." I locked my eyes onto hers. "These books are yours to read whenever you want. The doctor had a great love of learning. It's no mystery that you share that love, Luben. And by the grace of God you have seen the way to sharing that love with Peter--and now he, too, possesses it. When the doctor was alive no one but him ever came in this room. There is no question but that, now that he is gone, this room should be open to those members of his family who wish to partake of the great feast of knowledge waiting to be had inside these walls. I'm not sure it's fair to restrict access to this room only to family members--but we'll start there for now, won't we?" Her smile was positively beatific.

No words that worked came to mind.

"Mrs. Zaharov," I finally began, "I'm honored that you would think to allow me to--"

She lifted her fingers off her lap. "Please, Luben," she said. "You are and always will be a member of this family. Peter looks up to you; Boyan is grateful to you; and I hardly know how to begin telling you what you have meant to me. You're like an angel to this family." She looked around the room. "Who better to share these books with than you? Nothing would please me more--and nothing, I know, would please my husband more--than if you and Peter began using this as your study."

She looked about the room again.

"So much learning has taken place in this room," she said. "It should go on."

It was in Dr. Zaharov's library that I felt the irresistible pull of medicine. Time and again, I would find myself drawn to the doctor's great number of medical books, unable to resist the powerful allure of discovering exactly how, for example, the leg bone's connected to the thigh bone. The human body is surely God's most wondrous creation; amongst the books of the doctor's library seemed to lay the keys to unlocking the workings of that wonder. I didn't know how long it would be before I would ever again have such open access to so many books; it is, in the balance, fair to say that I took advantage of Mrs. Zaharov's kind offer to use her husband's library. And I know that this pleased her.

I was pleased when later that year one of my teachers, Mrs. Zacharoff, told me that, as the president of our school's Red Cross organization, I'd naturally been chosen to represent our school at a special one-month camp the Red Cross was going to run throughout the upcoming August for its campus representatives from high schools all across Bulgaria.

The camp was to be held in Banki, a resort village about twenty-five miles north of the Bulgarian capital of Sofia. When I heard of this, my breath caught in my throat.

First Pleven! Now this!

It was almost too much to bear. For quite a while now my world had been expanding on what seemed like an almost daily basis. But it had never, in one fell swoop, grown with the exponential power it would if I went to a special, one-month camp so far from home--where I would be surrounded by the best students from high schools all across the country!

I didn't even try to imagine what such an experience would be like; I knew I couldn't.

And yet I couldn't, of course, stop my mind from trying, anyway.

I saw the pain it caused my father when I told him about the camp. Not only would transportation to and from Banki be expensive (everything else, though, was paid for!), it meant losing my labor during the critical last month of summer, when everything must be prepared for the upcoming harvest.

"But I'll be back at the very start of September," I pleaded. "And I'll cut back a little on my studies at the beginning of grade twelve, to make sure everything gets done here. You'll see, Father. It will work out."

Finally, he said, "All right. Go. Of course--go. My son, parading about the famous resort town of Banki, known throughout the world for its mineral baths! His arthritis will be cured! His heart disease--gone! His skin--like a baby's bottom! What a strong worker Luben will be when he returns to us after this month of soaking with the rich!"

My father, the comedian.

In truth, I did expect Red Cross camp to be a bit of a vacation. The wealthy and social elite really *did*, after all, go to Banki to soak and forget the worries that then (if not now, for that matter) I couldn't imagine having in the first place. But instead of any sort of junior-level spa and resort, Camp Banki--comprising about 100 tents erected on a green grass plain--turned out to be decidedly more like a combination school and military camp.

This was, let us not forget, August of 1939. Already Hitler was in Austria, Czechoslovakia and Poland. On September 1, Hitler, with his massive invasion of Poland, would let the world know his intentions and purpose.

And the Red Cross, tending to its own concerns relative to the challenges so clearly visible ahead, thought it might be a good idea to teach young leaders from across Bulgaria all it could about things like how to help average citizens respond to and defend against, say, gas warfare.

So we learned how to quickly don and use the heavy and awkward gas masks--and how to strap them onto the heads of strangers, too, and get them used to using them, but quick.

"Before attempting to help anyone else," we were told, "first be sure that your own gas mask is secure and functioning properly. It is not advisable to begin assisting another person until you are certain that you yourself are safe."

Not bad advice generally, I suppose.

The regime at Camp Banki was certainly reflective of a mentality concerned with wartime preparation: up at six; breakfast; physical exercise; lectures beginning at nine o'clock; break at noon; lectures and demonstrations again from two to four o'clock.

So, actually, we had a two-hour break at noon, and then were off every day at four.

And I have to say what we all kept saying: the food was *outstanding*.

So in a way it *was* like a vacation, after all!

And in a way it wasn't, too. One little dynamic that worked itself out at Camp Banki proved to be a microcosmic presaging of the whole of World War II. At the commons one morning after breakfast, the director of the camp announced that on the following day a group called Hitler Youth from Germany would be coming to our camp to stay for a week. The next day a busload of scrubbed young men arrived, wearing their black shorts and brown shirts with the swastika on the sleeve. They did not speak Bulgarian; we did not speak German.

The one language we all understood, though, was the universal language of aggressive assertiveness. This was heard very clearly throughout our camp the first morning after the arrival of the Hitler Youth, when they arose quite early in the morning, and made a point of running their flag up the camp's only flagpole--the same one we'd been running our Bulgarian flag up every morning. Throughout the course of that first day, there was nothing for it but to allow the Bulgarian flag to fly beneath the German.

That evening, furious at this "Teutonic impertinence," the director of Camp Banki instructed some of us to get up before *anyone* else the next morning, and run the Bulgarian flag up the pole first.

The Germans got the hint: From the second day onward their flag, after its ill-gained, short-lived reign atop ours, became, again, the lesser flag.

Another event occurred during my month at Camp Banki that wasn't in any overt sense dramatic or earth shattering--but that for me was nonetheless profoundly significant. I happened to be manning the camp's first aide station when a boy who had been outside playing lurched up the steps of the little cabin and burst into the room, clasping the bleeding index finger of one hand with such fervor it was as if he feared the thing might at any moment leap to the floor and get away. I calmed him down, and then cleaned and put iodine and a bandage on his cut; realizing it was nothing to be concerned about after all, he then smiled broadly, profusely praised me, and then happily ran off to rejoin his friends in whatever fun they had been having.

Watching that boy leave--seeing the wholesale transformation that took place in his attitude and mien between the time he burst into the office and the time he bounded back out of it again--suddenly brought my entire life into very sharp focus.

At that moment, I knew what I'd certainly suspected during my many hours pouring over Dr. Zaharov's medical texts: I was born to be a physician.

Because of me--because of my calmness, and the almost weird way I have of being able to detach myself from the immediate emotionality of pain and concentrate simply upon its physical manifestations and implications--that boy's life has been very quickly, and very significantly, enhanced.

And do you know what? It felt good being the one who worked that little miracle of healing. It felt *really* good.

It sounds too supercilious to even say, but the truth that at that moment settled over me like a warm blanket was that I was born to heal people's bodies when something had injured or in some way gone awry with them.

This wholly unexpected realization of the purpose and fate for which I was put on earth did not in any way make me feel exalted or specially gifted, or anything along those lines at all.

What it made me feel was humble.

People's bodies were designed to be naturally healthy. When something interfered with that God-given state of physical equilibrium, *other* people could get involved, and set things right again--or come as close to it as humanely possible.

I wanted to *be* one of those other people.

I already *was* one of those people!

The rest was just a matter of getting the education it would take to bridge the gap between where I was, and where I was now absolutely sure that I was headed.

Understanding this fundamental truth about my life and future brought me a feeling that was at once excitement and peace: it was as if I were a train that had always been driving at full force, violently plowing through farmlands, over fields, across rivers, into forests--and now, finally, had dropped onto its proper track, and for the first time was running smoothly, and in control. It was a wonderful feeling.

To this day, whenever a young person asks me for almost any kind of advice about their life, I almost always tell them, "Discover what you want to do with your life. Choose a path--or, better, find the one that's waiting to choose you. But put in the time it takes to discover, once and for all, God's purpose for your life. And then bend your will to accomplish that purpose. Without that solid, inspiring grounding, you can only float through your life. But with it, you know who you are, what you're doing, and where you're going. Then you have done the impossible: You have put yourself in control of life. Even better: You have made a *partner* of life. For nothing in this world is more true than that once you start moving toward the place God intended you to go, life begins to *help* you get there: Opportunities arise from thin air; doors you never knew existed suddenly fly open. Discovering and deciding what you're going to *do* with your life is the only sure way to stop fighting life, and to start befriending it."

Our month of distinctly *un*resort-like camping passed quickly enough, and it wasn't long until I was back on our farm, doing my best to make good on my promise to my father that upon my return I'd make up the difference in the work I *should* have been doing the month I was away. Balancing that account was, of course, impossible--but no one could say I didn't try.

And doing so definitely reconfirmed for me what an outstanding idea it was to become a doctor, rather than remain a farmer.

The following school year--the twelfth, my last of high school--passed quickly enough: nothing, but nothing, gobbles up time like constant studying. I also stayed active in various cultural and professional organizations--always steering clear of anything having to do with politics. Many of my friends and associates at that time were sympathizing with Hitler and the Nazis; I never hesitated (none of has had any reason to, yet) to say I was against them both. It was amazing to me that anyone could approve of Hitler's invasion of his neighbors, of his outrageous declaration of war against Poland. I believed he was manifestly insane: Who else would dare to provoke into a war France, England and the United States? How could Germany hope to prove victorious over such enemies?

On July 13, 1940, I graduated from high school, and turned my eyes out onto the world.

Chapter Six

Calling Dr. Walchef

What I wanted to see upon graduating high school was a medical school beckoning me with open arms (and, frankly, an open wallet). What I found instead, of all things, was the language of *Latin* insisting I stop by and visit for a while: It turned out that no medical school would even consider me unless I passed a Latin exam I never even knew existed.

I would like to say, "So, just like that, I learned Latin." And that is, actually, true--but only if for "just like that," you substitute, "I found a Latin tutor who would teach me for almost no money and bled my brains out studying with him every night for about half a year before I passed that stupid Latin exam."

Actually, I was pleased to learn that ancient language. I knew how likely it was that my studies would take me through Europe: Latin is about as close to the language of "European" as one can get. Not a bad item to have in one's bag of traveling tricks.

Armed with my Latin certificate, I then applied to the Sofia Medical School, at that time the only such college in all of Bulgaria. It was a relatively small institution that accepted only about one hundred twenty new students each year. I could barely imagine that I would fail to be counted among that number for the upcoming semester. After all, I'd been the president of my senior class! I was Ruler of All Things Red Cross on my campus! I was (very nearly: I never was fully able to grasp the intricacies of Russian) a straight "A" student!

I'd been manager of the *school cafeteria,* for goodness' sakes! (Oh, you scoff now. But at my high school, guess whom you had to come see if you wanted that extra piece of cherry pie, or that little cup of sugar to take

back to your room? If you'd missed lunch because you were off gallivanting around downtown Pleven and now realized you'd have to starve until
dinner, whom did you know you had better track down? That's right:
Kitchen Master Luben.)

I was sure I'd be admitted to the Sofia Medical School. My academic
and extracurricular resume had too much going for it for me to be refused.

Except, as it turned out, what it *didn't* have on it, anywhere, were the
words, "Son of a High-Level Government Official," or "Son of a Wealthy
Landowner," or "Brother of an Army General," or … well, you get the
idea.

"Yes, of course they rejected you," said my ex-French teacher, Mrs.
Tzeckova. "That school is where the wealthy send their children to see if
they would like to study medicine. Admissions there are given out like
prizes from the elite to the elite."

So, as it turned out, I couldn't compete after all.

After I got my rejection letter from the Sophia Medical School, my
father found me out in the barn, squatted down in a corner with the letter in my hands, losing my struggle not to cry.

He put his hand on my shoulder. "Son," he said, "It's not the end
of the world. There are other medical colleges in the world. Think about
it: The school in Sophia is clearly uninterested in forging doctors from
the best young minds it can find. That leaves no doubt but that you'd
receive a second-rate education there. It isn't that you're not good enough
for them; it's that *they're* not good enough for you. You haven't studied
as hard as you have to now receive anything less than a top-notch education.

"Let me ask you this," he continued. "If, knowing what you now
know about how the hallowed Sophia Medical School chooses its students, would you want a doctor who graduated from there operating on
you?"

Through my tears I smiled at my father.

It sure was hard to argue with that kind of logic.

The next day I went to the Pordim library, and began researching
other medical schools to which I might apply.

One day soon afterward I was back in Pleven, visiting with some of
my erstwhile high school friends, when I met a young lady who had graduated the same year as I. She very nearly knocked my socks off by telling

me that she had just been accepted to a medical school in Germany. This impressed and excited me, not only because Germany was known for the quality of its medical colleges, but because the research I'd done thus far had me believing it was nearly impossible to get accepted into a medical school outside of one's own country: All colleges, I thought, admitted only native students, people who spoke their language and, if nothing else, could actually *read* through the mountains of paperwork simply applying for medical school entailed.

"How did you do it?" I cried. "Please tell me!"

"Well," she said, "there is a man who is staying at our house named Dr. Otto Kaiser."

"*Otto Kaiser?*" I said. "Wait, let me guess. He's Italian. No, wait! Chinese! He's Chinese!"

"No," she laughed, "he is a German. He works with the cultural attaché corps translating letters and documents between government officials in Germany and Bulgaria; he's fluent in both languages. When he heard that I wanted to apply to a medical school in Germany, he was extremely gracious about assisting me. He knows everything there is to know about such matters. In a matter of weeks I was accepted to the first school I applied to."

"Do you think he would help me do the same?" I blurted.

"I don't see why not," said my new savior. "If you'd like, we could go home right now, and I could introduce you to him. I'm quite sure he's there."

I looked gratefully toward the sky. If someone up there was watching out for me, they were doing one heck of a splendid job at it.

Trying not to sound insane with desperation, I said, "If you're sure that wouldn't be too much trouble to you, your family, or to Dr. Kaiser, I would appreciate that very much."

"Not at all," she said. "Let's be on our way, then."

My heart was beating so fast in my chest I could barely walk--much less carry on a casual, easy, not-going-to-where-your-every-last-dream-might-come-true sort of conversation.

But I did all right, I suppose--and before too long we arrived at the young lady's home.

Just before we stepped inside, my new friend turned to me, and said, "My father is a priest in the Orthodox Church. So he can seem a little .... well, you'll see."

The moment I saw her towering, dour-looking father, I thought the word she must have been searching for was "extremely frightening."

Except, not really. He was a *serious* man, that much was clear; but when he heard what I was there for he seemed to immediately lose interest in me, and his daughter and I proceeded up a flight of stairs and down a hallway to a shut door.

"Dr. Kaiser?" she said, tapping on the door and leaning into it a bit. "Are you in?"

The doctor was, indeed, in--and was more then willing to see us now.

The young lady introduced me to him, and then said, "Well, let me leave you two alone to get acquainted, while I go down and help mother with dinner."

And then I was alone with Dr. Otto Kaiser in his bedroom inside the home of a young lady whom I wouldn't have known from Eve a half hour before.

A bald, bespectacled man who radiated good health and cheer, Dr. Kaiser was as friendly and willing to help as any man could be. After I had told him a bit about myself and my situation, he readily suggested that I apply to a medical school in Wurzburg, a venerable old city in the northern part of the German state of Bavaria.

"It's a wonderful medical school," he said. "One of the best in the country. It won't be any trouble to secure from them an application for admission. In the meantime, bring me your high school diploma, your birth certificate, and two letters of recommendation. I will translate these and a few other documents you'll need into German; then together we will fill out the application; and then we'll make sure that it gets into the right hands! This will all go as smooth as butter!"

I did everything the good doctor told me to--and then, unbelievably enough, three weeks later, in the middle of August, I received a letter informing me that I had been accepted for admission to the University of Wurzburg: I was, it said, to report to the school that January for the beginning of the winter semester.

I leapt for joy.

I cried from relief and excitement.

I ran about the barn, whooping and hollering and doing an exceedingly thorough job of disturbing our horses.

And then I stopped all that, got myself together, and headed for the library, where I checked out some books on how to speak and write German.

Being accepted to medical school was one thing; being able to actually *afford* going to medical school was another thing altogether. I'd been invited to run a million dollar marathon--but couldn't afford shoes.

"I'm proud beyond anything I can tell you," said my father, "to have a son who has been accepted into a medical college. But I feel a bit like a man with no shovel who's been told where a secret treasure is buried. How can we *get* to this great thing? How in the world can we afford to send you to medical school? As you know, Luben, we can barely afford to bleed, much less educate a doctor."

"How did we afford to send me to high school in Pleven?" I replied. "How did I attend two years of high school at the same time? I'll make it work. I'll get a job. I'll work and study, same as I've always done. It won't be any different."

"Except you don't speak German, Luben. That doesn't exactly look good on your applications for German jobs! And medical school isn't like high school. You're going to need more time to study than you'll have if you're also holding down a job that makes you enough to live between tests. I can help you a little, but not nearly enough. You know our situation here. We're not exactly storing away barrels of money in our cellar."

It was my ever-supportive grandfather who suggested a way by which the Walchef family of Pordim, Bulgaria, might send one of their own to medical school in Germany.

"We'll sell the old home!" he declared. "The one you were born in, Luben! That home gave you your first start--and now it will give you your second!"

"But that's your home, Grandpa." I said. "You can't sell that. It's too much. But thank you."

"Nonsense!" he cried. "What does an old man need with two homes? I can only live in one. Besides, your uncle and stepson are still living there. They need a home to call their own, too. What better place for them than the one in which they've already been living for so long?"

When my uncle heard the idea, he slapped his hands down on the course wooden dinner table before him. "Of course we will buy this house," he said with his characteristically robust resolution. "Then my son and I will own our own home, and Luben can go to Germany and become a famous doctor! It is the perfect plan! Yes! It is done!"

It was my uncle's stepson--by now doing very well with the market he owned in downtown Pordim--who actually put up the money for the sale of the house. Being a generous, good man, he insisted on paying more than a fair market price for the place he had called home all his life.

And that was that: I was going to medical school. I wasn't exactly flying there first class in one of my new silk suits--but I was going. It was enough to get me started. I was confident--in a way, perhaps, that only the young can be--that, once there, I would find a way to keep going what my dear family had managed to begin.

As the summer moved into fall, I began eagerly awaiting the beginning of my new life in January. I tried to imagine what things would be like in a foreign country: what they ate there, how they dressed, what they did for recreation. I found the contemplation of such matters both exhilarating and intimidating. And, needless to say, I did not find exactly comforting the fact that the country in which I'd soon be living was led by a manifest madman who seemed bent on dominating the world. I couldn't help but imagine Germany as an entire country of people who wore stubby little black mustaches, and screamed whenever they spoke. Housewives, old men, children, dogs: all with little mustaches, all screaming like maniacs. That fantasy, of course, never lasted long, but I certainly did wonder to what extent everyone in Germany support Nazism. Did they all? Was such a thing possible? Had Hitler somehow managed to brainwash an entire country of people?

Well, I found it easy enough to put such concerns out of my mind. Strange people; strange ways; strange ideas; distant lands. None of it mattered. What mattered is that I was going to medical school. Everything else was something that in a very, very fundamental way did not concern me at all.

And then something happened which could not possibly have concerned me more.

It was September 24, 1940, around noon. I was on our front porch, just sitting there thinking about one thing or another, when I heard a loud thump coming from inside the house. I turned, and saw through the open front door my mother, who had been descending the stairs and was now stopped about half way down them. She was hanging onto the stair's railings with a kind of swaying desperation that told me something was terribly wrong. When I rushed to her side she looked into my face with an expression that said she had no idea what was happening to her--but that, whatever it was, it was bad. Supporting her, I guided her down the stairs, and then out into the front yard, so that she could lie down on the cot beneath the walnut tree where my father took his breaks.

"What's wrong, Mother?" I said, keeping my voice calm as she lied down. "What is it?"

She could not answer, though: she was incapable of doing anything but murmuring and moaning a little.

"Shh, shh," I said. "Just rest here, Mother. Everything will be all right." I was very relieved to see that she did, in fact, seem to relax a little as she laid her head back upon the pillow. I held her hand and smoothed the hair away from her forehead.

At that moment one of my sisters came into the yard. I rushed to her, and quietly told her what had happened.

"Where is father?" I said.

"He's out working in the field."

"Okay," I said. "Stay with mother. I'm going to run to town and get a doctor." It was not the first time I wished we had a phone--but I'd never wished harder. With my sister kneeling beside my mother under the shade of the walnut tree, I tore off for town.

The doctor with whom I returned examined my mother, and reported that she had had a stroke: There wasn't, he said, much to be done about such a thing. While he was there my father returned from the fields: He, my sister and I watched as the doctor gave my mother an injection of something meant to help her heart.

"Take her to her bed," said the doctor. "Rest is the best thing for her now. See that she remains undisturbed. After that," he said, "there is not much more any of us can do besides pray and hope."

We all fervently did both, of course.

Forty-eight hours later, my mother left this life for a better one.

To people who have lost someone near and dear to them, no words about the shock and grief of such a loss are necessary. To people who have not experienced such a loss: God bless you, and I hope you never do.

The funeral for my mother took place at our house. Flowers from relatives, friends and neighbors abounded throughout the house and front yard, where we placed tables covered with white linen and food for everyone to partake in.

As cruel as death is, it has one redeeming value: It brings the living closer together.

The day of the funeral was long and trying--and yet I seemed to move through it all as if in a dream.

People hugged me, and kissed me.

So I hugged and kissed them, too.

It seemed like the thing to do.

I really had no idea what I was doing. Inside of me--which is where I was--it was simply too dark to see.

One evening a month later I was sitting on the back porch steps when my father came and took a seat beside me. We were both quiet for a while, watching the shadow of our house grow long across the yard and the field just beyond our fence. A rustling breeze came around the house, cold enough to let us know that winter was coming.

Finally, my father spoke. "Luben," he said, "We need to talk about you going to school."

I reached down between my feet and picked up a slender twig lying on the step. The subject of my attending medical college hadn't been brought up since my mother had died.

"I don't want you to go," he said. "Of that, I am absolutely certain." He sighed heavily. "And yet, at the same time, I *do* want you to go." He turned to look at my profile for a moment, and then again fixed his gaze back out on the field. "I just don't know how I can get along here without you, Luben." He looked at me again. I held his gaze for a moment or two--and then looked back down at the step between my feet.

I remembered when my father and uncle had built those steps. They'd been so careful about getting them just right. Same as they had the whole place.

"I know," I said. "It's so hard to think about leaving, ever since … ." I couldn't finish my sentence. I didn't have to.

My father laughed morosely. "It's so hard to think about anything since then," he said. "You hear your sisters, still crying themselves to sleep every night. And when day comes, they do almost nothing. And the rest of us are barely keeping pace." He sighed, and lifted his eyes to slowly gaze about our back yard. "The whole place feels like it's falling apart."

"It's not," I said. "We're all right. We'll be ready for winter."

There was a long stretch of silence.

"And that's when you'll leave," said my father.

With the twig I drew a circle on the porch between my feet. "That's the plan," I said.

My father looked off to his right, away from me. Then he looked forward again, and kept his eyes focused upon something far off at the horizon. "Is it still?" he said.

I began drawing straight, evenly spaced lines between my two shoes. "I don't know. Things are hardly the same."

"Hardly."

I looked out at the distorted, elongated shadow of our home. "I don't know what to do," I said. "I want to go to medical school. It's a dream I've been working my fingers to the bone for for so long I can't even remember when I started. And then it came true. What shouldn't have happened, happened. Even the money that shouldn't have been there for it arrived almost by magic."

My father laughed heavily. "Almost," he said. The he added, "Your cousin is a good boy."

"A man now--and he sure is. I still can't believe he was willing to in-vest in my future like that. How can I ever repay such a debt? Or the one I owe grandpa, for being willing to sell the house in the first place?"

"You don't owe anyone anything, son. We're family. That's what family does."

"It seems like such an awful time to leave."

"That's because it is."

I leaned back on my arms, and looked up at the flat, gray sky. It took me a while, but I said it.

"I'm staying. I won't leave you alone here at a time like this."

My father dropped his head for a moment, and then looked back out at the horizon. "Good," he said. "I need you here." He nodded a few times to himself, as if confirming the rightness of such a decision. Then he stood, and extended his hand to me.

"C'mon," he said. "Let's get the horses set for the night, and then eat."

I took hold of his hard, calloused hand, and let him gently pull me up. We were just walking side by side around the house and moving toward the barn when I realized he was no longer beside me. I stopped, and looked back to see him gravely regarding me. With his eyes locked on mine, he said, "You know what, Luben? I don't think you should stay here. You have worked hard to go to medical college. We've all worked hard for you to do that. And none of us--I don't even think you--wanted that to happen more than your mother did. The thought of you becoming a truly educated man brought your mother real joy, Luben. Real joy."

He took a step toward me. "If you don't go, then all her hopes were for nothing. Then everything you and we have done for so long now means nothing."

"I can go later," I said. "I can go next year."

"No. You're already two years behind everyone else. Besides, you know how things go: You can wait all your life for tomorrow to come. We'll be all right. I'll hire a man to help us out around here." He smiled a bit. "And he won't have to live in the barn, either. After all, now we'll have a spare room."

I felt my heart swell with excitement.

"Are you sure?" I said. "Because I meant it when I said I would stay."

"I know you did. I think that's one of the reasons I most want you to go. You're a good boy, Luben. And you'll make a good doctor. Besides, it's what your mother wanted. And you know her: One way or another, what she wants seems to happen. I'm sure she's up in heaven right now, arranging your future. And it looks like a good one. I think it best not to resist."

I nodded. "Resisting Mother is not usually the best idea."

He looked at the ground. "No," he said sadly. "It's not." He looked back up at me again. "It's what your grandfather wants, too." I nodded that I knew that was true.

"It's decided, then," he said. "You're going."

"I ... I don't know what to say," I said. "I want to do what's best. I ..."

"What's best is that you go." He closed the gap between us, and as we resumed our walk he put his arm around my shoulder. "Dr. Walchef," he said. "You know, I do believe I could get used to that. It doesn't have the ring *Farmer* Walchef has--but it's not bad, in its own way."

So on the morning of January 7, 1941, my father and I loaded my two suitcases onto our horse buggy--and then we and my two sisters headed off for the Pordim train station. Everything was in order. I had my visa and passport. I had the money from the sale of my grandfather's house. My father had wended his way through the legalities imposed upon him by the Bulgarian government, which amounted to a bond arrangement stipulating that if I failed to return to Bulgaria from Germany after graduation in order to serve my obligatory military service, the ownership of all 200 or so acres of my father's land would automatically transfer to the government.

"So you *will* be coming back," my father said upon signing the final paper of this agreement. "And if you decide not to, be wise, and don't *ever* return."

I had even learned what I hoped was enough German to get me by-- or to at least get me started in the country I'd soon be calling home.

There was nothing left to do now but endure the freezing, bumpy ride to the train station.

The night before, my grandfather, then seventy-five years old and suffering from the effects of a stroke which had left his left leg paralyzed, had called me into his bedroom.

"Luben, Luben!" he said in his crafty, us-versus-them whisper I so loved. "Come in, come in! Shut the door!"

I entered his small, neat room, quietly closing the door behind me. "What is it?" I said. He had been reading while propped up in his bed; he now put his book aside, and swung his legs over the side of the bed.

"I have something for you," he said. "Open my closet there. On the floor of the closet is a board, two from the back and all the way to the right. If you press on the left side of that board, you'll see the other end lift."

I wasn't so old (is *anyone?*) that I didn't thrill a little to hear that my grandfather had a secret storage place in the floor of his closet. I did as I was told--and sure enough, the board he told me to press was, suddenly, loose.

"Now lift that board all the way out," he said. "Then reach your arm in there, and feel along the bottom of the two boards next to it, closer to me. You'll feel two latches at either end of those boards. Undo them. Then you can lift those two boards out, too."

I did feel the latches. They were closed tight--but when I popped them open, I saw that what looked to be two separate floorboards was actually one piece "divided" by a straight groove; that piece, along with the third I'd just removed, formed the top of what amounted to a cedar box sunk into the concrete of our house's foundation.

"Grandfather!" I whispered excitedly from inside the closet. "What do you have here?"

"A sense of history," he said. "You'll see a metal box down there, with a lock on it. Take it out." Holding my breath I reached down into the box and pulled out a heavy gray metal box. "Bring it over to me," he said. "And fetch my keys there on my desk, please."

"I can't believe this," I said, handing him the box and his keys. "Who would have thought you were a man who harbored secrets?"

"Anyone who's ever lived in an occupied country," he said. "When I was a boy my family hid three men--Bulgarian revolutionaries fighting the Turks--in our attic for two months. *That* was a secret. This is a small box in the back of my closet--a box that doesn't have to eat or any of the things that accompany eating. I could practically hide this box in my hair. Besides, only a fool keeps everything he owns out in the open. What the wind can't find it can't blow away."

He unlocked the box, and removed from it a sheaf of bills that turned out to be about one thousand Bulgarian livres (roughly two hundred American dollars). "I want you to have this money," he said. Moving things about in the box, he then pulled out a bill worth fifty Swiss francs.

"And I *really* want you to have this money," he said.

"No, grandpa," I said. "I have enough. You've already given me more than I need. Keep your money. I'd feel better being in Germany just knowing you've got this secret money stashed away in your secret box beneath your secret closet floor. Please: Keep it."

"No, Luben," he said. "You don't understand. I have had this fifty-franc bill for a very, very long time. I always told myself that I wouldn't resort to spending it until every other single option was gone from me. And now, all these many years later, I feel this bill is a kind of good luck charm! I feel as if God, determined to never put me in the position of having to spend it, sees to it that I'm never that desperate."

"Then keep it!" I said. "Why part with something that might be protecting you from trouble?"

"Luben, look at me. What protection do I need at this point? I'm seventy-five. I can't move my left *leg* anymore! As poor as my eyes are these days, I'm happy to say that from here I can at least see the end-- and, frankly, the rest of the road promises a fairly smooth ride. I'm done with this franc, is what I'm saying. This bill has already worked for me! It needs a new challenge!" He reached out my hand, and pressed the bill into it. "I want you to have this, Luben. I've been waiting a long time to give it to you."

"But grandfather--"

"But nothing," he interrupted. "Listen to me for a moment, Luben. You are young, and so don't have the sense of history you will one day--of the way generations unfold, one after another, from the beginning until we don't know when." He took both my hands in his cool, rough hands, and squeezed them tight, his sinew and bones seeming to send energy right through me. "My blood is in you, boy," he whispered intensely. "And so is the blood of my father, and his father, and his father, and all the Walchef fathers from as far back as time reaches. And great many lives! And look what they've all come to, boy. *You!* You are the new Walchef! And look what you are doing! Look where you are going!

"You're going to college to become a doctor!" he cried, releasing my hands and holding his up to the sky as if he were holding an invisible beach ball between them. "A doctor! A healer! When people are hurt, they will come to you, and you will heal them! You will make them better! This is as close to the work of God men can do on this earth!"

He picked the fifty-franc bill off the bed and, with shaking hands, pressed it into my palm.

"This is nothing," he said. "Although, compared to truly nothing, it may turn out to be the something that saves your life! But I want you to have it. It's a symbol of good fortune I've had with me more years than

I can remember." He looked down at the bed, sighed a heavy sigh, and looked back up at me again.

"I love you, Luben. I'm proud of you. Your father is proud of you. Your mother, God rest her precious soul, is proud of you. Your sisters are proud of you. Everyone in your family is proud of you. Of course I give you my lucky fifty-franc bill. Of course I sell my house to give you the money to go to Germany to study. Of course your uncle's son buys that house for much more than it's worth, so that you can benefit from his largess. Because you're a Walchef, Luben. And because it's clear that you're going to do what so many Walchefs before you did: You're going to make sure that that *means* something. You're going to give a whole host of Walchef men looking down from heaven a good reason to smile."

I had tears in my eyes as I wrapped my hand around my grandfather's lucky franc.

"Thank you, Grandpa. I'll try my best to make you--" I rolled my eyes heavenward--"and everyone, proud of me."

"Too late," he said. "We already are."

Sitting on the edge of his bed and holding one another's hands, my grandfather and I held back our tears. I searched for the words to tell him how much I loved him, how much I appreciated everything he'd done for me, the extent to which I knew that, for the rest of my life, he'd be my model for everything a good man should be.

I tried to find words to communicate all of that.

And didn't even come close, of course.

I sure did try, though.

And riding next to my father in our buggy the morning I left for Germany, my Grandpa's weathered lucky bill was folded up in my wallet, where I expected it to remain for a very, very long time.

It was my father's idea to arrive at the Pordim train station at eight in the morning--even though the train wasn't supposed to arrive until nine. "You must arrive early!" he'd declared. "These trains don't wait for people to arrive, you know! You're there; you're not there; it leaves all the same! Better to wait one hour than twenty-four!" And so there we were--I, my father, and my two shivering sisters--sitting upon the roughhewn bench in the little wooden shelter of the Pordim train station, a small building on the outskirts of the village far from any other buildings at all. The sun was just coming up over the trees, bright and shining on the snow.

"Now you have everything, right?" asked my father for what seemed like the hundredth time. His breath turned into quick little cloud bursts in the cold, crisp air. "All your papers? Your visa? Your passport? Your admissions papers? You have it all, right?"

"I have it all. Everything is in order."

My father seemed energized--he was in an upbeat, lively mood. As my sisters and I sat on the bench he paced back and forth before us, apparently uninterested, or even incapable, of sitting down.

"Now, the thing is, son, you've got to be careful," he said, walking past us. He almost seemed to be talking to himself. My sisters and I looked at one another questioningly: Who *was* this chatty fussbudget? "You've got to be very careful, indeed. Because you're used to doing things in a certain, shall we say, Bulgarian way. And that's our way--and it's a good way. But you're going to Germany now." About ten feet away from my sisters and I he stopped, and looked at me. "Germany," he repeated, and then looked back at the ground before resuming his big-booted, over-vigorous pacing. "And they're not going to do things in Germany the way we do them here," he said. "They will have ways you can't even *imagine*, Luben. Completely different ways of doing everything."

"And they're at war!" cried my younger sister.

"With everyone!" cried my middle sister. "Even America now!"

"Listen to your sisters, Luben," said my father. "Because the Germans *are* at war with everyone. It's clear to everyone in the world except the Germans that Hitler is a madman. And so you've got to be very careful about every single solitary thing you do in Germany, son. All of it: you can't for a moment let down your guard. On top of all the natural differences that exist between two very different countries a long way from one another, the Germans have decided to let a lunatic run their country. That's going to make them crazy: A runaway horse has a runaway rider. So move and speak cautiously. You didn't know the rules going in--and it's a sure bet that those rules are now changing daily. So beware!"

And so on.

It was as if my father was intending to give me, in one hour, all the advice he thought I would need for the rest of my life.

My sisters, however, had a more direct means of expressing how they felt about my leaving. They cried. They hugged me. They kissed my cheeks and implored me to write them constantly.

I had always loved my sisters. Now, with our mother gone, the three of us were closer than ever.

When the train arrived, I embraced my father and sisters with a kind of fury, really. All at once, it seemed, the magnitude of what I was doing struck me, and I felt I might never let them go.

And yet I did, of course: A train is a train, and as sad as I was to leave the protective arms of my family and the life and town I knew so well, I was also eager to embrace the mysterious, exciting life awaiting me.

Once on the train, I stored my suitcases and then took a window seat facing the station, so that I could wave goodbye to my father and sisters, which I continued to do until the movement of the train finally pulled them out of my vision.

I looked out the window as it ran alongside the village in which I'd spent my whole life. I saw myself as a child walking its fields, climbing its trees, running to and fro with friends I knew I'd never forget.

And then, despite my efforts to keep looking, Pordim, too, slipped from my view.

I turned in my seat, and faced front.

I was twenty-one years old.

Whatever was coming, was here.

Chapter Seven

Wurzburg

The train's first stop was in Pleven; I spent the short break off the train gazing at what I could see of the city from the station, again feeling nostalgic for a past that I knew would soon enough seem further back in time than it actually was. Following that the train stopped at a good many other places--mostly small towns I'd heard of for one reason or the other but never seen--before pulling into its final destination for the day at Sofia, the capital of Bulgaria.

The capital!

Already, I was feeling like a true world traveler!

Imagine how I felt, then, by the end of the following day, when I had taken a train that stopped in such places as Belgrade in Yugoslavia, and Vienna in Austria. *Vienna!* The crown jewel of Europe! I didn't get to see much of the city during our brief stop there, but what I saw dazzled me beyond anything I'd ever seen before.

And during my brief walk around the part of Vienna near the train station, I couldn't help but notice that no matter where I looked in the city, I never saw so much as a single sheep or goat.

This was, truly, a different world.

At last, we arrived where I was headed: the great city of Munich. (And I do mean "at last." In the course of our train ride, I had good reason to remember that Germany was at war: At the border crossings between Bulgaria and Yugoslavia--and then again at the border of Germany--the train stopped for a very long time while officials inspected everything and made sure everyone's papers were in perfect order. The whole process had an ominous, anxious feeling to it. I don't mind telling you that I felt no small relief when my own papers were deemed in order.)

With suitcases in hand, I stepped off the train in Munich into a station so vast and bustling I felt instantly lost.

The first thing of which I became aware is that I couldn't understand anything anyone around me was saying. This was an amazingly disorienting experience: Until that moment I had no comprehension of how much I took for granted and was even comforted by being able to simply understand what those about me were saying--even if they weren't necessarily saying it to me. And at this particular moment I found it acutely problematic to be suddenly surrounded by people who, as far as I was concerned, were babbling nonsensically, because I knew that in quite short order I needed to find which of the seemingly infinite number of trains about me was the one I needed to board, the one heading for Wurzburg.

The signs meant nothing to me.

Peoples' words meant nothing to me.

I was flooded with a sense of regret that before leaving Pordim I hadn't more assiduously applied myself to my German lessons.

It is, I think, a measure of just how disoriented I appeared that a man in a business suit saw fit to approach me and ask if he could help. At least, I think that's what he asked; this was a Good Samaritan who, alas, spoke only German. Still, it was someone willing to help--and I knew that if ever I was going to get the nerve to try out what little German I had managed to learn, this would be a very good time to do so.

And yet, I choked.

"Wurzburg!" was all I could manage to say. "Wurzburg!"

"Ah!" said the man. "Wurzburg!" He pointed to a sign suspended above a train that said, "Wurzburg."

Good!

Then I remembered: "Danke schon," is German for "thank you."

"Danke schon!" I practically yelled at my benefactor. "Danke schon!" He said something back in German that I am confident meant something very nice; I nodded enthusiastically, picked up my bags, and hustled off to toward the proper train.

A porter approached me and asked (I assume) if he could help with my bags. Smiling, I am sure, in a somewhat insane fashion, I shook my head in what I hoped was the universal sign of "Thanks, but no thanks"--not only was I afraid he would talk to me some more, but I also hadn't yet had time to exchange any of my money for German currency.

Before getting on the train, I did my best to ask a man wearing what seemed to be the uniform of those associated with the railway if the train I was about to climb aboard was, indeed, headed for Wurzburg.

"Wurzburg?" I said, pointing to the train. "Wurzburg?"

He nodded enthusiastically, pointed to the train, and smiled. "Ya, Wurzburg!" he said.

Good enough.

I hoisted everything in the world I owned, and climbed aboard the train I was now reasonably confident would drop me off within walking distance of my new college.

The first thing I noticed about my fellow train passengers was that they fell into two categories: people who were well dressed, and soldiers--who as a matter of fact were also well dressed, but of course in an entirely different way. I found myself a seat, and settled back amongst people speaking a language I couldn't have understood less if it were Venusian, or the clicking, high pitched songs of whales.

It wasn't too long before the train pulled into the Wurzburg station. Hoping to *never* again feel as helpless as I had at the Munich train station, I spent my time on the trip memorizing the German phrase, "Wo is die university Wurzburg?" which means, "Who killed the University of Wurzburg?" (I'm kidding, of course: it means, "Where is the University of Wurzburg?") So when the train stopped I gathered together my luggage and stepped out into a city that six months earlier I hadn't even known existed.

I looked about for a bus that I understood had the university on its route. I saw one idling nearby, and thought I'd start off with it.

"University Wurzburg?" I asked the driver.

"Kommen sie, kommen sie," he answered. I couldn't imagine what he meant--and then could, once he began nodding and waving me in.

Thank God for the universal language of gestures, I thought, and made my way up the steps into a bus that could scarcely have been more crowded if there were people strapped atop its roof. As he closed the bus door the driver said something that I took to mean, "Stand right where you are and grab hold of this metal pole right by my seat." So that's exactly what I did.

Keeping a firm grasp on the bar, I bent to look out the bus windows as we drove down what I later learned was the city's main street. What I

saw zipping by were more shops, showing in their windows more mer-
chandise, than I ever imagined existed anywhere in the world.

Shoes! Suits! Furniture! Food! Glassware! Women's clothes! Office
equipment! House wares!

I stood straight again, to give my eyes and brain a break.

And here all this time I'd been thinking that Pleven was a pretty big
city.

When I looked out the window again, I was struck by the sheer
beauty of the buildings. They were large, old, as intricately ornate as
could be--and clean. Really clean. *Freakishly* clean, in fact. To my mind,
the whole place looked less like a city than it did some kind of grand,
wonderful museum display.

Were all big cities like this, I wondered? Did only villages and small
towns look … well, *lived* in?

The bus stopped at the end of the city in front of a large park. I was
nearly lost in the beauty of the grounds outside the bus door when the
driver said to me, "Da ist die universität."

I turned to him, my mouth agape. *"That?"* I blurted in Bulgarian.
Had I accidentally enrolled in, and arrived at, the Louvre? Or some sort
of College of Versailles?

This--the most beautiful grounds I'd ever seen in my life--was the
university?

I looked back at the driver with an expression that in any language
can only mean one thing: "I'm too amazed to believe anything other than
that you're kidding me."

He made it clear that he wasn't, though: That this was the University
of Wurzburg, and that I needed to get off the bus now.

So--*barely* remembering my suitcases--I thanked the kindly driver,
and stepped off the bus.

And there I was, on the grounds of my new school.

The park-like area I was in was covered in a light layer of snow. It
was somewhat cool, but not cold; instead of early winter it felt like early
spring.

What it felt like was an absolutely perfect day to be starting a whole
new life.

I walked onto the campus proper, and before too very long at all
found the registration office. Upon opening its door I saw a middle-aged
man sitting at a large workhorse of a desk; it was to him that I presented

my letter of acceptance to the university's medical school. Being a sharp-minded fellow, it didn't take him long to realize that I knew about as much German as he did Bulgarian. Indicating with a raised finger that he had an idea, he picked up his phone and called someone with whom he engaged in a conversation. Then, looking satisfied, he hung up the phone, made it clear to me that I should sit in a chair off to one side and wait, and returned to the work on his desk to which he'd been attending when I arrived.

After about a half hour, a smiling young lady entered the lobby, went straight to the desk, and engaged the man in a short, friendly-sounding conversation. She then turned and walked toward me with her hand extended.

"So, you must be the new student from Pordim," she said. "I'm Illania. I'm very glad to meet you."

And she said it *in Bulgarian!*

Instantly, I wanted to have her babies.

Okay, my feelings weren't perhaps *that* extreme, but I did instantly feel more at ease than at any time since pulling out of the station in Pordim.

Illania, it turned out, was from Sofia; she was, she said, a dentistry student who had been in Germany three years.

"How long did it take you to learn German?" I asked her (in Bulgarian, of course).

"Oh, you'll pick it up so much sooner than you might think," she said. "When I first came here, I was in tears every day from not knowing what anyone was saying. In a month, I began to understand some, at least. And then, before I knew it, it seemed like I was able to understand more and more of what people were saying. It wasn't long before I was all right. Trust me: You'll catch on very soon. In the meantime, there are enough people around who speak Bulgarian to get you through."

To say I was relieved would be an understatement. *I* almost started crying--but from the joy of learning that there were others nearby who had been in my predicament, and who would help me get through what I had already begun to think might be too difficult a time.

With Illania's help my registration went quickly. When she asked where I was staying I shrugged my shoulders, and again this saint of lost Bulgarians volunteered to help.

"Rooms in the city are difficult to find right now," she said. "But I know a pension downtown that rents to students. If you'd like, we can go down there right now, and see if anything is available there."

We did; there was (the very last room available!); and before I knew it I was placing my suitcases down upon the floor of my new living quarters: a small room outfitted with a small bed, a small desk, a small chair, a small window overlooking the same street that had so amazed me on the bus, and a wash basin in the corner. (The bathroom, shared by everyone on that floor, was located down the hall. The good news is that it wasn't located out behind a *barn*.)

"Perfect!" I said to Illania and my new landlord.

"Wonderful!" clapped Illania.

"Rent is due the first of every month," said the landlady with considerably less enthusiasm. "You're late, you're out. Included in the rent is a good dinner I serve every night at six. Don't be late for that, either." And with that she turned on her heels and bustled out of the room.

I profusely thanked Illania for all her help. "To say I couldn't have done it without you is like saying things get wet when it rains," I said. "Without your help, I'd still be back at the registration office, driving that poor man crazy."

"I'm glad to have been of assistance," she said. "These are strange times in Germany. It's a good time to be associating and keeping close to those from your own country. There are a lot of Bulgarians in town. I'll introduce you to some of them."

When Illania left to return to the campus, I almost immediately fell dead upon the bed--where I stayed, sound asleep, until the next morning, the beginning of my first day as a medical student at the University of Wurzburg, Germany.

And now, if you please, it's time to step back for an historical break, concerning the history of Wurzburg itself:

A smallish city rich in ecclesiastical and cultural history, Wurzburg was founded when St. Boniface established a bishopric there in 741 A.D. By the 12th century, bishops held ducal authority throughout the region of eastern Franconia, in which Wurzburg lie. In 1803, the city was ceded to Bavaria and fell under the rule of Ferdinand III (formerly the grand duke of Tuscany in Italy), who thereafter took the title Grand Duke of

Wurzburg. In 1815, the Congress of Vienna restored Wurzburg to Bavaria; it then became the capital of Lower Franconia, one of the seven
government districts of Bavaria.

Despite the ravages of many wars (not the least of which was the
Second World War, during which an Allied bombing that lasted about a
minute completely destroyed eighty percent of the city--much of which
has since been restored), many of the Wurtzburg's finest old buildings
and other structures have remained intact. Chief amongst these is one
of the country's great prides, a 650-foot long, 15th century stone bridge
across the Main River, which is adorned with statues of saints. Another
of the country's unique and treasured buildings is the Fortress of Marien-
berg, which stands on the Leistenberg (which is to say, the mountain of
Leisten). It was in this fortress that the ruling bishops resided from 1261
to 1720.

Many of the everyday houses one sees in Wurzburg date from medieval times. Sundry ancient churches throughout the city remind one that
for many years Wurzburg was the capital of an ecclesiastical principality.

The main church in the city is a Romanesque cathedral, the basilica
of which was begun in 1042 and consecrated in 1189. The cathedral's
Rococo facade dates from 1719, and the dome from 1731. The ducal
palace, the Residenz, located on the large square in the center of town,
was an alternate residence for the city's bishops and grand dukes. (It is
now a museum.)

The hillsides on either side of the Main River are terraced and planted with grape vines. The local white wine is as excellent as the round,
flat-sided green bottle in which it comes is unique. Sadly, this delicious
wine does not travel well.

So that gives you some idea of what Wurzburg represents to the
world in general. What it represented to *me*, of course, was a place where
I needed to learn as much German as I could in the shortest amount of
time possible so that I wouldn't flunk out of the only medical college to
which I'd managed to gain acceptance.

At that time, earning a degree in medicine took a six-year commit-
ment. The first three years of pre-med were spent learning physics, chem-
istry, botany, biology, anatomy, and physiology; during the second three
years one covered surgery, internal medicine, obstetrics and gynecology,

pediatrics, ophthalmology and otolaryngology. (Say "otolaryngology" three times, quickly! Or even once!) In the final three years, we used actual hospital patients as study aids.

Following those six years was a seventh of internship--and then you were a doctor.

The institutes at Wurzburg where the medical lectures took place were located in an area not far from the building in which I lived. Except for anatomy and physiology, most of what we went over my first year were subjects for which my high school studies had prepared me well. The schoolwork was not my primary problem--*that* was my near illiteracy in German. As such, German is what I truly bent myself to study. Every day, for instance, I made a point of memorizing twenty German words. Most of my teachers, aware of the challenge I was facing, were kind about doing whatever they could to keep me caught up with the material. I remember particularly the many kindnesses of my botany professor, Dr. Bulgeff. (When he found out that I was from Bulgaria, he opined that he believed his name was Bulgarian in origin. What, if anything, he asked, might "bulgeff" mean in my language? When I replied it meant a carpenter's tool, he seemed a tad disappointed--but then he rallied, and speculated upon the distinct possibility that one of his ancestors had invented something which at one time or another had proven absolutely invaluable to no less a personage than Jesus.)

Botany was relatively easy because (oh, happy day!) I knew Latin.

Physics was relatively easy because in high school I was, if you recall, a veritable physics wiz. What was special about studying the subject at Wurzburg was that I took my lectures at the Institute of Physics, where the incomparable W. C. Roentgen discovered the X-ray. (The institute at which he worked is now a museum, where one can view the first X-ray Roentgen ever took, of his own hand.)

Though I'd never taken an anatomy class, the subject was made infinitely easier by the truly gifted artist who was its professor: With his hand moving across the board at something near light speed, he would render giant, precise, eminently skilled drawings of every bone, muscle and nerve in the human body you can imagine (and several I can *still* barely imagine). I always made a point to sit at the front of his classroom so that I could see and hear everything this consummate scientist and artist had to present. The man was nothing less than inspiring.

Physiology turned out to be the subject that presented me the most formidable challenge. Yet again, however, the material was rendered highly compelling via one of the most popular teachers at Wurzburg, one of those lively, genial geniuses of communication who could make a phone book seem like the most fascinating literature ever written. Like all natural born teachers, this one made a habit of enlivening his lectures with wonderful stories and examples which would make the lecture hall--always packed beyond capacity when he spoke--resound with heartfelt laughter.

Here, for example, is one of the stories he told us during the part of his course concerned with blood groups: An English king had hemophilia, the hereditary blood disease which can cause massive blood loss after even the smallest of cuts since its primary effect is to stop the blood's natural propensity to clot. As it happened, this king once found himself in need of a blood transfusion. His was the rare blood type AB, however, which is difficult to find under the best of circumstances, and particularly rare in England at that time. Luckily, a transplanted Scotsman with AB blood was located in the nick of time (so to speak). The man was, of course, pleased to be of such direct and vital service to the august ruler of England

After the transfusion the grateful king paid one thousand pounds to the Scotsman, who, no worse for the wear at all, returned home a happier, wealthier man.

A few months later His Royal Highness suffered another cut--and this time, of course, the king's caretakers knew where to find the Scotsman. Knowing good fortune when it pulled up to his cottage in a royal entourage of carriages, the Scotsman was of course all too glad to again be of assistance. This time, however, the king only paid him seven hundred and fifty pounds for his trouble. The Scotsman frowned a bit, but said nothing.

A few months later the apparently clumsy king found himself in need of yet another transfusion, and again the Scotsman was summoned. This time the king only paid him five hundred pounds for his blood. Upon taking his payment the Scotsman looked so disappointed that the king asked what was bothering him.

"Well, sire," said the Scotsman, "I don't mean to be ungracious, and goodness knows I'm honored to do anything I can to ensure the health of God's king on earth, but ... well, sir, the first time I gave you my blood, you paid me one thousand pounds. The second time, you paid me seven hundred. And now you've paid me but five hundred. It's the same blood, for the same purpose. I can't help but wonder, my liege: Why does the price go down every time I give you my blood?"

"Because," said the king, "Every time you give me your blood, I become more and more like a Scotsman!"

See? *Pretty funny!*

Then again, it's possible you had to be there.

In any account, I passed all my classes that first year--all of them, that is, except anatomy, which I had to repeat that summer.

The killer for me, of course, was that on top of the extensive Latin and Greek all medical students at that time had to learn, I was also still desperately trying to learn German. Imagine attending lectures in which you miss ninety percent of what is being said. Not to sound immodest, but by the end of my first year I counted it a blessing that I'd only failed one of my classes.

By about half way through my first year I'd at least learned enough German to survive socially--and once I knew that much, I employed a key survival trick I'd learned back in high school in Pleven: Always get a job where the food is.

And presto-hey, there I was once again, working in my school's cafeteria.

During my first summer break in college--during the one in which I had to retake anatomy--I also found a job in a garage that serviced Opel cars. I was thrilled to become a word I'd never heard before-- a "stock boy"--whose responsibility it was to keep shelves filled with parts and in general try his best to be as helpful as possible. For someone raised in a household that depended for all its transportation needs upon two horses and a wooden buggy, I suppose I did all right. Either way, the people with whom I worked were exceedingly kind to me, and I took advantage of my time there to learn as much as I could about car mechanics.

Summer in Wurzburg was absolutely gorgeous. Besides my class work, my job, and my frantic studying of German I had little free time--but spent as much of it as I could walking along a nearby river with Irmgard, a bright and beautiful German girl I'd met in one of my classes. Irmgard taught me a great many things about German art and culture. She pointed out to me the rococo and baroque designs in the local architecture, for instance, and taught me how to tell them apart. I cannot in all honesty say that I absorbed as much from her lessons as she may have believed I did--but (especially given our language difference) she can surely be forgiven for sometimes mistaking my interest in her for my interest in the valuable observations and insights she was kind enough to share with me.

She and I also went together to hear concerts in the open theater at the Residenz, and to slowly walk through the beautiful gardens surrounding the palace. On some weekends Irmgard and I took long walks from Wurzburg along the river all the way to Veitshöchheim. One time in that town we came across some workers tending a large garden of fruits and vegetables. Something about seeing those men working so hard and carefully at the same thing I'd spent so much of my life doing back home made me want to talk to them. So I did--and was amazed to find out that they were all from Bulgaria!

It wasn't long before I understood that it was hardly unheard of for foreign workers to be in Germany at that time. The war had created a boom market for labor: There's nothing like a war to empty factories of men at the same time production needs increase. People from across Europe flowed into Germany to take advantage of the economic opportunities afforded by the country's undertaking of war.

And at that time it seemed like a gamble that would pay off for the foreseeable future--for on September 1, 1941, Hitler invaded Poland.

Two days later, Britain declared war on Germany.

Suddenly, there was work for all.

Naturally enough, no one in Germany at the time seemed to be talking about anything but the war. Some were pessimistic, thinking Hitler a madman who at the very least was going to destroy Germany. Others felt he was the savior of a country still stinging from the deep humiliation following the First World War. Everyone had an opinion, either way. One day, for instance, I stepped into a Wurzburg radio shop (it's a measure of how vital it was at that time to keep abreast of world events that, on my budget, I felt a need to buy a radio, the primary means of mass communication at that time), and entered into a conversation about the war with the store's owner, who then invited me to dinner so that he could hear more about my life in Bulgaria. At his home that night, this merchant expressed his conviction that before too long Germany would invade Russia and occupy the Crimea, a very popular resort on the Black Sea. When that glorious day came, he said, he would relocate to the Crimea, and open a business there. He looked very forward to the time when German was the language spoken throughout the Russian Empire.

I nodded, and said yes, that would be some time, indeed.

In the months forthcoming, Hitler followed his invasion of Poland by occupying Holland, Belgium and half of France, including Paris and Normandy.

On December 7, 1941, Japan bombed Pearl Harbor, and America joined Russia, England and France (the Allied Forces) against the Axis of Germany, Italy and Japan.

The Second World War was happening with a fury and speed no one could have anticipated. In Wurzburg, as across the Western world, we relied for information upon radio and the half-hour newsreels that were shown before movies. The government of every country, of course, produced newsreels showing its own efforts in the best possible light: When the German army was advancing into Russia, for instance, my friends and I saw footage of large numbers of Russian soldiers being taken prisoner and sent to work in German labor camps.

It was this sort of information that delighted what seemed to me the great majority of Germans, that had them feeling utterly confident that no other outcome of the war was possible besides a total victory for their country.

As a foreigner (if not, as I thought then, as nothing more than a person possessed of his sanity), I saw things quite a bit differently. On the very face of it, it seemed manifestly untenable that such a relatively small country as Germany could defeat the combined powers of the Soviet Union, Great Britain, France and the United States. Already Germany was spread between France and Great Britain on the west, and the Soviet Union on the east. And that was *before* the Japanese had awakened the sleeping giant of the United States. After that, how in the world could the Axis powers ever hope to win?

We in Wurzburg, along with the rest of the world, waited to find out. In the meantime, life in Germany remained relatively normal. Food, however, was scarce, unless more than anything in the world you loved to eat baked and steamed and mashed and fried potatoes--with a delicious side of potato bread. In that case, Germany was the best place in the world to be. If, however, you craved meat, butter, fruit and vegetables, then it was best to crave no more than the two hundred grams (about a fifth of a pound) of meat and butter per week the government allowed each person. To this day, to me the term "food coupon" still means a government-issued ration ticket.

By June of 1942 I had completed my third semester of college at Wurzburg. Only days before school let out that summer, I received the heart-stoppingly good news that I'd been awarded a scholarship from the Von Humbold Foundation, a long-shot for which I had nonetheless applied a good many months before. (Mr. Von Humbold was a renowned naturalist and writer who did the bulk of his work in South America; upon his death his great wealth went to the creation of a trust fund intended to provide financial aid to deserving foreign students in Germany.)

I figured no one could argue that I was a deserving foreign student studying in Germany, so I had applied for the scholarship. (It was a process which turned out to be more exhaustive than I'd anticipated: I had to get letters of reference from just about everyone I'd ever known, from the director of my high school in Pleven to Boris, the alpha male in the sheep herd back on our farm. In truth, though, the letters I received in response to my request for references gave me reason to pause for not the first moment in my life to reflect upon how fortunate I'd been to have known so many good people who were willing to do so much to help me realize my goal of becoming truly educated. It reminded me again that one can certainly fail alone, but never succeed.)

Given my ever-precarious financial situation, you can imagine what it meant to me to receive a letter from the foundation stating that I had won a scholarship for what amounted to free room, board and full tuition for a year.

"You got *what?*" said my father when I told him the news. I had meant to tell him the moment he picked me up from the train station-- what better way to begin my visit back home for the summer?--but then, riding beside him on our old buggy, decided to wait until we were back home to let him know of our newfound fortune. It's easier to have a real conversation when you're not testing the durability of your internal organs by bumping along a dirt road in a wooden horse buggy.

"I think I must have some dust in my ears from the ride home," he said. "Say that again, please?"

"Just before coming home I received a scholarship from the Von Humbold Foundation giving me free room, board and tuition for one full school year!" I cried. *"And the scholarship is renewable every year for as long as I stay in school!"*

Moving slowly, my father took a seat at our family's roughhewn dining table. "You're such a funny boy," he said. "It's always one joke after another with you. Very entertaining. But you shouldn't joke about some things, Luben. Some things may sound humorous when they're inside your head, but then, when you actually say them out loud, you discover they're really just a way to give a poor innocent old man a heart attack. And there's nothing funny about that, Luben."

"I'm not joking, Father! Look! Here is the letter!" I pulled out the paper and slapped it down on the table before him. "Right here! This is real! I won a full scholarship! From now on, my going to school won't cost you one single penny!"

My father looked at the paper, took a sip of tea, and regarded me with an entirely nonplussed expression.

"So, you're not kidding me, then."

"No!"

"You're serious."

"Yes!"

"You've been awarded some sort of ongoing money from ... from who?"

"From The Von Humbold Foundation!"

"From The Von Humbold Foundation. And these people at the Von Hamburger Foundation--"

"Von Humbold!"

"Von Humbold Foundation, they've decided, out of the goodness of their hearts, to simply hand over to you, my son, Luben Walchef, all the money you need to continue going to college, for as long as you want."

"Yes, Father!"

"For free."

"Yes!"

"They've given you this money for free."

"Yes! It's a scholarship! They've awarded me a scholarship!"

"And if you take this money from them, they won't show up here four years from not wanting to break my legs because I can't pay it back to them. Nobody is going to come steal our sheep for repayment. They're not expecting to ever see this money again."

"No, father! Never! They awarded me the money because that's what they *do!* They find a worthy student from outside the country who is studying in Germany, and they give them money to help them continue their education."

"For free."

"Well, that's it. I give up. Okay, one more time: Yes, Father. The money is mine for free."

"They've chosen you," he murmured. "These people, at this foundation, have chosen you to award all this money to."

"Yes," I said softly.

He looked at me in a gleaming, dazed sort of way. In the spellbound tone of one whose conscious mind has only just begun to comprehend what his heart already knows, he said, "This is fantastic. This is truly fantastic. This is real, right? This can't be taken away? There's nothing left for you to do? No final steps that need to be taken? You don't have to … I don't know…take a physical, or pass any test, or…do anything else? This thing is done?"

"Yes! It's done!" What had happened to my father, who had once been so … *sane?*

He stared at me for a moment, and then raised his hands and brought them banging back down upon the table. "This is fantastic!" he yelled "Exceptional! This is the best day in the history of the Walchef family! In the history of Bulgaria! In the history of the *world!* Angelina! Angelina!"

"Who's Angelina?" I said.

My father's eyebrows raised. "Ah," he said. "Right. You don't know who Angelina is. Come, Luben," he said, rising from the table and extending his arm as if to put it about my shoulders. "Walk with me a bit."

As we walked out our front door and down the path through the garden my father remained silent. It wasn't until we were out near the fields that he spoke.

"Luben," he said, "I've remarried."

My heart seemed to stop in my chest. *"What?"*

"I've remarried. I waited the customary year--and a year beyond that, not just because it's the right thing to do but because my heart wouldn't

have it any other way. But then I met this woman, Angelina, from Plev-
en, Luben--where you went to high school."

"I know where I went to high school, Father," I said. It came out
sounding more cross than I intended, but if my father noticed he didn't
let on.

"She's a widower," he continued, "like me. So she knows. Her children are grown, have gone off to lives of their own. When I met her she
was living alone above a bakery." He stopped walking. I turned to face
him.

"She's a good woman, Luben."

I held his gaze for a moment, and then turned to look out over the
fields growing soft in the waning afternoon light. Then I looked back at
him, and said, "How could you do this without telling me?"

"I wanted to write and tell you, Luben. I did. But, as you know, I
don't write so well. And the truth is I didn't want to bother you at school.
I know how important your studies are to you, and I was afraid ..."

"You were *afraid?*" I cried. "You were afraid that if I learned you
married another woman, I wouldn't be able to *study?* And *that's* why you
haven't told me about this until now?"

"Yes," he said, as if not understanding what about that I might find
troubling.

"You thought that it was more important that my studies remain undisturbed than it was to know that there was a different woman sleeping
in my mother's bed, a different woman cooking meals in my mother's
kitchen with my mother's pots and pans, a different woman acting as
the mother of my sisters. You thought my knowing that just wasn't as
important as my being able to continue studying as if my life back here
in Pordim hadn't radically altered."

"Yes. This is what I thought. And, Luben, it wasn't that long ago. We
only married at the end of April. And I knew you'd be coming home for
the summer."

"When did you meet this woman?"

"In January. She was visiting her relatives in ..."

"In *January?* You married a woman you'd only met--what, three
months before?" I was practically screaming now. "How could you do
such a thing?"

"Hey!" my father boomed at me, his eyes ablaze with anger. "I'm
your father! Who do you think you are to ask me how I could or couldn't

do something? You're off living at college! I am glad you are getting this money, but that doesn't erase the fact that you do *nothing* for us anymore! When you're in your room at college--which *I* pay for! which *I* allow!--do you ever stop to think for a moment what things must be like on our farm back here in Pordim? Do you? Does it ever cross your selfish mind to think, 'I wonder how my father is getting along now that he has to do twice the work? I wonder who is helping him with his chores? I wonder who is cleaning, or sewing, or doing the millions of things a wife does to keep a home and farm going?' Does it ever occur to you to think about such things, Luben?" He was yelling now, full force. "Do you ever wonder who is doing the *cooking* for us now, Luben?"

He looked furiously into my eyes, and switched his tone to a low, seething voice.

"I'm glad you're learning so much in college, Luben. And I know that to you I must seem like an ignorant peasant farmer. But please believe me when I say you have got a great deal yet to learn about life. A man needs a wife, boy. And your sisters need a mother, whether they know it right now or not. And I know it must hurt you to think of another woman taking the place of your mother. But that's not the way it is. No woman can ever take the place of your mother. Don't forget: I loved your mother for years before you ever came into our lives. Angelina isn't your mother; no woman could be. But she's a good woman, and she's been a good friend, and she knocks herself out trying to get your infernal sisters to at least be polite to her. And she'll win them over yet, because she's exactly that kind and patient. And because she is trying very hard to do exactly that."

He looked away out at the fields, and took a deep breath. "Your sisters have been an embarrassment to me, Luben. Angelina's been very kind about saying how she's looking forward to meeting you, but in her eyes I see her fear that you'll be another of her husband's children who hate her for something she can't help.

"Don't be that child, Luben. Be a man about this. Make Angelina feel welcomed in our home. She's my new wife. I married her because I find her admirable, and because life on a farm without a wife is a kind of hell I assume you wouldn't want me or your sisters to live with. I know you've been away a while, now. But surely you haven't already forgotten how difficult life out here in Pordim is."

"No," I smiled. "I haven't."

"Well," he said, putting his arm about my shoulder and turning me back toward the house, "Let's see if we can't refresh that a little in your mind, just the same."

Instead of going straight home, though, we walked alongside the fields some more, talking. He told me that while I had been away, the political situation in Bulgaria had grown very tense. The communists in the area were trying to organize themselves and develop into a viable power; I was told by my father and some of my friends that many of them had taken to the mountains, only to be arrested and even killed when, seeking to further their cause, they dared to return. "Though the government is very strict with them--even cruelly so," said my father, "the communists persist, believing that if Germany loses the war, they can then turn for help to a communist Soviet Union, and take over Bulgaria. It's a dangerous gamble--but one they're taking." (And one that paid off when, in fact, Bulgaria became a communist satellite country of the Soviet Union after the war.)

"What I'm saying, son, is beware of everything you do and say in Germany. These are troubled times, and they don't seem likely to get better before they get worse. And you're living in the very stomach of the beast now. So you've got to be wary of everything you say, and of everyone you speak with. Don't relax your tongue. Stay as neutral as you can, boy."

I assured him that I couldn't have less interest in politics--that then, as always, my singular reason for being in Germany was to study medicine.

Before our evening walk ended, I apologized to my father for snapping at him about his new marriage. He was right, I said: It was good for him to remarry. And I promised him I'd talk to my sisters about giving Angelina a chance.

Oh: and I liked her. Over the course of the next few months I came to agree with my father that Angelina was a good woman. By the time summer ended she and I had become quite close--and by then my sisters had not only backed off her, but had begun, however reluctantly, to accede that she did, after all, have some good points, and may just possibly be possessed of a character that it wouldn't exactly kill them to admit wasn't entirely evil.

"Apologize to her," I told them both on my last night at home. "How would you like to move into your husband's home, and have to put up with the likes of you two? She's had a hard life--she loved her husband as much as we loved our mother. And now she's married our father. Apologize for the way you treated her--and start cooperating with her. You've seen how happy she makes Father. That should be enough for all of us."

My sisters hugged me, and kissed me, and promised they'd make it all up to Angelina.

It was with a light heart that I waved good-bye to Angelina and my sisters the next morning as my father and I rolled off to the train station.

Chapter Eight

Berlin

The end of that fall's semester--my fourth at Wurzburg--meant that I was done with premed and now prepared to begin my clinical studies. It also meant I was free to change universities: In Germany at that time, all college classes were standardized--the same classes, the same lectures, the same textbooks--which meant that students could transfer from any college to another without their grades being in any way effected.

I'd been at Wurzburg for two years. I loved the college; I loved the city; and I loved the friends I'd made there--particularly Irmgard, to whom I had become especially close.

Still. Two years.

All my life I'd dreamed of the next big thing to come my way.

The next big school.

The next big college.

The next big city.

And now I found my mind moving toward one of the biggest cities of all: Berlin.

Berlin! The very capital of Germany!

The moment I imagined it I wanted it. And not just because I knew that Berlin, one of the world's great cities, offered more culture, art, cuisine and, well, more *everything* than Wurzburg ever could, but also because it was home to one of the Europe's greatest medical colleges, the Charite Medical School at Von Humboldt University. And *that* is where the renowned pulmonary surgeon and lecturer Dr. Saubruch practiced and taught.

Life was short, I thought: Why settle for anything but the best?

"But Luben," said Irmgard when I told her of my plans to begin the following semester in Berlin, "all your friends are here." We were strolling together in the park when she stopped and fixed me with her beautiful eyes. "I am here," she said.

"I know," I said. "I know." Just her saying it--and especially with those eyes--was enough to rattle my resolve. "But it's one of the best medical schools in Europe," I said, spinning away and almost pleading with her. I held my arms wide in an attempt to explain. "You know my background. You know how important it is to me that I get the best education I possibly can."

"There are other things in life besides education, Luben. Not everything can be learned from books."

I dropped my arms.

She did have a point.

And at the end of our walk together, I knew I had some more thinking to do.

"You're more than just a friend to me, Luben," Irmgard had said, taking my rough hands in her own soft ones. "Quite a bit more."

I can't say I got a lot of sleep that night. My room, which had always seemed more than big enough for my needs, suddenly felt stiflingly small.

One moment I'd be lying on my back, staring up into the darkness, imagining my new life in Berlin--the teeming crowds! the opera! the museums! the vast, monumental, humming, vibrant city!--and the next I'd be sitting on the edge of my bed, while thoughts of Irmgard swam through my fevered heart and head. And at those moments Berlin might as well have been the capital of Antarctica.

"Can't you come to Berlin?" I asked her the next morning.

"Luben," said Irmgard, touching my shoulder. "Are you all right? You look as if you haven't slept a wink."

"It was a long night," I confessed. "Quite a bit to think about. But I'm serious, Irmgard: Can't you come to Berlin? Think of it! Berlin!"

"You know I can't," she said. "My family is here. And here I am getting as good an education as I could anywhere: The foreign language program at Wurzburg is one of the best in the country. You know that."

"Oh, sure," I said, defeated. "Your family and your education. Like that's such a huge reason to stay."

She smiled sadly at me. "Stay in Wurzburg, Luben."

"Oh, Irmgard, I can't. I just ... can't. I want to. I want to stay and be here with you, and with all our friends here. But ... but there's something else in me, something that I'm afraid is bigger than my desire for things to stay the same. I've always had this ... drive. I don't know what it is. It's as if I'm .... I don't know ... genetically programmed to keep moving ahead, or something." I sighed, and looked down at the ground. "You cannot imagine what life on a farm is like, Irmgard," I said softly, looking back up at her. "You just can't. And do you know why you can't? Because you *have* an imagination. And that's because you didn't grow up on farm. If you had, the imagination would have been wiped out of you by the grueling, grinding, brain-killing sameness of every wretched day, which is so much like the one before it and the one that will come after it that in no time at all you know your *only* enemy in life is to ever hope or in any way imagine that things will ever be any different. Every day the fields need tending, the machines need fixing, the animals need feeding. It turns *you* into an animal, Irmgard. What's the difference between an animal and a man who never dreams? They're the same. People become what they do."

I looked down at the ground for a long time. Irmgard silently kept her hand resting on my shoulder.

"I have to go to Berlin," I finally said, looking up into her soft, loving eyes. "It's insane, I know. Wurzburg is a wonderful city, and the thought of leaving you is like a dagger in my heart. And yet, as compelled as I am to stay here, this city ... this place ... it's just not, somehow ... ." I looked heavenward, in hopes of perhaps there finding the words I sought.

"It's just not far enough away from Pordim," I said.

How to begin writing about Berlin? The history of this fabled city, which first appeared in the record of mankind in 1244 after merging with its sister city, Koln, reads like the history of all mankind. It begins, surely, at the beginning (man first appeared in the area around 50,000 BC.); over the centuries the city, situated athwart the natural east-west commercial and geographical axis of the Spree River (a position which affords it natural dominance over the North European Plain--which is why empires from the kingdom of Prussia to the Third Reich made it their capital), has seen all manner of upheaval, prosperity, war, devastation, renewal, disgrace, and triumph. It is an inspiring monster of a city.

At the time I arrived, in February of 1943, Berlin was in the midst of one the most difficult times in its history--and had just begun a year that was, literally, devastating to it. The Second World War was, by this time, about three and a half years old. The German army had just experienced a crushing defeat at the Battle of Stalingrad, one of the largest, bloodiest battles in all of history: Raging for over 200 days, it brought death to more than 1,200,000 Soviets; 300,000 Germans troops; 100,000 Romanians; and 87,000 Italians.

It is difficult to imagine the horrible magnitude of just that one battle--let alone of WWII overall.

And Berlin, of course, was the capital of the Third Reich.

Although lack of any positive news about the Stalingrad offense had many Germans doubting Hitler's screaming declarations of invincibility, no official word of the disaster in Russia came until the very month I arrived in Berlin. It was on Thursday, February 18, at Berlin's massive *Sportsplast,* that Hitler's infamous Nazi propaganda minister Joseph Goebbels gave his famous "Total War" speech, broadcast to millions and largely credited with inciting the Germans to continue for another two and half years the war which had turned so decisively against them: His mobilization slogan, "Let the storm break loose!" called for Germans to forgo virtually all "luxuries" for the good of the war, and mandated into the law the enlistment of all German women in the war effort.

It was the first time the German government publicly admitted that the war wasn't, in fact, going as well as it had led the German people to believe. (Notably, what Goebbels especially didn't want to talk about was what, exactly, had gone so wrong with the German war effort: "Now is not the time to ask how it all happened," he proclaimed. "That can wait until later, when the German people and the whole world will learn the full truth about the misfortune of the past weeks, and its deep and fateful significance. The heroic sacrifices of our soldiers in Stalingrad have had vast historical significance for the whole Eastern Front. It was not in vain. The future will make clear why. When I jump over the past to look ahead, I do it intentionally. The hour is at hand! There is no time for fruitless debates. We must act, immediately and decisively, as has always been the National Socialist way."

Typically, Goebbels, the mastermind behind the Final Solution, blamed the Jews for the disaster at Stalingrad--the war against Bolshevist Russia, he declared in his speech, was nothing less than a war against the Jews, who lived only to enslave the world through craven capitalism. ("International Jewry," he said, "is the devilish ferment of decomposition that finds cynical satisfaction in plunging the world into the deepest chaos and destroying ancient cultures in which it played no role in building," and so on.)

From its inception, the Nazi party had made no bones about its desire to persecute and eliminate anyone of Jewish descent. By the time I arrived in Germany, there were maybe twelve hundred Jews hiding throughout Berlin.

Ten years before, one hundred and sixty thousand Jews lived in the city.

In 1939, about seventy-five thousand were left. That year 50,000 of those were removed to concentration camps, where most were murdered.

Before the Summer Olympic Games of 1936 were held in Berlin, Hitler ordered all of the "Forbidden for Jews" signs throughout the city removed, in order to avoid offending the sensibilities of foreign visitors.

Berlin, at the beginning of 1943, was about as strange a place to be as existed in the world at that time.

My first goal, upon arriving in the city, was to secure a place to live. Through an ad in the paper I was fortunate enough to find relatively near to the university a good-size, quiet room on the second floor of an apartment occupied by an elderly couple, Mr. and Mrs. Mueller. My new landlords were kind, delightful people whom I was very glad to get to know. The Muellers had no children of their own; it seemed that right from the beginning Mrs. Mueller was happy to consider me the son she never had. By day her husband worked in an insurance office; at night I would often see him in his room, hunched over a small table equipped with a strong light, gazing through a magnifying glass at a disemboweled pocket watch someone was paying him to repair. Moonlighting as a watch repairman brought Mr. Mueller a nice second income (I purchased a watch from him that I gave to my father)--though his extra work also,

I think, kept him so busy that oftentimes his wife was glad to have me around to talk to. And, God bless her, the good woman did more than talk to me: She also, for free, washed my clothes, cleaned my room, and frequently brought food up to my room while I was studying.

"Eat!" she would say. "Who wants to be treated by a skinny doctor? People want a doctor who looks like he knows how to take care of himself!"

Becoming a doctor was, of course, the primary activity of my new life in Berlin. I knew the war was raging--one couldn't walk on the street for one moment without hearing this person or that expressing this or that opinion about it--but, in a sense, I simply didn't care. I couldn't afford to: Studying took virtually all my time and energy.

Wars, I knew--even the worst of them, even this one--passed. What I was working on was my future.

I don't see how I could have picked a better medical school than Charite College. I found it to be a college truly worthy of it international reputation: A total of 29 Nobel Prize winners came from the scientific work that was done there.

And yet, as grand a learning institution as it was, on May 10, 1933--the date Hitler assumed control of Germany--students and professors alike there burned books deemed to in some way antithetical to the "glory" of the Third Reich.

Also, from that time until 1945--the end of Hitler's reign--the university was "cleansed" of all of its Jewish academics and students.

So, then. We see how relative the term "higher education" can be.

Nonetheless, at Charite I found the education I needed to become the very best doctor I could. The clinical subjects I was required to study encompassed surgery, internal medicine, obstetrics and gynecology, pediatrics, ophthalmology and otolaryngology. In order to gain real-world experience we studied hospital patients inflicted with diseases or ailments in each of these areas: I was required to make medical rounds with the professor of each discipline every day. We went from patient to patient, discussing diagnosis and treatment.

I very much enjoyed the medical lectures; the professors were excellent teachers. In the discipline of surgery, I was honored and thrilled to hear lecture and see operate the famous pulmonary specialist, Professor Saubruch. Throughout Europe at that time there were a great many people suffering from tuberculosis; the treatment of choice was to either go to Switzerland--where a lot of the best work in that field was being done--or to be operated on in Berlin by the renowned Professor Saubruch.

At that time, pulmonary surgeons were consistently faced with the terrible problem of patients' lungs collapsing after surgery. In order to solve this problem, Professor Saubruch designed a special operating room with all sealed walls. Following a surgery, he would use negative air pressure to create a vacuum within the room: This caused the patients' lungs to expand. Though ultimately too unwieldy to regularly depend upon, it was an exceptionally creative solution to a very real problem, and directly led to many innovations which became fundamental to the field. Fortunately, it was at about this time that anesthesiology began to improve dramatically; eventually, a machine was invented that allowed air to be pumped into the lungs via a bag, which made it possible for a trained anesthesiologist to expand the lungs following surgery. This is the technique for post-operative lung expansion that is still used today.

When I wasn't studying, I did everything I could to explore and see as much of Berlin as possible. In short, I fell in love with the city. It was a splendid place, with unimaginably vast and ornate buildings, shopping streets, parks, churches, plazas, museums, concert halls, monuments. It was during this time in my life that I developed the passion for opera that is with me to this day. Only the very finest of Europe's singers made the Berlin opera companies. (Then, as now, it was true that opera is not for everyone. One night a friend of mine invited me to see and hear "The Flying Dutchman" by Wagner. "It is the finest opera!" my friend declared. "It will do our souls good to be stirred by the masterful, poetic genius of our greatest composer!" I found the performance absolutely riveting. At one point, when the music had very nearly brought me to tears, I looked over at my friend, and found him looking at the stage with an expression one would expect to see on a person who had been duped into paying a great deal of money to watch a man pet a dog, or perhaps to watch two people play checkers. It wasn't long before this would-be patron of the arts leaned over to me and said, "I can't stand this music. We've suffered enough. Let's get out of here! I *hate* Wagner!")

In one of my classes I met the son of a pediatrician in Berlin; this friendly young man kept a sailboat on Potsdammer Lake, which he invited me to sail with him on weekends. What a wonderful time we had out on the water, admiring the city's skyline and dazzling lights. Having never sailed in my life, I cherished every moment of it. Those Sunday afternoon excursions onto the lake remain among my life's most precious memories.

What is surely *not* amongst my most pleasant memories is what, soon enough after my arrival in the city, became an all too regular reality in Berlin: Bombing. The city had become a target of Allied bombings only a month before: Following the January 20th daylight raid by the German Luftwaffe of a school in London which killed forty-four children and one teacher, the RAF bombed Berlin with a Mosquito air attack during the celebration of the Nazi party's tenth anniversary.

And that was just the beginning.

I finished my first semester in Berlin in the summer of 1943--when I was lucky enough to be accepted as a resident in a private hospital for diabetics in the city.

Sounds nice, right? My first posting as a doctor--a joy to be relished, right? That is right--until you consider the bombings of Berlin that happened on the following dates during 1943, beginning that August:

Monday, August 23: 1,700 tons of bombs dropped by 727 RAF bombers.

Tuesday, August 24: Berlin is covered with smoke from the previous night's bombing in a blanket that reaches 20,000 feet into the air. Initial estimates put the Germans killed in the bombing at about 6,000.

Tuesday, August 31: The RAF, using over 600 planes, pound Berlin with over 1,000 tons of bombs, killing about 5,000 civilians.

Thursday, November 18: The RAF instigates "The Battle of Berlin" by dropping 700 tons of bombs upon the city, part of the largest RAF bombing of Germany to date.

Monday, November 22: In less than 30 minutes, the RAF drops 2,300 tons of bombs on Berlin

Tuesday, November 23: The RAF once again targets Berlin, rendering it the most bombed city in Germany, with 12,000 tons dropped upon it in 1943 alone.

Wednesday, November 24: Berlin reported as a "sea of flames" the morning after the previous night's bombings, estimated to have claimed the lives of between eight and ten thousand German citizens.

Friday, November 26: The RAF executes its fifth consecutive night raid on Berlin.

Thursday, December 2: Allied bombers continue the "Battle of Berlin" by dropping 1,500 tons of bombs on the city.

Thursday, December 16th: Another bombing blitz on Berlin brings the total amount of bombs dropped on the city to 18,500 tons.

Wednesday, December 29: On the third anniversary of the German's first fire bombing of London, the RAF drops 2,000 tons of bombs on Berlin.

Berlin was bombed 24 times between November 18, 1943 and March 1944, and sporadic hits continued until the city was captured by the Russian army in April of 1945. By that time, the city had been reduced to 98 million cubic yards of rubble. Each of the later bombing attacks involved over 1,000 planes and the dropping of up to 2,000 tons of bombs. Half of the city's bridges were destroyed; all the underground railway tunnels were flooded. There was no gas, electricity or water in the central portion of the city. The pre-war population of 4.3 million had been reduced to 2.8 million, as people were forced to flee the city; some 1.5 million people became homeless when their homes were bombed. One out of seven buildings destroyed in Germany by Allied bombing raids were in Berlin; Berliners jokingly referred to the American and British air raids as "Baedeker Bombings"--Baedeker travel guide books were used by tourists to locate famous and historic buildings. Out of a total of 245,000 buildings in Berlin, 50,000 were completely destroyed, and 23,000 were severely damaged.

Some 80,000 Berlin residents were killed by the bombs.

Chapter Nine

Heidelberg

I may not be the sharpest knife in the drawer, but even I knew enough to begin, way back in August of 1943, to consider where, besides Berlin, I might like to consider continuing my medical education. By then, I had already seen (and heard!) enough of the war to last me a lifetime. The hospitals and clinics that were part of my daily life were increasingly filled with soldiers returning from Stalingrad: People in the medical profession throughout Germany surely knew how the war was going before government officials had to tell them. I saw endless numbers of soldiers suffering from malnutrition, or with their noses, toes and fingers frozen off from frostbite.

No matter how one felt about the ultimate cause these soldiers were fighting for, it was painful to see so many young men so severely damaged. You could see the damage to their spirits it in the shocked daze of their eyes, in the way the pain in their bodies had forced their minds to detach from almost anything physical. They had left their homes knowing they were in for something, but had never imagined it would be for this.

Closer to home, the nightly air raid sirens meant a trying physical ordeal for Mrs. Mueller, who though generally healthy was no longer young. She suffered from mild asthma, which was nightly aggravated by the arduous climb down the four flights of stairs it took us to reach the basement of the building in which we lived.

Our building had no elevator. So most every night, with me supporting one side of her and her husband the other, the poor woman had to make her long way to the basement--and when the danger had

passed, she had to climb her way back up the stairs. It would have been a
workout for anyone; on many nights, this kind, thoughtful women could
barely draw her breath after the strain. It wasn't easy to watch someone
who was so kind to me suffer in this manner.

Not, of course, that there was any lack of suffering to be seen in Berlin in 1943. Or in so many other places throughout Europe, of course.

Every night from our windows we watched nearby buildings burn,
and listened to the screams and cries of women and children.

I knew I'd never enroll for another semester in Berlin. Enough was
enough.

But where to next, I wondered? I still had my scholarship money
(which would follow me anywhere), and so was free to enroll for the fall
semester at any college in Germany. I went to the library and began researching Heidelberg and Freiberg, because I knew they were both beautiful cities with outstanding medical colleges. I read about the beauty of
Heidelberg and its famous castle. I read that its university was the oldest
in Germany (founded in 1386!), and that many famous professors were
doing incredible work there.

So I decided to take a train to Heidelberg, and see what I thought of
the city and the college. If I didn't like what I saw or wanted something
else to consider, I would then continue on to Freiberg, also a very real
option.

I left Berlin the first part of September and arrived in Heidelberg the
same day. When I saw the city and the castle of Heidelberg, I found the
whole place so beautiful, and so captivating, that I immediately forget
about Freiburg.

It didn't matter what the competition had to offer: this, I knew, was
my new home.

Heidelberg, which lies on the river Neckar, is located in Baden-
Württemberg, Germany, about halfway between Stuttgart and Frank-
furt. Founded in 1196, it is a relatively small city, long and narrow, but
as rich in history--and history you can see, everywhere you look--as any
place on earth. Perched 200 meters above the Neckar on the sharply
rising wooded hill of the Konigstuhl is the famous medieval Heidelberg

Castle, which dominates the city it looks down upon. Surrounding this awe-inspiring relic from another time are beautiful park grounds where poets and thinkers of the likes of Goethe have strolled for their inspiration.

Though steeped in tradition, Heidelberg has always been the center of education and learning. It is home to one of the oldest educational institution in Europe, the University of Heidelberg, founded in 1386 and still going strong today. Among the prominent thinkers who considered the college their intellectual home are the great dialectic philosopher Hegel; the critical theorist Jürgen Habermas; Hans-Georg Gadamer, who pioneered the field of hermeneutic philosophy; and the discourse philosopher Karl-Otto Apel. But Heidelberg has nurtured thinkers of a decidedly more mechanistic bent, too: One of its most important students was Karl Drais, whose self-propelled two-wheel invention of 1876 heralded the forthcoming age of the automobile.

Work in the arts and sciences has always flourished throughout Heidelberg; even today, there are many important research facilities located in or around the city. With one foot always firmly rooted in the past, Heidelberg has also never failed to point to the future.

I knew some or even all of this before I reached Heidelberg, but nothing had prepared me for the sheer dazzling display of the city itself. The Heidelberg castle alone is enough to make even the most experienced traveler stop to catch his breath--and that's *before* he's made the long climb up to the place itself. Making that climb was one of the first things I did upon arriving at the city; from there, surrounded by the somber, romantic mist of days long gone, I gazed down upon the city from a stone wall at the edge of the castle garden. There I saw the sight that has been moving viewers for centuries: the golden Neckar River valley, with its lush wooded hills and picturesque stone bridges leading into and away from the perfect, small city of Heidelberg, with its sea of amber rooftops dancing below a dozen or so church steeples which rise above it. At the moment I was lost in this view a cacophony of bells began ringing from the belfries of those towers, creating an ancient, stirring symphony of worship, community, and even alarm. I let the sound swirl and dance around me, and felt I had traveled back in time.

That sense was in no way diminished by walking through the cobbled, winding medieval streets of the town itself. I tried to imagine how many generations of people had walked those same streets: people pondering and wrestling with problems I knew that I, with my modern mind, couldn't even imagine. Everywhere around me rose up from the streets the intricate Baroque architecture for which Heidelberg is renowned, and which makes one feel like a child who has inadvertently stepped into some gilded, romanticized fairy tale of old. Ancient, looming castles; monumental gateways that look as if they've been cleaned up and transferred to earth from the grounds of some medieval giant who lives in the clouds; ancient, perfectly arched stone bridges that invite pedestrians to leave one world, and cross over into another. All of it leaves one looking about, lost in a wonder of inspiration.

In Heidelberg, one century mingles and glides into the next--and each offers inspiring, heart-pounding visions of its own. Here is a medieval church; there a Renaissance plaza; here an ornate gateway from the 18th century. It's as if one is simply strolling through time, stepping as easily as can be from one epoch into another. There is not, I believe, any place similar to it in America.

Like untold millions before me, one of the first things I did upon arriving in Heidelberg was to pass through the famous arched gateway of the Karl-Theodore Bridge. On either side of the bridge looms one of the gigantic cylindrical Baroque towers (each of which holds several dungeon cells!) that were once integral to the medieval city's fortification. Today, they seem to welcome visitors to come onto the bridge and stare up at the Heidelberg castle--though they do seem to be intoning that you watch your step, and mind your manners. The stone bridge itself--a marvel of functional grace and durability--is as old as the city, and over the centuries has been built a rebuilt many times.

Another classic(al) Heidelberg experience that I made sure to partake of right away was a stroll up the famed Philosopher's Road--the *Philosophenweg*, in German--a woodland walking path winding its way up a hillside across the Neckar from the castle. Named for its best-known perambulators, the apparently fit and hale Goethe and Schiller, this "walk" turned out to be a seemingly vertical climb up a steep path made of ancient, roughhewn steps. Benches situated along the way invite one to stop and ponder the mankind's most enduring conundrums--or to simply sit a moment and wonder where one ever got the impression that philosophers weren't known for their physical prowess. The *Philosophenweg* is a challenging hike, but more than worth it once the ground, way up high, levels out, the trees suddenly part, and the breathtaking vista of

Heidelberg and the sparkling Neckar River valley spreads itself below.

It is at that moment that any man or woman would become, in an instant, a philosophizer.

Oh, there is so much to see and do in and around Heidelberg! The fabled, majestic Church of the Holy Ghost! The *Grosse Fass*, or Great Vat, in the Heidelberg Castle, a 58,000-gallon barrel that once held the wine of Karl Theodor (a man who, one presumes, really knew how to throw a party), the top of which was for centuries the *dance floor* of choice for courting couples.

Countless odd and exotic little museums! Parks and public grounds so well kept they seem to have been waiting and preparing all these centuries only for *you* to appear and enjoy them! Innumerable churches, hotels, homes and civic buildings, each boasting a richer and more storied history than the last! Restaurants that once served men and women of the Enlightenment, people who never dreamed their special little eatery would still be selling bratwurst all these many years later!

A person could spend their life--and any number of lives after that one--exploring and marveling at the wonders to be found at every turn throughout Heidelberg.

A person could also lose their scholarship doing that.

It was time, once again, to put my nose to the proverbial grindstone.

The first place I stayed in Heidelberg was at a hotel at the railroad station. The next day I registered at the university; I then found a room in a fraternity house for foreign students in the center of town, and close to everything. It was here that I constantly found myself facing the gut-wrenching choice familiar to anyone who has ever tried to study at college while surrounded by a great number of his fellow naturally-rambunctious peers (much less a crowd consisting of young people from all over the world): Fun, or Study.

I, being yet a farm boy from the country and now in the middle of one of the most exciting cities and times imaginable, found myself often choosing "fun."

Not good. I was quite sure the powers-that-be at the Von Humbold foundation, pleased though they may have been to discover all the ways in which my social life and skills were improving, would nonetheless have been constrained to chastise me financially if I continued to choose "Going To The Movies" over, say, "Memorizing Enzyme Catalytic Processes."

So after a month of fevered, all-night political debates, rooftop dance parties and spontaneous, full-squad games of soccer (some of them indoors, in hallways, laundry rooms, *living* rooms …), I moved to another room I found in a much quieter area of town: This was a small, humble room, with a bed, chair, table and wash basin.

At the fraternity house I had become especially good friends with a lively young man from Luxembourg named Marcel, who was studying to be a teacher of German. Marcel stopped by my room one afternoon as I was packing my things in preparation of my move across town.

"Luben!" he said. "Where are you going? How can you leave this exciting international assemblage of the brightest young minds in Europe? We have friends here from France, Belgium, Italy, Spain, Czechoslovakia, Holland! I had this amazing Italian fish soup yesterday, a dish I couldn't even have dreamed of before I tasted it--and one I know I will now crave for the rest of my life! And who do you think prepared it? It wasn't just any sweaty culinary cretin, my friend! No! It was the girl with the hair of wavy silk and the midnight eyes Michelangelo couldn't dream up! Yes! That girl from the library you've been admiring! Carlina! Carlina made us soup yesterday, Luben! And where were you? Off studying! And tonight there's going to be a giant party over at the commons, with everyone bringing an instrument from their own country. What beautiful cacophony is sure to result! And the food! Already I have smelled something that chap from Greece is bringing--you know, that one-browed bear of a fellow, what's his name? Xerses, or something? Apollo, maybe? Well, you know the fellow! He's cooking something that smells like licorice and leather! I myself will be bringing a sweetbread that, I am here to tell you, I am imagining will cause our dear Carlina to swoon! Oh, you must be there, Luben! It's the chance of a lifetime!"

"That's what I'm afraid of, Marcel!" I said. "I'm afraid that if I keep taking advantage of so many chances of a lifetime, I'll ruin my lifetime! You know I've got to keep my grades up in order to continue qualifying for my scholarship. I don't know if my grades can take one more dinner party, or musical celebration, or political debate fueled by beer and cigarettes. I'm afraid I don't have your stamina, my friend."

"And I'm afraid I don't have your grades, " Marcel sighed. "What is life, if not a series of calculated compromises? And, you're right: We must own up to the results of our actions. It's true that too many of us act as if one day doesn't follow the next. You are destined to be a great doctor, Luben, and are right at sticking to that goal, no matter what delicacies the wondrous Carlina may invite you to partake in.

"Well, now, about Carlina," I began.

"No! No!" said Marcel, dramatically flourishing his hand in the air and turning his head away. "Speak no more of her! Carlina is a siren whose seductive call you, a Bulgarian Odysseus set on his course, must not heed! Forget that fragrant flower of the Mediterranean, my friend! Stay the course! Abandon the Carlinas of this world to the likes of dissolute scoundrels such as myself, men who are so busy eating dessert they forget the sound nourishment of a good meal! Go! Learn! Study! Succeed! I and my ilk will, alas, take whatever comfort we may find, wherever, and with whomever, we might."

I hurled one of my shirts across the room at him; and even though it landed on his head, completely covering his face, this didn't stop him from continuing exactly the sort of tirade that, truth be told, was one of the chief reasons I was so fond of him.

Marcel and Carlina or not, however, I had soon enough returned to my life of monkish intellectualism: In my new room across town I was alone, able to study (and rest!) whenever and however I pleased. In contrast to my short stint in Berlin, in fact, the silence of Heidelberg was almost disorienting: There was absolutely no bombing of the city, as the large number of foreign students living and studying there had resulted in it being declared a "no-bomb" zone.

In the fall of 1943, Heidelberg was *the* place to be in Germany. Less comforting a place was Mannheim, about thirteen miles west of Heidelberg on the Rhine. Every night we could hear the bombs being dropped on this jewel of a German city. It was, to say the least, a dispiriting sound. (And as a reminder to us all of, if nothing else, just how close thirteen miles can be, one night an RAF bomber lost its way, and accidentally dropped some bombs extremely close to Heidelberg. Much rattling resulted; but no one, thank God, got hurt.)

As I was settling down to utterly dedicate myself to my medical studies at Heidelberg University something ominous occurred of a much more political nature. One afternoon while I was studying in my room I answered a knock at my door, and found there a taut looking gentleman wearing a perfectly pressed suit and round, rimless eyeglasses.

"Are you Luben Walchef?" said the man in the crisp tone of one who is hardly making a social visit. I allowed as how I was--and the man reached into his dossier, pulled out a couple of sheets of paper which he held out to me, and informed me that he was a representatives of the German government. He had come, he said, in order to secure my signature on the declaration he was proffering me, which stated that, as a foreigner living, studying, and working in Germany (and so to that extent indebted to the German government), I would, if called upon by the government to do so, willingly become a mobilized soldier of the German army.

"It is now a requirement for all foreign students in Germany," he said, the papers still in his outstretched hand.

I looked at the papers, and then at him.

"But studying is all I do," I shrugged, trying to sound relaxed--and remembering my father's advice about choosing my words about such matters with utmost care. "I am simply not politically inclined. Besides, the German army doesn't want the likes of me fighting for it. What kind of soldier for the Third Reich would an ex-Bulgarian farmer turned lowly college student make, anyway?" I laughed, hoping the government representative would do likewise.

He did not. "Are you saying that you refuse to sign this promise to serve in the great German military, even though you have been living and going to school in this country for such a long time now? Is that the position you are taking?"

"No, no," I said, sensing that for this moment it would be best to play the very soul of cooperation and gratitude. "That's not what I am saying at all. Of course I am very grateful for all the German government has done to help me in my studies. And if the German government felt it truly needed my services in order to achieve its noble goals, then it would be my pleasure to serve." (I prayed that God wouldn't strike me dead, right there.)

"Good," said the man, thrusting the papers forward. "Then sign these, please."

I took the papers from his hand. "This is a pretty long document," I said. "Of course I would like to read it before I sign it. I'm a fairly good student, I suppose, but I'm fairly ignorant in the ways of the world yet:

As such, I made a ironclad promise to my dear father that I would never sign anything detailed or serious without first reading it carefully--and, actually, asking his advice on the matter. I don't think I need to ask his advice on this--though I would like to. But in any case, I want to read it first. I'm sure you understand that."

"Of course I do. I can wait."

"Well, the thing is," I lied, "I have a class that I'm already late for. It's a lecture I cannot afford to miss. Is it possible that I can read this, sign it, and then bring it somewhere? Is there any office in the city to which I could return this signed document?"

He studied me for a moment or two while I did my absolute strongest impression of an Earnest Innocent. And then he told me where to take the document once I'd read and signed it.

"I'll do that," I said. "Thank you very much."

"Heil Hitler," said the man.

"Heil Hitler," I rejoined, and then closed my door.

Not good. This was not good. Of all the things in the world of which I was sure, none was more sure to me than that I had not come all this way to end up a German soldier waiting to die somewhere in a fox hole. Even if my knowledge of history hadn't already drummed from my conscience any sense of the romance of war, seeing as many broken and wounded soldiers returning from this particular war as I had was more than enough to convince me that taking their place was the last thing in the world I wanted to do.

And yet the German government, it appeared, had other plans.

And they knew who I was, and where I lived.

And the German government, as virtually everyone living in Germany at that time, was extremely methodical about getting whatever it wanted.

I knew I had to move.

Chapter Ten

Dossenheim

I waited about a month so that if anyone came checking it wouldn't appear as if I'd simply bolted from my address as soon as the representative from the government had visited me--and then I moved to Dossenheim, a small village about five miles away from Heidelberg along Bergstrasse, a street that extends from Heidelberg far alongside the Neckar Valley and is famous for the fragrant, wonderful fruit orchards it meanders by and though. To get to school every day I rode a small old train that ran between Heidelberg and the villages along Bergstrasse.

There may be more romantic things to do than ride a quaint train in the spring through the miles of lush blossoming fruit trees along the Neckar's Bergstrasse--but I can't imagine what those things might be.

And such rides were certainly not rendered any less romantic by the occasional accompaniment of my girlfriend from the University of Wurzburg, Irmgard. Irmgard had seen fit, after all, to transfer to the University of Heidelberg, where she was continuing her education in languages. It was a very good thing to once again be reunited with such a good and loyal friend.

My landlords in Dossenheim were Mr. and Mrs. Hans Stoer. He worked in Heidelberg. I liked everything about the room I rented from this kindly couple; the bed in particular was memorable, in that, being very firm, it afforded me truly refreshing sleep. The Stoer's had two daughters who worked with their mother in the garden, which yielded delicious fruits and vegetable of all kinds. (Especially delicious were the apples from their few apple trees, which were wonderful and lasted all winter.) As the Stoers had more than enough yield from their garden and were not at all inclined to sell their excess, they generously shared their produce with me. Quite a boon to a struggling ex-student (who used to be a farmer, and who never *would* get over his love of fresh produce!) Fruit and vegetables were the lion's share of the meals we and everyone else in Germany ate during those times, as the government has rationed meat to only 200 grams a week. Still, we got meat when and how we could: When it rained, for instance, and the snails were in the open, I would take a bucket and collect great numbers of them, which I would then cook by boiling them with some salt for 5 or 10 minutes, after which I would clean them, and then cut the resultant meat into smaller pieces and fried them with butter.

Delicious! It was the same thing I had done as a boy in Bulgaria.

I recall another means by which, for short time, I was able to enjoy some meat without causing the German government to come crashing to a halt. While at Heidelberg, I worked in the university's clinic as an intern, and there became acquainted with a patient I was taking care of who lived on a farm in the mountains not too far away from Heidelberg. One day this kind fellow invited me up for a visit to his farm. The following Sunday I got on my trusty bicycle and rode along the river and up the mountain to his farm. It was a splendid place, filled with gardens and fruit trees I smelled before I saw. It being fall my friend had lots of pears and apples, which he generously loaded me up with.

"Come!" he said. "I'll show you the newest additions to our family!" I followed him out into the yard and to a little pig house, which held, I saw, a mother sow with five little piglets who were each about one month old.

Is there anything in this world cuter than a baby pig?

At that moment it seemed to me there couldn't possibly be, so I asked him if he would sell me one. He said he would, and so I paid him just a few German marks, and gently placed the little piglet in my ruck-sack, along with some straw to keep him comfortable. With the piglet nestled into the main part of the sack, and the pockets on either side bulging with fruit, I drove away from my friend that day like a whole little farm on wheels.

Although it was in the light of the afternoon that I waved goodbye to my friend, it had become dark by the time I had bicycled down the beautiful hill and made my way back to Heidelberg--a trip I enjoyed, as it offered me the splendid passing scenery of the river, the city and, of course, the great castle.

Things became distinctly less enrapturing when I arrived at the famous old Heidelberg bridge. There a policeman who was standing guard called at me to stop. I did, of course, and he came over to inform me that I was not allowed to ride a bicycle at night without a light. In my friendliest tone, I explained to this no-nonsense guardian of the public good that it had simply gotten late sooner than I had anticipated, and that it would not happen again.

My heart went to my throat as I saw him eyeing my bag, as at that time it was against German law to buy or transport any meat or animals within the country.

"Was haben sie in deinem ruchsack," he said--"What do you have in your rucksack?"

I again made sure to maintain the persona of the most innocent, eager-to-please young man in the world.

"It's fruit my friend gave me from his farm!" I said. I reached into one of the side pockets, hoping that in the dark it would appear that I was reaching into the sack's main compartment. I prayed the piglet would remain quiet as I pulled out a pear. "Would you like a piece?" I said. "It's delicious!"

"No, thank you," said the policeman, softening a bit.

"Are you sure?" I said, still holding out the pear. "Maybe for later?"

"No, I'm fine. Now move along. Walk your bike across the bridge, and don't ever let me see you bicycling along here after dark without a light. That's dangerous."

"Yes sir," I said, climbing off my bike. As I began to walk my bicycle away I kept the pear in my hand; I didn't want to jostle the bag any more than I had to by placing the fruit back in its pocket.

"Goodbye, now!" I called merrily.

And then, walking just as casually as any relaxed country boy ever did, I held my breath until I knew I was far enough along the bridge to be out of piglet-noise range from the officer.

"Thank you, pig," I whispered to my secret cargo.

Mr. Stoer was very pleased to meet the newest addition to his household. He let me make a little house in the corner of the garden, where I kept the pig as a pet--until it had grown large enough to serve the Stoers and I another purpose altogether.

It was during the meals in which that pig played such a central role that I found myself (almost) missing life back on my family's farm.

The relative peace I found in Dossenheim was shattered in the first months of 1945, after Germany was defeated in the war and American soldiers occupied Heidelberg and its surrounding communities. They announced their arrival in Dossenheim by shooting flares into the air and calling out through bullhorns from the streets, "Attention, German citizens! We are the American army! We are issuing an order that every single resident of this town stay within their home for the next forty-eight hours. Repeat: no one is to step out of their home for the next forty-eight hours! At the end of that time, we will announce when it is okay for you to again resume your daily activities! The United States Army thanks you for your cooperation!"

Boy. Talk about getting people's attention.

The first night of the American occupation, the only doctor in Dossenheim was called to come to the aid of a patient who was apparently having a heart attack. This doctor, responding to an authority that he must have recognized as higher than the American military, took his bag and headed out on the street toward the home of the suffering man. When the American soldiers saw him they ordered him to stop. When instead he simply continued on his way, the Americans, after having called a few more times for him to stop, shot and killed the doctor, who was very popular throughout the town. It was one tragic moment in what of course was an almost overwhelming series of tragedies, but it resonated deeply throughout the hushed, scared little town of Dossenheim.

The morning we were first free to move about outside our homes I caught an early train into Heidelberg, eager to get back to the college and resume my work and studies. On the way there, I saw a sight that haunts me to this day. As we were peacefully rumbling along I looked out the window at the passing trees and saw something hanging from them I did not at first recognize. It's funny how when a person sees something for which they have no prior frame of reference, they try to fit what they are seeing with something they've ever seen before. It wasn't long before that tact failed, however, and I was forced to realize that I was, in fact, seeing what I couldn't believe I was: dead men hanging from trees.

I gasped, and sat bolt upright back in my chair. I heard the other passengers react at what they, too, saw. Pulled to do so by the sheer will of unbelief, I looked back out the window. There was no mistaking what I'd seen.

Later, I learned that the bodies we'd all seen on the train that day were of German soldiers who had been caught fleeing from the front lines of battle. The German SS had hung the bodies there as a warning to other Germans who might be inclined to betray the interests of the government. The Americans would discover the bodies soon enough, and take them down.

When I arrived at Heidelberg University, I found that it had been surrounded by barbed wire, and was being policed by American soldiers. At first these soldiers wouldn't let me into my school; they relented, however, when I showed them my ID and explained to them that I was a medical student who worked at the university's infirmary.

Once in the hospital I saw some of the last of the returning German soldiers. The human body is an amazing machine, capable of continuing to function despite almost unimaginable abuse and distress. And it's a funny thing about the politics of warfare: you can feel one way or another about whatever political realities resulted in one group of people waging war upon another; but no matter how you feel about either side, seeing the results of that war--seeing what it has done to the bodies and minds of the young men who willingly took upon themselves the brunt of whatever decisions their leaders made for them--wipes from the mind any and all "political" considerations.

A young man without a nose, or missing a leg, or blinded by shrapnel, makes one forget all about whom the "bad" guys are, and whom the good.

No young man deserves to have happen to him the type of things I saw in the hospitals in Heidelberg.

It's an old adage that will never grow stale as long as wars are fought anywhere: If the people who made the decisions to go to war had to actually *fight* the wars, the world would be a very different place.

At least I could help the returning soldiers.

There are some times when being a doctor is infinitely more awful--and infinitely more rewarding--than others.

It was about this time that I got a letter from Mr. Mueller, my beloved old landlord in Berlin, with whom I had made sure to stay in touch. He told me that a few months after I left their home his wife, who had always treated me as if I were her son, had died during one of the bombings in Berlin. The stress of it had been too much for her, he said: During one of the hurried trips I knew so well down the four flights of steps toward the basement, she had stopped, while the bombs rattled the walls of their building, and clutched her chest, falling upon the steps. She did not rise again.

Heidelberg changed a great deal after the American occupation began. Everywhere throughout the city were American soldiers: One saw them on the streets, in the market places, everywhere on public transportation. The Philosopher's Way along the Neckar River, which was meant to inspire reflection in thoughtful pedestrians, became a roadway for American jeeps: Whooping and laughing, they tore up the hallowed pathway driving their Jeeps up and down the mountain. They didn't hurt anyone physically by doing such things, but it was greatly disheartening to see such active disrespect for something meant only to inspire peace. As abominably as its doomed and demented government may have acted during the war, Germany is, after all, a place that throughout time has bequeathed to mankind some of its richest cultural accomplishments. It was disheartening, to say the least, to see so much of that rightfully proud heritage be so callously disrespected.

But. To the victor, as they say.

In keeping with what seemed to be Fate's desire to forever at the last moment thwart my educational plans, the University of Heidelberg, at the end of 1945, closed. I was one semester away from graduating from medical school.

What *was* it with me and schools being closed?

Fortunately, instead of the school being closed for three years as had happened at my old high school in Slavianovo, *this* school--due to the Herculean efforts of surgery professor R. H. Bauer and the philosopher Karl Jaspers--reopened after six months. (When it did so, we students found missing from campus all the professors whom, we were in some cases very surprised to learn, had been Nazis.)

The good news is that the university re-opened; the very bad news, for me, was that at the end of the war the Von Humbold Foundation ceased operations. I knew that without that financial assistance, there was no way I would be able to finish even the six months standing between me and graduation. Desperately, I brought my case before the American authorities, and was deeply pleased to discover that I was going to be allowed to continue my studies under something called the UNRA, an organization that had been set up to subsidize the studies of foreign students in Germany. It was hardly going to supply me with the funds I'd been receiving from the Von Humbold Foundation: But it did cover university fees and one free lunch a day.

And that's what I lived on throughout my final semester of medical school at the University of Heidelberg, from which I graduated on July 13, 1946.

Chapter Eleven

Physician, Heal Thyself

I was, of course, delighted to have finally arrived at the position of a pedigreed medical professional; I was decidedly less thrilled to realize that I'd never in my life been poorer. I needed work, and quickly. The problem was that many doctors who had been serving in the military were now pouring back into Germany, looking for the same jobs as I. Nobody in Germany at that time was having an easy go of it: Jobs quickly became exceedingly difficult to come by; at the same time, the cost of food seemed to rise daily. Most food (and most everything else, for that matter) was being sold on the black market at high prices.

Because I couldn't find a paying position and needed the work in order to produce my final dissertation (which would allow me to get my Doctor of Medicine degree), for two years I became a medical researcher at the university's hospital, where, in a study involving eighteen patients, I did clinical research on a sulphur injection treatment for polyarthritis. From the results of this research I was able to publish a paper, "Treatment of Arthritis With Colide Sulfur," in the medical magazine, "Practice," published in Munich. This paper was the core of my dissertation, which I soon thereafter presented to the University of Heidelberg's medical certification board. The result was that I was awarded, *cum laude,* my Doctor of Medicine degree.

Even with this advanced degree, however, I could find no work. I was still living with the Stoer family in Dossenheim; and though they were, as ever, exceedingly kind to me, I felt that I could no longer continue living there without paying rent. But where to go? What to do? There were simply no jobs to be had.

Finally, though, one turned up: a job as a surgical resident in a city hospital in Ludwigshafen that had been damaged during the war, but was apparently restored enough to be back in business. Although the job offered no pay it did come with room and board; at this point too desperate to turn down anything, I packed my bags and moved from Dossenheim to Ludwigshafen.

I was given a small room in one corner of the hospital; exceedingly humble though it all was, I was happy in those hard times to have a roof over my head, a bed and meals. Where for so long my view had been of beautiful Heidelberg and the Neckar River, now the view of my room was of Ludwigshafen and a bit Mannheim, both of which had been 95% destroyed in the war. It was a change for the worse, no doubt: But at least I was surviving, and working in a field that surely promised a brighter future.

For the present, however, my job, though it certainly kept me busy, was also barely keeping me alive. As such, I found myself searching about for some other means of income. Low and behold, in a conversation with some American soldiers one afternoon in a café, I discovered that they had access to as many upright carpet sweepers as they cared to buy from their military supply houses.

Aha! If there's one thing I knew German women liked, it was a clean house.

I had just enough money to buy, at a reasonable profit for the soldier involved, one carpet sweeper--which I immediately sold to a German housewife for about four times what I'd paid for it. And just like that, I had a way to make enough money to cover my transportation and personal needs.

And before you knew it, there I was: a doctor, busily buying and selling, at truly amazing profit, black market carpet sweepers.

My *other* job, as a doctor, proved to be of great interest for me, in that it brought me into working contact with a professor very well known for his work on varicose veins. He was preparing a book on the subject, which I tried my best to help him with. His work concerned the relief of varicose veins without surgery: His method utilized elastic bandages, and the elevation of the legs. When this more benign treatment failed, he had to use surgery in order to remove the veins. This process entailed passing a wire upward from a small ankle incision through the vein to the inguinal area, where the wire was found by palpation. The wire was pulled out through a small incision at that point, bringing the vein with it. This was called "vein stripping."

It was, as I say, interesting work. I was happy to help this knowledgeable doctor, and to learn from him.

I was not happy, however, to have my primary source of income derive from my moonlighting as a market-savvy trader on the black market; this was hardly the life I'd been working toward for so long. But there didn't seem any way out of the mess Germany had become. In the postwar negotiations, the Allied powers had divided Germany was divided into four zones, the largest going to the Soviet Union. Berlin itself was similarly divided: France took the area west of the Rhine, Great Britain occupied northern Germany, and the U.S occupied the southern part, including Heidelberg, which became headquarters of the American occupation force.

All things considered, I felt the time had come for me to leave Germany. I knew, right away, that I did not want to return to Bulgaria, as it had become a communist country. Since for so long my goal had been to move to America, the first thing I did after deciding to find my way out of Germany was to register to immigrate to the United States. As popular a country as I knew it to be, I was shocked to hear that I was now on a ten-year waiting list for people desiring a visa for America.

Clearly, I would need something to do until my name came up.

I next decided to try my luck in France. I had, after all, studied French for six years in high school, and was fluent in the language. I wrote a letter seeking employment to the Hospital Cochin in Paris. In return I got a very nice letter inviting me to work in the hospital as a "volunteer assistant." I wasn't sure exactly what that meant--but I did notice that nowhere in the letter was there any mention of pay.

The first thing I did was to write my friend Marcel, who I knew had returned from Heidelberg to his home in Luxembourg. His response was an invitation to visit him for a two week stay. An agency called the International Refugee Organization (IRO) had the power to issue passports for people currently in Germany who, after the war, did not want to return to their home countries. However, the German regime had rendered my Bulgarian passport invalid, which meant, I learned, that I had to travel to Stuttgart in order to obtain a "stateless passport." At that point I learned that I was, technically, a stateless refugee in Germany.

Stuttgart was about 100 miles from Heidelberg, but I had a small motorcycle (a hybrid motorcycle/bicycle, really: The handy, sensible contraption allowed one to pedal in the occasion of it running out of gas), and one day decided to ride it to Stuttgart. I went through a mountainous area on the way, which was very nice going down and less nice walking up. Still, having left very early in the morning, I arrived in Stuttgart around noon, which allowed me enough time to go to the IRO office, apply for, and obtain the passport on the same day.

A good day, indeed!

That night I said my goodbyes to my second family, Mr. and Mrs. Stoer and their daughters, knowing that for the rest of my life I would miss them, Dossenheim, and the city that for so long had meant so much to me, Heidelberg. Throughout the horrors of the war, Heidelberg had never relinquished its air of the good, old German fairy tales: It remained a wondrous place of mystery and magical transformation. For six years I had been a part of that magic; I, too, had been transformed there, from a boy with few resources to a grown man with a medical degree from one of the finest colleges in the world.

I could only hope the rest of the world would be as good to me as Heidelberg had been.

The next day I packed everything I owned back into my two old suitcases, and caught a train for Luxembourg.

The Walchef family, Pordim, Bulgaria, 1922. Sitting, from left to right: My father Simeon (holding my sister Veska); my other sister Vassilka (in the sailor's cap); Simeon's mother (my grandmother); my grandfather Valcho (with me between his legs); my adopted cousin; his adopted father, my uncle; the son of our live-in hired hand. Standing, back row: My mother (wearing the gold necklace given to her by her father on her wedding day); my aunt; my uncle's wife; our live-in hired hand.

Foreign Couple Fascinated By TV
... Simeon and Angelina Walchef of Pordim, Bulgaria

Bulgarians Visit

From The Iron Curtain To TV In Living Room

The Cincinnati newspaper article about my father Simeon and his wife, my stepmother Angelina.

My class at Pordim Elementary School. I am in the very middle of the front row, on my knees just between the two reclining boys. On the far right is the math teacher whose bicycle inspired me to go to college.

The home and medical clinic in Pleven, Bulagria, where I lived with the widowed Mrs. Zaharov and her son Peter, whom I tutored.

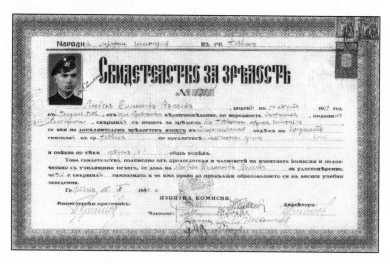

My diploma from the high school in Pleven. That's me in the picture (and yes, that hat was part of our high school uniform). The big text across the top of the document, written in Bulgarian, translates literally into "Certificate of Maturity."

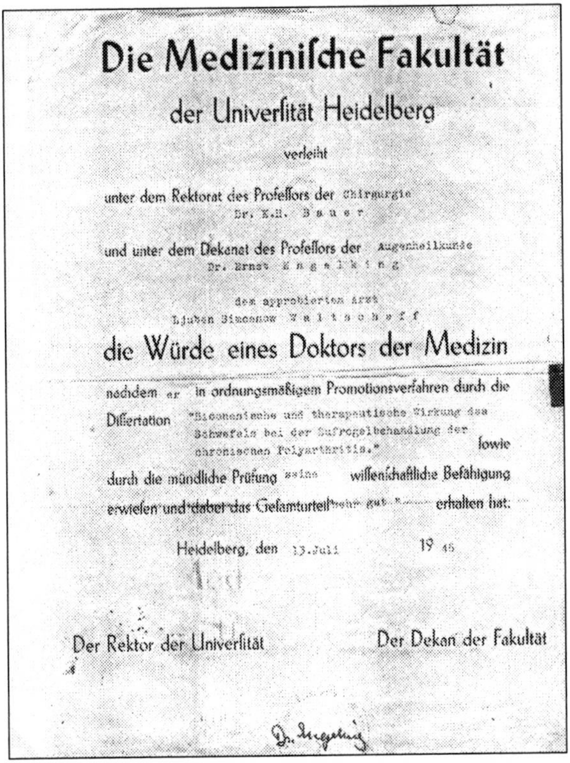
Die Medizinische Fakultät
der Universität Heidelberg
verleiht
unter dem Rektorat des Professors der Chirurgie
Dr. K.H. B a u e r
und unter dem Dekanat des Professors der Augenheilkunde
Dr. Ernst E n g e l k i n g
dem approbierten Arzt
Ljuben Simeonow W a l t s c h e f f
die Würde eines Doktors der Medizin
nachdem er in ordnungsmäßigem Promotionsverfahren durch die
Dissertation "Biochemische und therapeutische Wirkung des Schwefels bei der Sufrogelbehandlung der chronischen Polyarthritis." sowie
durch die mündliche Prüfung seine wissenschaftliche Befähigung
erwiesen und dabei das Gesamturteil "sehr gut" erhalten hat.
Heidelberg, den 13. Juli 1945
Der Rektor der Universität
Der Dekan der Fakultät
Dr. Engelking

My medical degree from the University of Heidelberg

With my friend Marcel (left) in Luxembourg, 1949.

My immigrant's card to Canada

Staff, physicians, residents and professors at the Royal Victoria Hospital in Montreal, Canada. I am in the front row, third from the right. Dr. Penfield, who became renowned for his work on epilepsy, is on the far right in the row directly behind mine.

My first Bulgarian friend in America, the restaurateur and sculptor, Dan Boteff.

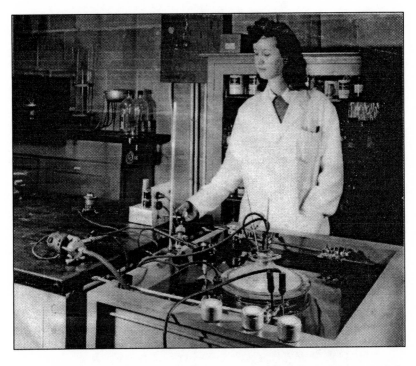

My wife Elizabeth, before I met her, at a summer job making use of the knowledge that would lead her to become a high school physics teacher.

My family in San Diego: (from left) my wife Elizabeth with our children Boyan, Luben and Lisa.

Me (sitting, with camera around my neck) in front of the Taj Mahal with my fellow travelers from San Diego. Later that night, I alone would see the Taj Mahal glow blue in the moonlight.

The home, eighty years later, built in Pordim by me, my father, and my grandfather.

My grandson Shawn and I before the Great Vat at Heidelberg Castle.

Me standing outside my Alpine Caste in Warner Springs.

Chapter Twelve

Luxembourg

I wasn't, of course, at all sure what the world might bring me by way of wonder and magic; I *knew* it had to bring me something by way of a job, as I'd spent very nearly my last dime on the train ticket to Luxembourg. It was not quite, but almost, the case that I needed to essentially walk off the train in Luxembourg and directly into a hospital or clinic (preferably one right across the street from the station), where I would immediately start my new job as a doctor. Not, of course, that that was going to happen. But if something like it didn't, I feared for the limits of my friend Marcel's hospitality.

When I got off the train Marcel was waiting for me, and his ebullient welcome put me in the best possible spirits.

"Luben!" he cried. "Look at you! You look fantastic, my old friend! It is very good to see you--very good indeed! Here, let me help you with your suitcases. How was your ride? Are you, as I finally was, glad to once and for all leave Germany behind? What a terrible place that became in the end, no? Well, now you are here with your old friend in Luxembourg--which, thank God, is still Luxembourg, and *not* part of Germany, as the Nazis tried to make it. What arrogance! They took over our country--they changed its name; they installed a Nazi leader as its head; they forced the inscription of our young into its wretched army; they killed anyone who resisted them--they even outlawed our native language! They tried with all their might to change our heads--but they couldn't change our hearts.

"Oh, you should have seen how we welcomed the American liberators, Luben! As if they were angels come to deliver us from hell--which they were! But all that nastiness is now behind us, 'eh, my friend? And now you, too, have left Germany behind, and come out into the real Europe! Oh, you are going to have a wonderful time, Luben! My parents--I told you I live with my parents, right?--are very eager to meet you. They've been waiting to meet the young genius doctor who took Wurzburg, Berlin and Heidelberg by storm!"

By the time we reached the impressively large home of Marcel's parents, my jaw was sore from so much smiling. It was not surprising at all that Marcel had been so proficient at learning languages: If anyone was born to communicate, it was he. His confidence and good cheer were exactly what I needed, and I was then, and will always be, grateful for it.

Driving to his home I realized that I felt truly free for the first time since I'd left Bulgaria. I'd been so busy in Germany, and so focused on my singular reason for being there, that I had, without realizing it, simply accepted the psychological burden that comes from living in the middle of a country furiously raging war on the rest of the world. While the oppression, fear, danger, and relentless suspicion had of course attended my every moment in Germany, I had effectively ignored them all, insisting that they stay at the outer fringes of my consciousness, where they were least likely to disturb my studies. It's what everyone in Germany at that time did. What *else* was there to do?

But now that I was out of that country, I felt a deep, abiding, joyous sense of peace and freedom infuse my soul. It fueled much of my laughter at Marcel's stories and comments; surely, that good young man never had a more appreciative audience.

That night, alone in the guest room Marcel's gracious, open-hearted parents had prepared for me, I slept like I felt I hadn't since back on the farm in Pordim.

"Come!" said Marcel the next morning, after we'd eaten the sumptuous breakfast prepared for us by his mother. "Before the cares of the world settle too heavily on your shoulders (for I know you must find work--and if I know you, my industrious friend, you'll be the head of a hospital two days after you begin looking for work), you must see our capital, Luxembourg City! We have parks, and beautiful wide streets, and all the splendor and history you'd find in Paris! You must see these things straight away, Luben! We leave at once!"

Marcel was right: Luxembourg City was gorgeous. I began to wonder if Luxembourg wasn't the place I might like to live.

The next day, however, Marcel, in the hopes of it perhaps leading to work for me, introduced me to a doctor friend of his. This man, impressed as he was by my background (I even showed him my diploma from Heidelberg), informed me that in Luxembourg at that time, foreign doctors were simply not allowed to practice.

"What?!" cried Marcel, saying what I was thinking. "That's absurd! My friend here is one of the finest medical minds in Europe! You're telling us that he can't heal the sick in this city, or anywhere in Luxembourg, just because he wasn't *born* here? What kind of travesty is this? If you were lying in the street bleeding to death, would you care what country your doctor came from, as long as you could save his life? Of course you wouldn't! What nonsense!"

"I don't make the rules," shrugged his friend. "I'm just telling you what they are."

"And here I've been telling Luben what a wonderful country we have," said Marcel. "This is embarrassing." Marcel pulled in a deep sigh, seeming deflated and sad. Then, being Marcel, he perked right up again.

"You shall go to Paris!" he cried. "A man of your vision and depth should be in Paris, anyway--instead of *this* apparently backward, provincial outpost. Paris, Luben! Think of it! There, I'm sure, you can find work. And everything else good that life has to offer!"

Going to Paris did, in fact, sound like a very good idea; that day I excitedly bought a train ticket to the City of Light--but it was a roundtrip ticket, just in case.

"Good luck!" Marcel waved to me as the train pulled away from the Luxembourg station. "See you soon! Though I hope not! You know what I mean!"

I laughed, and waved--and then settled back into my seat (underneath which was stored my two trusty *old* suitcases) and wondered what adventure was in store for me next.

I looked about at my fellow passengers. Everyone seemed very well dressed; and everyone was speaking French. I was happy to discover that I understood most of what they were saying, though a little intimidated that I didn't understand it all.

Well. It was enough.

The first thing I did upon arriving in Paris (after ogling everything in sight to such an extent I realized I'd best focus on what I was doing before I tripped or walked into a wall, and killed myself) was to look up some relatives of Marcel's.

"They will take you in!" Marcel had told me. "I've already called them! They are waiting for you--with a room and everything! It will be your home in Paris!"

Well, at any rate, it would be my attic in Paris: Marcel's relatives had nothing more to offer me than what amounted to a storage room along one wall of which had been placed a small bed.

It was plenty; I thanked them for their generosity, and promised I would only stay as long as it took me to find a job.

"There is no rush," they said.

I pulled the empty pockets out of my pants.

"There is," I said.

You perhaps recall that while still in Heidelberg I had received an invitation from a professor at a university hospital in Paris, the Hospital Cochin, to be a volunteer surgical assistant. The day after my arrival in Paris I went to meet the doctor; he remembered me, and on the spot accepted me for the position.

The good news was that I had a job; the bad was that it paid exactly nothing--not even a free lunch. I had made better money--*much* better money, actually--working in the cafeteria at Wurzburg. Still, it was a job in the medical profession, and anyone who has ever made anything of himself knows that it's always better to work than do nothing at all. And since my only option at the time was nothing at all, I showed up for work at the hospital, every morning at nine o'clock, to observe or assist with surgery. In the afternoons I was delighted to stroll about the capital city of France, with its historical monuments, beautiful wide streets, museums, theaters--and, of course, the famous French opera house. I especially enjoyed walking along the little path that bordered the gorgeous lake in Luxembourg Garden, where I would watch the happy fathers and their little boys playing with toy boats. It was here that it first occurred to me that one day I would like to have a son, and do the same.

One night, alone in my tiny attic-bedroom, I found myself doing something I never thought I would, something I hadn't done the entire time I'd been in Germany: considering cashing in the fifty Swiss francs my grandfather had given me the night I left Bulgaria. It hurt me deeply to even think of doing such a thing--but my wallet (and, frankly, my stomach) seemed to leave me no choice. I was barely making it in Paris; I was lucky to eat any other meal in the course of a day besides the bowl of soup and piece of bread I bought every noon from the cafeteria at the hospital where I volunteered. And I couldn't find any regular work at all. Goodness knows I tried. Not atypical of my experience in that regard was the time I was interviewed for a physician appointment at a small private hospital in Paris. The man questioning me was not only the hospital's chief surgeon, but its owner. The interview went well, I thought: I was not perhaps as fluent in French as I might have wished, but I answered all the man's questions in a way that I felt left no doubt as to my qualifications for the job.

Imagine my dismay, then, when the man asked to see my medical diploma from Heidelberg--and then laughed at it.

"I would throw this in the trashcan if I were you," he said, flipping it back toward me. "That piece of paper is worthless. I wouldn't hire you if you were the only 'doctor' left in all of Europe. Now please be on your way."

Later, I found out this doctor was Jewish. At that moment, of course, I understood why he might harbor so much resentment toward someone coming fresh out of Germany looking for work in Paris.

And so there I was after having been in Paris for a few months: as poor as I'd ever been, and as hungry.

And there was my grandfather's treasured fifty-franc bill.

I cashed it in. My grandfather was a survivor, and it was in the spirit of survival that he'd given me that money. I was to spend it when--and only when--I had to. He had trusted me to understand the difference between need and want, and I knew that I had not ever betrayed that trust.

If ever I'd been in a time of need, it was now.

As emotional as it was for me to cash in my grandfather's money, it was a tremendous relief to finally *have* some money. Determined to never again find myself in such a position, I (if possible) redoubled my efforts to finally find a job worthy of my degree.

It wasn't too long afterwards that I heard of a job opening for a doctor at a prison. I went to inquire as to the job, and spoke with the hiring doctor, who informed me that the job did not pay particularly well--though it was something.

"And you are to live at the prison," he said.

"Excuse me?" I said, fearing that I had not, in fact, misunderstood what he said.

"The doctor we are seeking will have to live in the prison itself," he said. "It's the nature of the position: He needs to be available day and night in order to care for the prisoners whenever they need it."

I swallowed hard, and said, "I'll take it."

"Very good, Dr. Walchef," said the man, extending his hand to me. "You may start tomorrow evening if you'd like!"

The next day I took one of my little suitcases (leaving the other behind with Marcel's relatives, so that I could easily return to them in case I really didn't like my new job), and reported to the prison.

As I passed through the main gate of the place, the thing I realized was that this was a *prison.* The moment I was on the facility grounds I was nearly overwhelmed by a sense of oppression and desolation. The staff of the office to which I had been told to report was expecting me; they took me to my room, which was of good size: It had a bed, a table, a chair.

I should rest now, I was told, and do whatever I needed to prepare for surgery the next morning. They closed the door, and then I was alone in my room inside a prison.

As the evening turned into night I saw and heard the massive main gate through which I'd come close and lock with a hard, thunderous boom. And then all was silent.

As I lie on my bed staring up into the darkness, I tried to grab hold of, and perhaps even take some comfort in, whatever differences I could conjure in my mind between my condition at that moment and actually *being* incarcerated in that prison.

My room was probably a little bigger than the average cell there. That was certainly ... a bonus.

Um ... and I was undeniably alone in my room. I wasn't sure in reality just how exclusive a privilege that was, but in the movies prison cells usually seemed to be occupied by more than one.

So. I had a bigger room, and I was alone.

Other than that, though, it felt, as far as I could tell, exactly like I was in prison.

Not good.

Really not good.

The morning after that first long, sleepless night saw me walking right back out the gate through which I'd arrived the previous evening. I didn't go to the office to say goodbye to anyone; I didn't talk to anyone; I didn't in any formal way at all process myself out of there: I just picked up my suitcase, and headed for the gate. They'd figure it out.

And do you know that from the second I passed that gate, I felt *exactly* as if I'd just escaped from prison? I could barely walk for fear of someone hollering out from behind me, *"You there! Stop! Stop before I shoot!"* And if *I* had heard that, I know what I would have done, too: I would have covered my head, and started running madly forward in a zigzag pattern.

I'd done my time, was how I figured it.

Now it's (sort of) funny; then, I was at my wit's (not to mention my wallet's) end. I went back to the home of Marcel's relatives (thankful that I *had* opted to buy a roundtrip ticket), and from there phoned Marcel and told him of my misfortunes in Paris.

"Come back to Luxembourg!" he said. "You have given Paris a chance, and that fickle damsel has left you hanging. Say goodbye to her, then, and come back here. Don't worry, Luben. We will think of a plan."

Marcel's plan was for me to next seek work in Brussels, Belgium.

"There is a man I know who works for my relatives driving a milk truck in and out of Brussels every day!" said Marcel. "This is perfect! All concerns about crossing from Luxembourg into Belgium will be eradicated by you simply sitting with my friend in his milk truck, as if you were assisting him! The border guards will give you no trouble at all! After all, who knows more about milk--and about *travel*--than you do, Luben? No one, that's who! No one! My friend will probably be worried that you'll take *his* job! It's the perfect plan! It gets you into Brussels without having to go through the bother of waiting for a passport and visa and all of that! And I am *sure* you will find plenty of work in Brussels!"

The very next morning I stashed my suitcase behind the passenger's seat of the milk truck driven by Marcel's friend (so low had my fortunes sunk that by this time I could fit all I owned into but *one* suitcase; I'd left its erstwhile faithful companion, empty as empty gets, back in Paris somewhere).

"Are you sure this is okay with you?" I asked the driver, a burly, friendly-looking fellow.

"No problem," he said. "A friend of Marcel's is a friend of mine. Hop aboard. I see the same guards every day; we all know each other. They won't give us any trouble."

And sure enough, they didn't--and before I knew it, I was in the third country I'd been in since leaving Heidelberg not four months before. Specifically, I was let out of the milk truck in front of a hotel in the center of downtown Brussels. I stayed that night in the hotel before finding, the next day, a small, inexpensive room through the newspaper.

That night, I counted what was left of my grandfather's money.

It didn't take long.

The next day, I asked my new landlords if there happened to be a hospital or medical clinic nearby. There was, as it turned out, and I headed immediately to what turned out to be a small Catholic hospital.

Imagine my joy when upon asking I discovered that there was, in fact, an opening for a surgeon there. Imagine it again when, on the very first interview for that position, I was hired! The job, being part-time, only paid fifty Belgian francs a month; it wasn't much, to be sure, but fifty full francs away from my previous earnings of nothing--and my room was only fifteen francs a month, which meant enough left over for food, transportation and entertainment.

Whew. Saved.

I phoned Marcel and told him the good news.

My work at the Catholic hospital left enough free time for me to feel comfortable approaching the professor of proctology at the University of Brussels to ask if he might also have any work for me. He greeted my overture with great friendliness, and accepted me for research at the university's institute of pathology. Under the professor's supervision and guidance, I researched transplanting bone to rabbits' kidneys. One such procedure involved taking a small piece of bone from a rabbit's leg, and then transplanting it back into the same rabbit, under the capsule of the kidney, which is richly supplied with blood.

After two or three months, I removed the piece of bone, and the professor and I sliced it into very thin pieces, which we mounted on glass slides and stained. Upon examining these pieces, we were surprised and very gratified to find the bone was growing and forming new bone cells.

This was good work that I was proud and pleased to be doing. I was enjoying other aspects of my life in Brussels, too. For the first time in a long time I had a little money for entertainment and other such (so-called) non-essentials. I met a young man with whom I became fast friends, a Swedish fellow who worked in the Swedish consulate; he and I had much fun gallivanting about the city together. I also got acquainted with Françoise, the secretary of my professor and mentor at the University of Brussels. She and I had spent wonderful time together, sight seeing on small trips, and going to the movies and theater.

All in all, in Brussels I enjoyed a good, healthy balance of work and recreation.

Still, you know me: After being in Brussels for two years, I found myself wondering not what life might be like in another country--I felt, by then, that I'd seen enough countries--but what it might be like on another *continent*. The one I had in mind, of course, was the one I'd always had in mind: North America.

Except I knew I still had--what, some seven years?--left on my ten-year wait for a visa to America.

And that left Canada.

Perfect! I'd always wanted to see Canada! (Well, all right: I hadn't *always* wanted to see Canada. But I had always wanted to see America--which actually *could* be seen from America. Good enough!)

So I applied for a visa to emigrate to Canada--and was told that would take two or three years.

Hmm.

In my mind, I pictured a map of the world.

What about *Africa?* Now *there* was a continent. I looked into it a bit, and found out that the Belgian Congo did, in fact, need doctors; it seemed that companies doing business there were paying high salaries for physicians. That was the good news; the bad was that, naturally enough, they were looking for doctors with training in tropical medicine. The closest I'd ever come to tropical medicine was scratching the occasional mosquito bite.

There was, however, a school in Antwerp (about 100 miles from Brussels on the North Sea) that offered a six-month program in tropical medicine. I decided to sign up.

"You're going *where?*" cried my Swedish friend. "To learn *what?* To go *where?*"

Despite my friend's protestations, I left my jobs in Brussels and moved to Antwerp, and for six months learned more than I ever imagined there *was* to learn about worms, parasites, malaria, yellow fever, typhoid, and a broad, broad range of venereal diseases.

Once the course was finished, I wasted not time applying for jobs in the Belgian Congo. Within a month I received a letter from a big company saying they'd like to hire me to come be their doctor in Africa.

I could already see the giraffes prancing across the sun-drenched savannah!

Except that on the same day I received the letter about becoming a doctor in Belgian Congo, I also received notification that, via some mysterious administration permutation, I had been granted the visa that would allow me to emigrate to Canada!

Now here was a puzzle. On the one hand, I had a job offer in Belgian Congo to make more money, by many times over, than I'd ever made in my life. On the other, I had a chance to emigrate to Canada, from which it would surely be easier to move to America than it would ever be from anywhere in Europe--not to mention from Africa. But I had no job in Canada. Going there would mean starting from scratch, a position I had barely taken a full step away from since ... well, since the day I was born.

A rich life in Belgian Congo, or a poor life in Canada?

Believe me when I say I put many long hours into thinking what to do--and then I decided on Canada. Because when I imagined myself in five or six years in Belgian Congo, I saw myself working at the same job I'd started when I arrived in the country, and making about the same amount of money. But when I imagined myself five or six years after arriving in Canada, I saw myself living in America.

And living in America was my dream. That was my goal. That was what I wanted.

Resolve is one thing; money, however, is (always) another. No matter how focused I now was on reaching North America, I lacked the funds necessary to buy a ship ticket to Canada. But, as happens so often in life, a dear friend came to my rescue: Françoise offered to lend me the price of the ticket. It was in truth a difficult gift to accept; but ultimately I did, promising to pay her back once I'd gotten my footing in Canada.

"Well, that won't take you long," smiled Françoise. "I'll look for a check a week after you've left."

"You're amazing!" cried Marcel over the phone. "I can't believe you are going to Canada--that is, I *wouldn't* believe it of anyone but you, my globe-hopping friend! I should have known a puny continent such as Europe wouldn't be enough to hold the likes of you! Good luck in the great Northwest, my intrepid wanderer! Tell the Mounties all their friends in Europe say hello! Don't forget about all of us stationary dullards back home, 'eh, Luben? We all depend upon you to tell us how the world is!"

And with a more-than-generous reference letter in my coat pocket from my professor and mentor at the University of Brussels, I boarded an old British military vessel named The Somalia in the French port of La Havre, and set sail for Canada.

Ten wavy, stormy, sea-sickly days later, the creaky Somalia was moving up the St. Lawrence River to Montreal, where we disembarked.

And there I was, in what, to me, was literally the New World.

Chapter Thirteen

O, Canada!

As always, the first thing I had to do was find a place to stay. And, as had by now become my Just Arrived routine, I went straight to the newspaper classifieds in order to help me locate that place. It didn't take long to find my way to a room listed as being near the Royal Victoria Hospital. In an extraordinary bit of luck, it turned out that the second-story room was being rented by a German family who took me in immediately.

So far, I liked Canada! I was in a part of it where French was common (as opposed to English, which I barely knew at all--though in Brussels, looking ahead to the possibility of life in America, I had studied it some); I was staying with a family who spoke German (in which of course I was fluent); and I was living near the Royal Victoria Hospital (in which, of course, I wanted a job).

Not bad for my first half-day in a country all the way across the Atlantic!

The following day, feeling (relatively) refreshed after my long boat trip (as it happened, The Somalia was retired immediately following the trip which had brought me to Canada--a stage in its career that I can say came not a moment too soon), I went to the Royal Victoria Hospital and looked up one Professor Selier, to whom my professional mentor back in Brussels had recommended me. Dr. Selier greeted me with great good cheer, and offered to show me about his laboratory. He was a pioneer in the field of stress and its physical implications; he was, in fact, one of the first doctors to even use the word "stress" in a medical context. I saw that in his laboratory he kept a fair number of monkeys, which were used for tests and experimentation.

After Professor Selier finished his tour of the facility, he said that he would be pleased to employ me as a research assistant--but only as a volunteer, since, as he explained, he then lacked the funds to afford me a salary.

"It is tempting," I said. "It's clear that you're doing new and important work here. Still, my stomach refuses to be satiated by that which delights my mind. It's a stubborn organ that way. So, I'm afraid I'll have to decline your offer, Dr. Selier, in the hopes of finding something that keeps both my stomach and mind satisfied. Thank you for the opportunity, though."

I wasn't fifteen steps out of his office, however, before I realized that I wasn't all that regretful about not being able to work with the great Dr. Selier. The research he was pioneering was certainly interesting enough, but I wasn't sure I had the necessary detachment for most effectively working with the monkeys.

The next day I went to search for work at another nearby medical institution associated with the Royal Victoria, the McGill University. I met there with a professor who told me that he had just started a year-long course in anesthesiology at the university. If it was something I was interested in doing, he said, he would be willing to register me for the course, which would then allow him to hire me as a resident in anesthesiology in the university's Department of Surgery, at a salary of one hundred dollars a month--*and* a free lunch every day!

I accepted his offer on the spot. It was hardly the kind of money I wanted to make, but it meant an end to all my immediate financial concerns--no small relief when you're new to a country, and aren't exactly sleeping every night on a mattress stuffed with money.

Besides being a comfort to me financially, the job also rewarded me intellectually. I was excited to be learning about the latest techniques in the formulation and application of anesthetics; I learned, for instance, how to administer nitrous oxide via a mouth mask or through a tracheal tube. Much of what I learned that year served me very well indeed later, when I had a medical practice of my own.

While at McGill I was also honored to observe major operations performed by professors famous the world over. I was able, for instance, to observe Professor Penfield, renowned for the work he was doing on patients suffering from epilepsy. His operational procedure was to remove scar tissue from the brains of epileptics, the result of which was a complete or near-complete cessation of their symptoms. It was breathtaking to watch this genius as he operated, and to realize the dramatic impact he was having on so many people suffering from that devastating disease.

As was my wont, I used my hours away from work to see and learn as much as possible about the city I was in. Montreal, I soon found out, was a city with as much to recommend it as any city I'd ever visited. Parks, theaters, movie houses, clubs, restaurants, art galleries--given all that, and the fact that everyone around me spoke either English or French (or, most charmingly, a combination of both) and this city of the New World seemed, to me, very much like a city of the Old. Perhaps the Atlantic wasn't as huge an ocean as my ten days on the Somalia had made it seem.

The summer months in Montreal were as balmy and warm as anyone could want--but the snow and cold of winter would be enough to send the Abominable Snowman himself packing for Hawaii. In clement weather my walk to work was but ten or fifteen minutes; the same walk taken in the cold and snow, however, became a fairly grueling trek that took twice that long. There were a few mornings when I couldn't even start that walk right, when to get outside at all I had to drop myself down from the bathroom window of my place because the snow had piled so high my front door was blocked shut.

It was during one such snow-caused acrobatic feat (straddling the window, one foot inside on the bathroom sink, the other dangling outside) that I resolved to get out of Canada. I'd seen plenty of snow in my life--in Bulgaria it was not uncommon during winter to have three feet of snow on the ground, and it got cold there--but I'd never even imagined snow like this. Just to go outside I had to wear so many layers of clothing once I *was* outside I could barely move.

There are a lot of things I admire about the Canadian people--their openness, their unfailing politeness, their energy and ingenuity--but I think what I *most* admire about them is their amazing ability to cheerfully weather bad weather. It's a testament to the great Canadian character that the country operates at all during the winter, much less that it never, from anything I saw, misses a beat.

I, however, was not Canadian, and--as I landed in a sweatery heap in the snow after having bailed from my bathroom window--I realized the unlikelihood that I ever would be, either. Which was fine, since my ultimate plan had always been to be (right after being Bulgarian, of course) an American.

And so, in June of 1951, as my year-long course on anesthesiology came to an end, I turned my gaze toward the south--which meant, in more prosaic terms, that I turned my gaze to a stack of the American Medical Association Journal I found in the hospital's library. And there, wonder of wonders, I found advertisements for positions as medical residents and interns in hospitals throughout the United States.

Bingo.

Within days I had sent letters seeking a position to six or seven hospitals--*two* of which summarily offered me jobs!

I can tell you: those were both exciting letters to receive.

And, oddly enough, they both came from the same place: Ohio. I'd barely *heard* of Ohio before, but I was instantly struck by what a happy, American-sounding little word it was, so bursting with forthright optimism and cheer.

"Oh, hi! Oh!"

Who *couldn't* like such a place?

One of the job offers was from a hospital looking for a surgery resident; that position, in Cleveland, paid $150 a month. The other was for an intern at the Deaconess Hospital in Cincinnati; that job paid $100.00 a month, plus room and board.

Hmm. Since they paid about the same, I had much to consider. I bandied about all the variables I was aware of relative to each job--intern versus resident; the one hospital against the other; the types of medicine I'd most likely be practicing in each facility--until I realized that, when all was said and done, what I *really* cared about was which city was further south--that is, which city would be *warmer*.

So I got out a map, and saw that Cleveland was on Lake Erie, which was surprisingly close to Canada, which meant it was entirely possible that people in Cleveland knew a thing or two themselves about bundling up and jumping out windows.

Cincinnati it was!

I wrote the Deaconess Hospital, and accepted their offer. When I explained to them that it might take up to three months for me to obtain my visa to the United States (a process I knew would be facilitated by a "physician's exchange" program then in effect between Canada and the USA), they said they would be happy to hold the position for me until I arrived.

Perfect!

Because I knew I had those three or four months to wait for my visa to be approved, I next applied for and was accepted into a residency of surgery program at Ottawa City Hospital, a position which I started immediately, and which paid $150 Canadian a month.

Perfect! I was in Ottawa before you could say "Goodbye, fantastic Montreal!" (though in French, of course).

Ottawa is a smaller, older, utterly charming city. I immensely enjoyed both the city and the work I was doing there.

What I *especially* liked about Ottawa was a young woman I met there named Barbara, a beautiful, intelligent employee of the Ottawa City Hospital's blood bank who, I was delighted, played one mean game of tennis. During my brief stay in Ottawa, Barbara and I became good friends; I often ate dinner with her and her proudly Scottish family.

In September of 1951, I received my United States visa, said my loving goodbyes to Barbara (and her family), packed my *two* suitcases (yes: in Canada I had come so far that it once again took two suitcases to contain my vast array of possessions), and set off for the gleaming, wondrous light that had been beckoning me ever since that moment so far behind me now it seemed like another life altogether--when, as a boy, I'd first stepped foot upon the grounds of the American College in Pordim.

Chapter Fourteen

Cincinnati

When, on October 1, 1951, I stepped off the bus in Cincinnati, I was not surprised to find no one waiting to greet me (though I had once again failed to stop myself, against all reason, forma at least momentarily hoping for it). I of course knew nothing about the great city upon whose ground I now found myself--nothing, that is, beyond what I'd learned from a city map about how, exactly, the ground was laid out for the short walk between where the bus dropped me off and the big, gleaming glass doors of my new employer, the Deaconess Hospital on Lincoln Street.

As I took my first walk in America I couldn't help but think of every home or business I saw along the way as a testament to the values and wonder of my new country. From what I saw, it was easy to imagine that America was everything I had hoped it would be--and more, I knew, than I was capable of imagining.

The hospital's personnel staff was, of course, expecting me: They welcomed me, and then took me up to the second floor of the residential building attached to the hospital--to the "room" part of my free room and board. There I was introduced to my new roommate, a physician who, as part of the same physician exchange program that had brought me there, had arrived at the hospital a few months earlier. And do you know what country this gentleman was from? *Germany!*

I can't tell you what relief and joy it was to speak German again, to be able to just let *go* when I had something to say, rather than, as I was by then so used to, struggling to make sure that whatever I said came out even close enough. (Though, that said, let me add that I was very happy indeed to in short order realize just how much English I had learned working in Canada at the Victoria Hospital; right away it was clear I wasn't going to have any trouble communicating with any of the staff or patients at Deaconess--a comfort if ever there was one.) From the start my new roommate and I got along famously; he turned out to be a very good man with whom I greatly enjoyed working and living. And because he already knew where everything was and how everything worked, he quickly made feel right at home.

Which, happily, didn't take all that much doing. The Deaconess Hospital was a small, friendly place. My roommate and I, as the new doctors, were on call all night in the emergency room; every night around ten o'clock we took a break (if we could, of course)--and every night around ten o'clock, one of the nurses would bring him and me a bowl of sweet, delicious ice cream, which had been made right there in the hospital's kitchen.

Any place that serves homemade ice cream to its employees on break had my vote, right off the bat.

"Now *this*," I used to think, twirling the soft ice cream around a spoon, "is a work break."

I got a break of a different sort altogether after I'd been at the hospital but a week or so, when one of my fellow physicians, having learned where I was from, told me of a Bulgarian restaurant in town owned and operated by one of my native countrymen. I called the restaurant and spoke with the man, a fellow named Dan Boteff, who was so glad to hear from me that he offered to pick me up in his car that very evening and treat me to a meal at his restaurant. And he invited me in *Bulgarian*, which sounded so sweet to my ears it almost brought me to tears. I accepted his gracious offer--and later that evening found myself dining with Dan and his wonderful wife, Tzetza. Over a superb, *truly* Bulgarian feast, Dan and Tzetza told me their story: how Dan had left Bulgaria as a young man, before World War II, and come to America, where he had worked hard, managing to save the money necessary to send back home for his beloved wife. United together in the land of opportunity, they took a chance, and decided to open a small restaurant--which over time they nurtured into the large, thriving establishment in which I was then being so graciously entertained.

It was an inspiring story, one that gave me confidence that I, too, could make it in America. At every opportunity--both that night and on the many nights thereafter when Dan, Tzetza, and their beautiful young daughter Victoria had me to their home for dinner--my new associates offered to do anything they could to help me reach that goal. And they did help me, too, in the greatest fashion in which anyone can ever really help another: They became my friends.

I was deeply pleased to have, through Dan and his family, begun something of a social life for myself in America--but things in that respect took a very swift uphill turn one night when, as was my wont, I wandered across Lincoln Street from the hospital onto the campus of the University of Cincinnati to have a look around. I've always liked college campuses, and tend, when I can (and especially when I'm in a place largely unknown to me) to explore them: One can learn a great deal about a place by reading the notices on one of its college's bulletin boards.

It was via one such notice that I learned of a night class in ballroom dancing being held on the campus. This caught my attention because I had always imagined that, in another life (one that most likely did not begin on a farm in Bulgaria), I might have been someone very much like Fred Astaire. Ballroom dancing is not now, I think, as common an ingredient in the social mix as once it once was--but when I was living in Bulgaria (and, indeed, throughout my time in Europe), *everyone* ballroom danced.

And I, if I do say so myself (and I think I must, as I'm quite sure no one else ever would), was quite good at it.

Anyway, lonely and alone in a huge, still-very-intimidating city, I figured it couldn't hurt if I stopped by the class, a session of which was being held that very night, to see what was what.

Well, what was up was one Elizabeth Betty, an Irish Catholic junior high school teacher wearing, on that particular night, a long, polka-dot skirt that swirled whenever she executed one of her smooth, graceful turns. I watched the class for a minute or two (well, I watched Miss Betty for a minute or two), and when the class took a break I made a beeline for the instructor, and asked her, in my most charming Bulgarian-French-

German accent, if it was possible for me to sign up for the class, right then and there.

It was; I was in.

Not five minutes later I was holding in my arms the enchanting Elizabeth Betty, spinning her about in a manner that I could only hope in any way reflected the way in which she had set my mind and heart spinning.

Naturally, during (and after) class that night we chatted--and then we did the same during the following Friday's class, and it came to pass, as one week rolled into another, that we were regularly dating. A piano player, Betty was always pleased to accompany me to hear the magnificent Cincinnati Symphony; I, being but a poor medical resident, was always pleased when the head nurse at Deaconess, who had season tickets at the symphony, couldn't go, and was kind enough to give her tickets to me.

The more I got to know Elizabeth, the more I liked her. I liked the whole Kelly family. As Elizabeth and I began seeing each other more frequently, her parents naturally wanted to meet me. Any number of times they had me over to their home for dinner, where I was pleased to get to know Elizabeth's father, William, and her mother Brigitte (both immigrated from Ireland at an early age; they met and married in Cincinnati); her two brothers, David and Bill; and her sisters Teddy and Bernadette (whom they called Bernie). Bernie was blessed with a beautiful singing voice; sometimes after dinner she would sing for us opera arias while Elizabeth accompanied her on the piano. Those evenings, of sitting around with this fine family listening to their girls regale us with the sweetest music imaginable, are as precious to me as any other I've known in my life.

Having completed my internship at Deaconess in July of 1952, I next accepted a position as resident in surgery at Good Samaritan Hospital. The change in jobs would have minimum impact on the mechanics of my life: Good Samaritan was located about two hundred yards down Lincoln Avenue from Deaconess. My new position would, however, somewhat enhance my financial condition: My new monthly salary was to go up fifty dollars to a whopping $150 a month--plus, still, free room and board.

During my first six months at Good Samaritan I worked in the orthopedic department, where we had a number of patients suffering from lower back pain, usually incurred through injuries. The typical method of treating the condition was to keep a patient lying on his back with elastic bandages wrapped about his legs; weights attached to the end of the bandages would gently pull on the leg and thus relief pressure from the patient's vertebrae. This was a good and sound approach lacking in but one aspect: the bandages along the patient's leg tended to loosen, making constant adjustment necessary.

It occurred to me that this means of treating back pain could be improved through the utilization of an aluminum straps attached to a sandal-like shoe, which could serve as a cradle for the leg and become the point at which the weights were attached: straps above the knee would connect the boot to the rest of the leg.

It made sense to me; so in my spare time I constructed this new "traction brace." Once it was finished, I showed it to Dr. Gienestras, the chief of the hospital's orthopedic department, who was impressed enough by it to suggest that I present it before a meeting of all of Good Samaritan's orthopedic surgeons. Such a meeting was called; I presented my brace, and was pleased to find myself the subject of much admiration and encouragement. The three main suggestions I heard at that meeting were that I should approach some of the companies that produce and make orthopedic equipment about putting my brace on the market; that I should exhibit the brace at the upcoming medical convention in Chicago; and that I should publish an article about the brace in a medical journal.

Wow! All of this, from a simple idea born of endless examples of my having to fix something that wasn't working back on the farm!

So I contacted one of the larger orthopedic device manufacturers, who said they would send someone out to see my device. In the meantime, I prepared two or three samples of my brace, and did in fact travel with it to Chicago, where I spent three days standing behind a desk in an exhibit booth and answering questions about it from the surprisingly large number of medical professionals who were interested enough to ask.

Back in Cincinnati, I had a meeting about the brace at the hospital with a representative from a large orthopedic supply company. The man seemed very interested in my invention: He asked detailed, specific questions; he scribbled furiously in his notebook; he snapped what seemed like hundreds of photos of the thing.

And then, smiling broadly, he shook my hand, and said that he would get back in touch with me just as soon as he'd had a chance to discuss my brace with his superiors.

While waiting for that response, over the next month or so I spent my spare time writing an article on the brace that I was very pleased to see published by "Surgery," a medical journal published in New Orleans.

Happy with my new prospects, I then bided my time, wondering when I would hear back from the orthopedic company.

And wondering.

And wondering.

And wondering.

Months went by--and I heard nothing.

And then one day I was flipping through a medical magazine, and there it was: an advertisement, from the same company that had sent someone out to learn about my brace, for what was, unmistakably, my brace.

My brace!

They had taken my invention, modified it just enough so that it couldn't be said to be *exactly* my invention, and claimed it as their own!

It wasn't very long at all until the brace that began its life inside my head became a standard hospital fixture for the treatment of back pain.

You can imagine the anguish this caused me, as, say, I wrapped my dinner roll in a napkin so that later on before I went to bed I might have a little something to eat.

On the other hand, it must be said that whatever money I might have received from my invention couldn't possibly compare in value to that which no one could ever take from me, which is the pleasure of knowing that I invented something that was instrumental in relieving the pain of countless numbers of people.

After I had been dating the lovely Miss Elizabeth Kelly, of Cincinnati, Ohio, for about a year and a half, she and I decided to get married. The only pothole in our road toward marital bliss was that I was raised in the Eastern Orthodox faith, while she was a Catholic so devout that at one time she had thought to become a nun. She told me of her hope that I would be willing to consider converting to Catholicism, so that our children could be raised in the faith which had for so long meant so much to her and her family.

It was not, in truth, a difficult decision for me to make: I told her I would be happy to become a Catholic. It is my own personal belief that though there are (goodness knows) many religions, there is but one God--and, in any case, it would have to be one awfully persnickety deity who would have too much trouble with anyone converting from Eastern Orthodoxy to Catholicism, since, as far as I could ever tell, the primary difference between the two is that Orthodox priests can get married and have families, whereas Catholic priests are supposed to remain celibate for life.

So it *could* be argued that leaving the Orthodox church in order to marry a Catholic was just one small way of further narrowing the gap between those two great branches of the same religion.

In any case, for a month I took lessons from Good Samaritan's chaplain, who then formally ushered me into the Catholic fold, which meant Elizabeth and I were free to get married in the beautiful old church where she and her family had long been communing with God.

So on December 27, 1952, that's exactly what we did. (Elizabeth chose that date because December 27 was also her birthday. I thought it an outstanding choice of days, as it ensured that for the rest of our lives together I would be able to buy her half the number of presents other men are usually compelled to buy their wives. This was a fine way of looking at it, maybe--what it was definitely *not*, however, was a fine idea to actually express. Funny how some things, while still in your head, sound one way--but then, in the glaring light of exposure, sound altogether different.)

The other troublesome snag in our wedding plans was that I would not be free for any kind of a proper honeymoon until I had finished my residency at Good Samaritan, which would not be until the summer following our wedding. Still, love trumps the calendar every time, and we decided to have a short honeymoon over the New Year's holiday--and then enjoy a real honeymoon in the summer, once I'd finished my year at Good Samaritan.

So for our mini-honeymoon I and the new Mrs. Luben Walchef, M.D. drove to one of the beautiful state parks near Cincinnati along the

Ohio River, where for three days immediately following our wedding we basked in the wonder and joy of our new relationship.

"Now, for our *real* honeymoon," I said as we drove back to Cincinnati, "let's go to Ottawa! It's the most beautiful city! It's like a real-life version of one of those idyllic little towns you see in the glass snow globes--although, thank goodness, there won't actually *be* any snow there when we're there. It'll be beautiful there--as warm as toast! What a time we'll have! And wait until you see the Laurentian Mountains! They're too beautiful to describe! What fun we'll have exploring them!"

And I am here to tell you: that's exactly what we did. In July and August of 1953, with my surgical residency at Good Samaritan completed, Elizabeth and I took the little money I'd managed to save and bought ourselves a (hold your breath, now) blue 1948 Nash convertible with reclining seats. Into the back of that royal behemoth we piled a ton of bedding and as many of our clothes as would fit--and then we pointed her toward Ottawa, Canada, by way of Niagara Falls.

Now *this* was the beginning of a honeymoon.

And it stayed a honeymoon, too, every single moment of every single day for the next two months.

We stayed in Niagara Falls for one day and night: We ogled the mighty falls until we were speechless--and *then*, wearing raincoats, we took a boat ride that sailed *under* the falls.

You may have seen pictures or even film footage of Niagara Falls. Didn't it seem like a lovely place? Well, forget that stuff: Sailing in a little boat that's drifting about behind the falls, you feel the full power of God roaring at you.

You also get pretty thoroughly soaked.

It is, all in all, quite the experience.

Still, nothing could too long keep us from our goal of Canada's mind-bogglingly beautiful Laurentian Mountains, which, even while strolling about the town of Niagara Falls, we could feel out there, waiting to help us revel in our only-slightly-late honeymoon.

And what a fine job they did of it, too.

I could see how a person might argue that camping is not the most romantic way a couple could spend their honeymoon. That person, however, would be wrong; having done it with Elizabeth, I feel confident in asserting that it's the most romantic way possible to spend a honeymoon.

We had a big, beautiful lake.

We had the sun on the lake.

We had the birds in the trees.

We had the fish in the lake, which did everything but fillet themselves and then jump straight into the pan we kept over the little fire we built on the shore.

We had full use of the nearby camping facilities--all the showers we could take, for a dollar a day.

We had each other.

It was the best two months of my life.

Still and all, romance or not, the call of a long hot bath and a soft bed after two months of camping makes for a siren song Conan the Barbarian couldn't resist. And so, as we were preparing for the drive back to Cincinnati, Elizabeth suddenly said, "Luben! I have an idea! Let's go to Ottawa and get a hotel room!"

I, of course, thought this was the greatest idea since warm towels--but was also aware that we lacked the funds for such diversion.

"Never mind about that! I've got some money in my pension plan at work I could have wired to us!" she said, proving to me once and for all that: a) she was a resourceful woman, and b) she was a woman who had just possibly had her fill of camping and was fairly desperate.

"Except," she said, looking crestfallen, "the money would take too long to get here."

"No," I exclaimed, "it wouldn't! Canada's not like America! In Canada, you don't pay for a hotel room until the *end* of your stay! We could get a hotel room in Ottawa, and then simply stay there for a day or two until your money arrives!"

And about .004 seconds later we were inside our trust Nash, heading for the best three *days* of my life, which we spent in a beautifully quaint hotel in Ottawa, where they had all the warm food, hot water and soft blankets anyone could ever, ever want.

After two months of being away it was good to be home again.

Unfortunately, in Elizabeth's case she really was *literally* home again: I had made so little money at Good Samaritan that her parents, taking pity on us, had been moved to invite us to come reside in a room on the second story of their house. This was, of course, exceedingly gracious of them--which made it some but not much less of a mortification for me. I was, after all, a medical doctor, trained at one of the finest medical schools in the world. And yet here I was, living in the home of my wife's parents. It was hardly the situation I had envisioned either for myself or my new wife.

Almost immediately upon our return, however, I obtained a position as a resident in pathology at The Jewish Hospital in Cincinnati. It wasn't phenomenal money, but it was (relatively) good--and it wasn't long after I began there that Elizabeth and I found ourselves with reason to believe that living with her parents might not be the worst thing in the world after all: Elizabeth, we learned, was with child.

Me! A father!

Elizabeth, a mother!

I thought I could not know a greater joy--I thought that, that is, until nine months later, on the morning of May 6, 1954, when, pacing back and forth in the hospital waiting room (for that was the custom in those days, even if the anxious papa-to-be was a doctor), I heard the cry of a new little baby who, as it turned out, was our son.

And then there were two Lubens, crying together.

One was born an American. The other was not.

I don't believe the foreign-born Luben stopped smiling for something like a year.

Chapter Fifteen

Practice Makes Perfect

When Luben, Jr. was about six months old, Elizabeth and I bundled him up and moved with him to Charleston, West Virginia, where I had obtained a position as a senior surgical resident at Kanawha Valley Hospital.

We rented an apartment.

Elizabeth got a job teaching at a local high school.

I immersed myself in continuing to learn everything I might ever need to know about performing successful surgeries.

Life was good--or it was, anyway, until poor baby Luben came down with a case of the measles so severe Elizabeth and I could see nothing for it but for her to take him back with her to Cincinnati, where they could stay with Elizabeth's parents while the child healed. It was hardly an ideal plan--but I was working, it seemed, around the clock, and Elizabeth could certainly use the help taking care of Luben so kindly proffered by her parents.

So we decided that she and Luben would return home, and that I would follow them once the final year of my residency had concluded.

Now *that*--being alone in West Virginia--was a difficult time for me: To say I missed my wife and child would be like saying a man stranded in the desert misses water. It *hurt* that they weren't there.

As much as a way of dealing with that pain than anything else, I resolved that if I was going to be without my new family for a time, then I was going to use that time as productively as I possibly could.

And I pretty quickly figured out how that would be, too: I would study for and take my Ohio State Medical Board Exams--which (assuming I passed them) would empower me to independently practice medicine back in Cincinnati, the place I now thought of as my American home.

So, late at night and during whatever time I wasn't working at the hospital, I studied.

And I traveled back to Ohio.

And I took the tests.

And lo and behold, I passed them.

And the next time after that my family saw me--when I walked back through the front door of my parents-in-law's house after having left behind Charleston, West Virginia and Kanawha Valley Hospital--I was a fully licensed doctor, ready to start my own medical practice.

Of course, the first thing I needed to begin my new business was an office in which to work and see patients. Even before that, though, what I needed to begin my new *life* was a place to live that wasn't in the home of my parents-in-law.

So, being the ever-resourceful type, I figured out one solution for both my problems: Elizabeth and I rented an apartment; and when we weren't sitting down and using it to eat on, I used our dining room table as an operating table.

Our coffee table doubled as an examination table. (The magazines were already right there!)

I used *real* Popsicle sticks as tongue depressors.

Okay, okay: It wasn't as bad as all that. But after we divided the two-bedroom apartment we rented on Clifton Avenue, just down the street from Deaconess Hospital, into one part home and one part medical practice, it sometimes *felt* as if it were that bad.

We really did turn the living room of our apartment into the reception area for my medical practice.

One bedroom became the examining room.

The other bedroom was where Elizabeth and I slept.

The kitchen remained the place where we made the food--and it doubled as Luben Junior's bedroom.

It's safe to say that we used up every square inch of that apartment.

And you can just imagine how cramped we would have been had I had any patients whatsoever. Thank God *that* wasn't a problem.

"No one is coming!" I cried to Elizabeth. "Don't people in America get sick? Don't they ever have accidents? When are any patients going to show up at my medical office-home?"

"Don't worry, Luben," she said. "You just opened. Give people a chance to discover you're here. Business will pick up."

Elizabeth, as always, proved right: Business did pick up, although not exactly in the way either of us hoped for. Financially, at least, things began to turn around for us once I joined The Academy of Medicine of Cincinnati--and then put myself on the emergency call list. Rather suddenly after that I had all the emergency hospital calls I could handle; it became not at all unusual me for me to be out of the house all night seeing to the care of people who had been in car accidents or for some other reason were in need of immediate and serious attention. Sometimes they even needed operations, which I was always more than willing to do.

The good news is that it was (something approximating) a living. The bad news was that my darling Elizabeth had to spend entirely too many nights alone in our bed.

Nonetheless, I made enough money so that in 1956 I was able to put down two thousand dollars against a seventeen thousand dollar loan for my first ever purchase of American real estate: a three-story brick corner house at 303 Mitchell Avenue, located in the residential area of a German community called Saint Bernard. (And I really do mean a *German* community: St. Bernard was one of those thriving immigrant enclaves in which seemingly *all* social and business affairs are conducted in a language other than the one predominate outside that community. In St. Bernard restaurant menus were in German. The community newspaper was in German. I used to attend a Lutheran church very near our home in which the entire Sunday service was held in German. I certainly can't say it was like being back in Germany--but at least no one was bombing the place.)

The previous owner of the house I purchased was a pediatrician who had passed away; part of what made his home ideal as my own was that a door in its living room connected the main house to the office the pediatrician has used for his practice (which had a separate entrance on the street around the corner). The first floor of the house itself (not counting the cavernous basement) comprised a large living room, kitchen, and dining area; the second the bedrooms; and on the third an attic and a couple of sleeping quarters for maids I knew it'd be a long while until we could afford.

All in all, the place was perfect.

Elizabeth was absolutely beside herself about it. "Now *this*," she said, her arms held wide as she spun about the living room, "is a home."

It was that; and, of course, it was also my business--which after a time finally began growing in earnest, primarily from patients coming to see me for follow-up visits after the emergencies for which I'd originally treated them. I couldn't afford either a nurse or a receptionist, so Elizabeth became a bit of each; a housekeeper helped pick up the slack this arrangement invariably left behind.

Both Elizabeth and I worked very hard, but it was worth it, because every night I went to bed knowing that whatever dreams I may have during that night's sleep, none could compare to the American dream I was living while awake.

I had a solid little practice going. I had my house. My family was thriving--and growing: On July 29, 1958, we were blessed with another son, whom we named Boyan; fourteen months after that, on September 24, 1959, our family was made complete by its final addition, a beautiful baby girl we named Lisa.

It was not, I knew, possible for my world to get any better.

I was a long, long way from our family farm back in Pordim.

And the more I felt that particular distance, the more I longed to close it. I had not seen my father, two sisters, relatives or any of my old friends from my home country since the summer of 1940, when as a student studying in Germany I had returned to Bulgaria on a summer vacation.

From around 1944 onward it was virtually impossible to get a message either by phone or post into or out of what had become communist Bulgaria. Most of the time I was in Europe, all the time I was in Canada, and not until around 1964 in America was I able to send or receive any mail to or from my family. Having to live my life for all those years ignorant of what might be happening in the lives of my family back home was a terrible emotional burden of a sort I wouldn't wish on anyone.

One time, in 1959, I learned that it had become possible to tele-
phone into Bulgaria from Switzerland, and though I could ill afford
to make the trip myself--let alone bring along my wife or any of our
children--I gathered together the necessary funds for one airport ticket,
locked the door to my medical office, and flew to Zurich, praying all
along that from there I'd be able to reach someone in Pordim who could
in turn get in touch with my father. From my Swiss hotel room I dialed
Pordim's only post office.

The man who answered at the other end understood my story, knew
my father (he still alive!), and said he would send for him.

"You stay there in your hotel room!" cried this good soul, "and I will
bring your father here, to the post office! From here he will call you there!
What is the number you are at?" I gave him my number. "Good!" he
said. "I have it here! Now you wait there! I will go get you father and he
will call you as soon as he arrives here! You wait there for that call!"

We hung up, and I began an hour of waiting so intense that I believe
I wore a path in the carpet with my pacing.

I thought feverishly of all I had to say to my father--about my life in
Germany, in Paris, Luxembourg, Brussels, and Canada. I tried to imagine
how he would feel when he heard I was now a doctor, living in America
with my own practice.

America!

Where he didn't know I had a home.

Where he didn't know I had a wife.

Where he didn't know I had three children.

What would it mean to my father to find that I'd made him a grandfather? Would mine be his first grandchildren? Had either of my sisters
married and had children of their own? Was I an uncle?

And what had happened to my father in all the years gone by? Was
he still on our farm? Had the communists taken it? How was his health?
How was his wife? How was--and then the phone rang.

And when over the crackling line I first heard my father's voice--
when I heard that voice, as known to me as the sound of my own heart-
-say, "Hello, Luben?" do you know what I said?

I said nothing.

Because I couldn't stop myself from crying.

That's what my father heard from me: my sobs.

And for a very, very long time that's all I heard from him, too.

Eventually, of course, we were able talk a little--enough for me to know that he was alive and well, and that everyone and everything back home was okay.

An hour after our phone conversation I was on my way back home to Cincinnati.

It's a funny thing to be on a plane when you already feel like you're flying.

About two years after that the relationship between Bulgaria and the United States normalized to the point where travel was allowed between them. Now my father and his wife could come visit us in America! I arranged for a six-month visa for them--and lo and behold, before too very long at all there they were, getting off a plane in Cincinnati, Ohio.

After hard hugs and long kisses all around I saw that my father, always the robust adventurer, looked hale as ever. Like a child he looked eagerly about him, his eyes agleam with a sense of vibrant curiosity.

His wife Angelina, however, did not seem to share his sense of ebullient well-being. Later she told me that she had never in her life flown before, and that the entire time she and my father were flying from Sophia to Amsterdam, then across the ocean to New York and on to Cincinnati, she had been absolutely paralyzed with fear. Given what the poor woman looked like when I first saw her at the airport, this was not difficult to believe: she appeared dazed, and not a little off her feed.

Once ensconced in our home, however, she livened up, and began a vacation that she later said--well, and that she said any of number of times during--was easily the greatest trip of her life.

During the whole time he was he in America, my father was ... well ... my father.

"I cannot believe this country!" he boomed. "It is beyond what a simple farmer like me can hold in his mind! Luben, do you remember that boy who when you were young left Pordim to come to America to seek his fame and fortune? Remember him? Remember how after six months, having failed, he returned to Pordim? Do you remember Mr. America, as we all called him? Do you know, he used to tell us all kinds of stories about what life was like here, what the buildings and people and food was like? Most of what he said seemed too fantastic to believe--we used to always joke with him that he was lying about all he'd seen and done here. But the things he told us about his time here in America have always been in my mind since then. And now that I'm here, I see that he wasn't exaggerating at all! It's even *bigger* than he said it was! There's even *more* here! No wonder for fifty years after he came here Mr. America couldn't stop talking it! I plan to tell every angel in heaven about it for the rest of eternity!"

And is sure didn't detract from my father's experience of being in America--nor did it particularly enhance his wife's--that while the two of them were visiting a huge article about them appeared in a large Cincinnati newspaper.

Leave it to my father to be in America less than one week before he becomes a star.

The way it happened is that on their flight in from New York, my father had somehow caught the attention of a reporter for this newspaper. (How odd, that my father should catch the attention of a reporter. "Unbelievable!" he was probably yelling. "Look at this plane! Nothing in the history of the universe could possibly compare to this flying building! Look at these seats! I have never been in a more comfortable seat in my life! I am sitting here, enjoying this soda, and yet as the same time I am flying through space like a bird! Like a man sitting in the giant belly of a bird! This is not to be believed! No human mind is capable of imagining such a thing! Yet here it is, happening!")

Somehow, the reporter managed to discern that my father wasn't from America.

So he started up a conversation with my father, and I guess came to feel that an old man traveling all the way from a small village in communist Bulgaria to visit his doctor son in America would make for a story that might be of interest to the readers of the newspaper for which he wrote.

And so this same reporter, accompanied by a photographer, came to my house the day after my father and his wife arrived, and interviewed them.

Two days after that, an article appeared about them on the front page of the paper's "Local" section.

"No," said my father when he saw the article, as if he had finally come up against something too fantastic to actually exist. "It cannot be possible. That cannot be a photograph of me and my lovely wife sitting in the beautiful living room of my son's beautiful home in this beautiful country. Such things do not happen. That is not a real newspaper, which thousands and thousands of people will read today as they eat their break-fast and sit on their buses and trains going to work. This is simply not happening. I know that in reality I am fast asleep and dreaming beneath my walnut tree back home. Please do not disturb my rest, as I am an old man who needs all the sleep he can get. When I awake, a sweetened cup of black tea with a little cream would be nice. In the meantime, let me continue to look at myself in this paper. What fascinating, unbelievable dreams I have!"

I found it a little hard to believe myself, to tell the truth. I didn't find it virtually *impossible* to believe--but it was a bit of a challenge.

At the hospital on the morning the article appeared, I suddenly found myself at the center of the attention of a great number of my col-leagues and associates. This proved to be a good thing, in that the article provided an opportunity for me to share a bit about my past with people I'd been seeing almost daily for years, but with whom I'd never had such a discussion. My co-workers seemed genuinely interested in my story: It turned out they had no idea (and of course there's no reason why they should have) that I had, for instance, attended medical school in Berlin during the war--or that from there I'd moved to Heidelberg, or any of it.

"My God, Luben," said one man, an orthopedic surgeon that I had several times assisted during surgery, "You're lucky to be here at all. And your father! How wonderful it must be to be with him again!"

My friend was right: It really was wonderful. As far as I was con-cerned, my father and stepmother could have stay with us forever if they had wanted. I believe my father would have gone for that, too--but his wife found herself terribly missing home, and her family and friends there. And so two months after they arrived, my dear father and his dar-ling wife returned home to Pordim.

"Good-bye my American son!" cried my father at the departing gate. He waved wildly at me; I remember thinking how strong his arms yet looked. "Pordim will never be the same after this! My life will never be the same after this! You have made a different man of me. God bless you, son!

That night, sitting in my home reflecting upon my father and his visit, I closed my eyes and said a prayer of thanks to God for bringing the two of us together again.

As time went on, I slowly realized that though I personally had more than I ever dreamed I could want, I did not have enough to one day send all three of my children to college. After all, I hardly wanted my children to struggle to become educated in anything near the way I had been forced to.

And so, in the natural manner in which I think being a father compels one to, I began turning my attention to ways of increasing my financial fortunes. As such, I more and more found myself reading books on real estate investments--and then, when that seemed insufficient, going to classes, lectures, luncheons and seminars on real estate. And my pursuit of knowledge in this area hardly isolated me from my professional associates: It seemed to me that doctors spent as least as much time talking about real estate than they did about medicine. The acquisition, development and sale of property was, I learned quickly enough, how the American moneyed set *made* its money.

And the two big things I learned about real estate were these: First, it isn't a subject one learns about easily or quickly--the *reason* I took so many classes and read so many books on the matter is because it's such a dense, multi-faceted subject. And the second thing I learned about real estate was that once you knew just about everything there was to know about it, all of that knowledge really *did* boil down to the same thing almost anyone knows is the most important thing to consider about any real estate purchase: Location, location, location.

Not a seminar went by, not an article was written, not a book on real estate seemed to be published without someone, somewhere in the course of what they were saying, proclaiming the same thing.

Location, location, location. It was the mantra of the real estate business.

And do you know what idea began to insinuate itself into my mind?

That Cincinnati wasn't all that great a location.

And it wasn't just the sagging, stagnant state of the local real estate market that gradually had me thinking that way, either. And it wasn't just my medical practice--which, though certainly decent, hadn't grown at anywhere near the rate I'd hoped or expected it would.

It wasn't those things that had me thinking it might be time to leave Cincinnati. I could live with those things.

It was Cincinnati's *weather* that was starting to drive me crazy.

The winters were cold and wet--and though there usually wasn't snow of the bathroom-bailing sort, there was still more of the icy stuff than, to my mind, any person should have to contend with.

And the summers, in their own way, weren't much better. They were as windy and hot as a hurricane in Hades.

One night at around two in the morning Elizabeth and I were awakened by a phone call from a frantic woman who begged me to come right over to see her brother, who was apparently in the throes of an uncontrollable violent rage. I anxiously drove to her home, parked my car, and, after having tapped lightly upon the front door of the home and received no answer, called out "It's Dr. Walchef," before stepping through the door to find a wild-eyed middle-aged man holding the butt of a rifle against his shoulder, the other end of which was pointing directly at my head.

I stopped just inside the small, cramped and very warm house, and remained perfectly still. "Hello," I said calmly. "I'm Dr. Walchef. I've come to help you."

"I don't need no help," the man growled. He waved the end of his gun, just a little. "Get out of my house before I blow your fucking head off."

"I want to," I said, smiling just slightly. "I would love to be back at home in my bed right now. And I will leave. But if I could, please, ask you just one question first. And that is: Are you sure you want me to leave? I'm a doctor. I don't like to see people suffer. I'm not saying that you are suffering, but it's just possible you are not right now experiencing the happiest moment of your life. Frankly, I don't see how you could be. It's hotter than a furnace in here."

The man's whole face softened, and he laughed. He kept the gun pointed at me, though.

"It is hot in here," he said.

"I thought maybe I died in my sleep and went to hell."

"And she keeps all the windows in the place closed," said the man in the almost pleading tone of one besieged by troubles he's powerless to deflect.

"Then why don't we open them?" I said.

"She won't let me!" he roared, and the way he then tightened his grip on the rifle made me think his words might be the last I ever heard.

"Who are you again?" he said suspiciously.

"I'm a doctor," I said. "Dr. Walchef. I came here to help you. I don't know why you're pointing a gun at me, because I promise you I'm on your side. And I'm definitely on the side of anyone who wants to open a window in here," I said, hoping to get him back on friendlier ground.

The man stared at me for a long time down the barrel of his gun while my heart jack hammered in my chest.

"Get out of my house," he whispered ominously.

"I will, sir. I'll leave right now. Thank you for having me over. I'm going to turn now, and just walk out the door."

With his cheek pressed against the handle of his rifle, he nodded slightly. "Do it," he said. "Or I'm liking your brains splattered all over the wall."

I nodded, and then turned as calmly as possible and pushed open the door. I stepped outside into the warm, silent early morning.

I gently closed the door behind me.

I stepped down his porch stairs and onto the path leading up to the door.

I walked down that path, and along the street a short way to my car.

And my mind was racing: Where was the woman who had called me? Was she dead? Had the madman killed her? Was there anyone else in the house? Were there any children involved?

I climbed back into my car and, almost as if I were wholly outside my own body, watched myself pull my keys from my pocket, slide the correct one into the ignition, turn it, and ease the car into the road and away from the home in which I'd very nearly been murdered.

I drove straight to the police station.

An hour or so later, soaked with and still reeking of my own adrenaline, I sat in the easy chair of my living room, cradling a glass into which I, a man who virtually never touched alcohol, had with shaking hands poured some cooking sherry taken from my wife's pantry.

I knew that what had happened that night could happen at any time, and in any city.

And I didn't care.

All I knew was that I now wanted, once and for all, out of Cincinnati.

Enough was enough.

As it turned out, the man with the gun had been recently released from a mental institution, and had failed to keep up with the medicines he'd been prescribed. He was apparently not anywhere near as dangerous as he had seemed: A police officer told me the day after my encounter with him that the gun the man had been brandishing wasn't even loaded.

And while of course during the succeeding months I got over the trauma of that night, my resolve to leave Cincinnati remained. I'd been in that one place long enough.

What my restlessness really boiled down to was that, crazed men with guns or not, I simply was not yet so old that I believed I'd already seen enough of the world.

That said, though, what I *was* sure of was that I'd seen enough of the world that wasn't America: A restless wandering spirit or not, I wanted to remain in America until my wandering spirit was wandering around the afterlife, wondering what might be around that next cloud, or somewhere over that rainbow.

Chapter Sixteen

California

As I began thinking about where else in America my family and I might enjoy calling home, the word that kept floating itself into to the front of my consciousness was "California."

There it was, in great, big, shimmering gold letters: CALIFORNIA.

California! It seemed more like a state of mind than a state of the union.

California! The vast, open expanses of the wild, wild west! The land of surf and sea! That wondrous, magical place, where both the sun and the stars shine around the clock! That place where the earth simply and willingly hands over its bounty, where fruit springs from the ground with such fecund alacrity that at any given moment a person might suddenly find himself atop a brand new peach or plum tree that just sprang from the ground!

California!

Was there any way to imagine it and *not* think of gleaming streets paved with gold?

Believe me, California holds real allure for a former farm boy from Pordim, Bulgaria. All my life I'd grown up with the belief that, just as America is the place where everyone else in the world wants to live, California is the place where all the *Americans* want to live.

As I understood it, the Golden State was the very best that America--indeed, that the whole *planet*--had to offer.

So, you know: I figured it couldn't hurt to at least look into it a little.

And then a little became a lot: I studied; I read; I researched and delved into all kinds of articles about California, and I asked everyone I knew about it, and before to very long I became convinced that moving my family to California was exactly the thing I should do.

Moving them before I had a *job,* however, would be something altogether different. So in August of 1963 I made arrangements to travel to Sacramento to take the week-long written portion of the California State Medical Board exams.

I passed those (grueling) texts--and was told to come back in a month to take the oral portion of the exams.

A month! That certainly didn't leave me the kind of study time I would have liked.

So I broke out my dusty old study habits, and spent every spare second of that month doing all I could to ensure that I would be as prepared for the oral part of the medical exams as I had been for the written.

At that time there was no medical school in San Diego, so the examination took place in a downtown Veteran's Administration hospital. I came into town a week or so before the exams began in order to secure for myself some private and dedicated study time. I took a room in a small hotel along the beach, and within minutes of putting my suitcase down in my room was so charmed by the warm, early evening air coming off the ocean that I immediately forgot why I was there, and followed my feet to the beach.

I hadn't walked through the fine warm sand all the way to the water's edge before I knew I'd found the place I wanted to call home. I'd buy that *hotel* if I had to--but I could see that wouldn't be necessary, that the shoreline stretched as far as the eye could see in either direction, and that somewhere--somewhere in this big, beautiful stretch of sunny North American coastline--there was surely a place for me and my family.

This was paradise. And as far as I knew, there was no law that said one had to pass from this world to the next before one is allowed to inhabit paradise.

While taking some pains to make sure that while the doctors on the examining board were questioning me I *didn't* let my vision wander out the window and toward the sea, I somehow managed to also pass the oral half of my medical board exams.

Almost upon walking through the front door back home in Cincinnati I yelled, "Pack up, everybody! We're moving to California!"

Almost--but not quite.

But I did talk to Elizabeth about it my first night home, and while she naturally had some very real reservations about leaving her lifelong home and all of her family so nearby, ultimately she gave in to the same excitement that had me so enamored of the state in which, we knew, so many of our friends and associates had always dreamed of living.

A few months later I received that all-important letter from the Medical Board in Sacramento, officially notifying me that I was licensed to practice medicine in the great state of California.

In anticipation of that letter, I had, through my professional contacts, already lined up a job for myself in a Los Angeles community called West Covina, where I would be working as an assistant surgeon to a Dr. Brown, a surgeon and family practitioner whose practice had grown to the degree where he now needed help keeping up with it.

So (to earn us a little income as we went along--and to keep the home for us, just in case), we rented our home to an earnest young intern from the Children's Hospital, packed our small Audi station wagon with our clothes and our television--and then the six of us (if you counted our beautiful dog Lucky, which of course you would) squeezed into whatever room in the car was left, and we hit the road.

In order to avoid the cold and icy roads to the north, we crossed the country via a southern route, driving through Kentucky, Tennessee, Texas, and Arizona. Even if we had turned around a week after arriving in California in order to drive straight back home again, just seeing that much of the country would have been worth it.

America the beautiful, indeed.

What a country this is.

Finally, we drove across a bridge over the Colorado River, and there we were: in California. Directly over the bridge beside the river was a little beach area; we pulled over there, and Elizabeth and I watched as our children and Lucky burst out of the car and rushed to the river, where with wild joy they all began playing splashing in the water and running about on the sand.

Standing in front of our car watching them, Elizabeth slipped her hand into mine.

"Oh, Luben," she said. "It's so beautiful."

As it happened, though, quite soon after arriving in West Covina my family and I *were* all ready to turn right around, to see the country in reverse on our way back to Ohio. Well, perhaps we were not yet entirely sure we wanted to leave California, but we were *positive* we could no longer continue to live in the amount of smog that was so unrelentingly thick everywhere around that us we felt like we were walking around in some kind of inverted planetary bowl of stinky, dirt soup. It was just unbelievable. Dr. Brown was a decent, kind man; we had a nice home in Glendora, which made for a short and convenient commute for me; our boy Luben was enrolled in a school he liked--everything about our new situation was ideal. We would have been absolutely delighted with our new lives, if only it hadn't been for the mildly inconvenient fact that we were all suffocating to death.

And actually, in Elizabeth's case, that wasn't far enough from the truth to even be funny. She suffered from asthma and was very prone to bronchitis; the smog really was too much for her. So within two months, we were very serious about finding another place to live.

"Let's just go back home to Cincinnati," said Elizabeth. "I've only been away for a little while, but I really miss air that's not *chewable*. Not that I'd want this stuff in my mouth. Or my lungs."

"Before we give up on California," I said, "Let me show you San Diego."

"No," replied Elizabeth. "It's not far enough away from Los Angeles. I'm sure the air there, like here, is so thick you could use it to tar a roof with. I'm sorry, Luben. I've got to get back to air I can breath."

"I know, I know. Me, too. But Elizabeth, you haven't seen what I've seen. I've *seen* San Diego. It's nothing like this. The air is clear there. Crystal clear. Perfectly clear. *Air* clear. I promise. Let's just take a vacation there. We've got Easter coming up: let's take the kids, and we'll get a hotel in San Diego, and if you don't think it's the most beautiful place you've ever seen, we'll leave for home the next weekend. I promise."

"Okay," she said. "But I'm telling you: If, when I go to open the car door, I have to push really hard against the thick brown air to get it open, I'm not getting out."

"Deal," I said.

So that April we rented a room for three days at the Bahia Hotel in Mission Bay. Today the Bahia is a truly world-class luxury hotel; then it was a much humbler single-story facility, with a nice little pool. But then as now it sat on the sparkling sands of Mission Bay: miles of flat, sparkling, clean water, as placid and enrapturing as any lake or bay anywhere in the world.

"See?" I said. "See?"

"I hate it when you're right," said Elizabeth, watching the children chasing Lucky along the shoreline. She turned and kissed me on the cheek. "And, oh," she said, "how I love it when you're right."

One of the first things I did upon returning to Glendora after our mini-vacation was to phone the San Diego Medical Society to inquire whether they knew of any surgeons in the San Diego area who might be seeking assistance. They sent me a list of those who were. I called a few of them, and found one, a urologist from Canada, who said he had prostate cancer and could no longer keep up with his practice in the manner he desired. Right there on the phone he and I worked out an arrangement whereby I would assume responsibility for half of his clients, while he would pay what amounted to virtually all the overhead for his practice-- including the fee of his nurse.

"You've got yourself a deal, sir," I said.

And I knew I had myself one, too.

The next day I put in my notice with Dr. Brown, and my young family and I prepared once more to move.

I found my job in San Diego very pleasant; personally I liked the doctor with whom I was now sharing a practice, and professionally I liked that so much of the work we did was at Scripps Hospital, then and now one of the finest hospitals in the country.

One day at Scripps one of my colleagues mentioned that a doctor in town with a thriving surgical and general practice had suddenly passed away. The doctor's business was at Garnett Avenue and Faunal Street in the heart of Pacific Beach, an idyllic little San Diego beach town. The doctor's widow, this fellow told me, was most likely going to want and need someone to take over her husband's practice.

I called the woman, and we arranged to meet the following afternoon at her husband's office. There I learned that she was indeed looking for a physician who could come in and keep her husband's business in the same robust condition in which he'd so tragically left it.

"I'd be honored if you would consider me, Mrs. Janis," I said. I could see no reason to beat about the bush about something so vital to the interests of her and her nine children.

"Well," she replied, patting me on the hand, "let's go to my house and talk about that, shall we?"

So in the living room of her spacious La Jolla home the widow Janis and I talked, and got to know one another. As the afternoon of our conversation grew into evening, she carefully placed down her cup of tea, and then looked at me and said, "I like you, Dr. Walchef, and I have great respect for all you've been through in your life. The life and business my husband built for him and our family was not handed to him on a silver platter, either: The man worked as hard as any man ever has to get to where he did.

"So I'll tell you what I'd like to propose, Dr. Walchef, formerly of Pordim, Bulgaria. If you feel that it is harmonious with your own interests, you can take over my husband's business: his clients, his referrals, his hospital work, everything. All I ask is that you pay me three hundred dollars a month; any income you generate after that is yours, and yours alone. If at the end of one year you find that you like my husband's practice and want to buy it, I'll sell the whole thing to you--including the office and building in which he worked--for $35,000."

"That's amazing," I said. "And I'm sorry, but how much am I to pay you between now and a year from now?"

"Three hundred dollars a month."

"Three hundred dollars!" I protested. "That's too little. Surely you want--"

"No," she cut me off. "That's all I want. That's all I need. I'm fine; our children are more than fine. Too much money in a person's life is a burden. You have a young family, and you're just starting off yourself. You need the money more than an old woman like me does. Three hundred a month, every month, is all I need. If you want it, at the end of a year his whole business is yours for $35,000. Is that something you think you might like to pursue?"

"Mrs. Janis," I said, "It sounds too good."

"Young man," she said, "you must know by now that there's no such thing as a deal that's too good. Your credentials are impeccable. You have exactly the kind of experience my husband's practice needs to keep it going and growing. The deal I'm offering you is the deal I'm offering you. It's your decision to make."

"Well, of course--yes," I said. "It's an amazing opportunity. I'm ... honored, and humbled, that you would extend it to me. I can't imagine how I will repay you such kindness. Thank you."

"You'll repay me by giving me three hundred dollars a month," she said, smiling. She extended her hand to me. "Congratulations, Mr. Luben: You are now the proprietor of a thriving medical practice in one of the most beautiful spots in California. I'll call my brother in Los Angeles tomorrow, and we'll make arrangements to do the paperwork next week, if that's all right with you."

"Yes, of course," I managed to say. "Of course. You have only to call. Thank you."

"No," she said, clasping my hand in both of her dry, warm ones. "Thank *you*," she said.

On the way home I found myself so unable to concentrate on driving that I pulled my car over to the side of the road, and turned it off.

My life, I knew, had just been handed to me.

I was now in possession of a medical practice it would have taken me at least ten years to build on my own.

I started driving again, maybe five minutes later.

Maybe ten.

It was a lot to digest.

"Wait, wait, wait" said Elizabeth, holding up her hand to me. "You're talking so fast I can barely understand you, darling! Now tell me again what you just told me."

I went over the day's events, explaining to her the nature of my new relationship to Mrs. Janis and the medical practice that had belonged to her husband. When I had finished my whole story, Elizabeth looked at me, smiled, and said, "Well, then. I think it's safe to say you had a good day, isn't it?"

Chapter Seventeen

Big Developments

Dr. Janis's business turned out to be every bit as successful as I had hoped it might be. At the end of my first year being in charge of the business I was more than happy to buy it outright for $35,000. It was the one investment in my life that I never had to think twice about: It was like trading a one dollar bill for a ten.

Things were going so well for us, in fact, that even before that first year was out I bought my second home ever; this time, I purchased (for nineteen thousand five hundred dollars--a reminder, in case you'd lost track, that this was 1965) a house with three bedrooms and a detached two-car garage at 5709 Waverly Avenue, near to both my office in Pacific Beach and the elementary school our children attended. It was ideal. And yet I thought it could be more ideal yet, so with that in mind I enlarged the house, converted the garage into guest rooms, and added a swimming pool.

Life was good.

Fully embracing the California lifestyle, I even purchased a boat-- along with some lobster traps. Every Saturday the kids and I would sail out to pull the traps, and if we were lucky we'd all enjoy fresh lobster that night.

It's a marvelous thing, to be a father and know that you're providing your children with a good, healthy life. It was good for the kids to be in California, swimming in their pool every day, attending a good school, going boating on the weekends. I felt proud of my kids--and proud, frankly, of what I'd been able to give them.

But never so proud, I suppose, then when I fulfilled the dream I daresay all fathers with daughters have at one time or another: I bought my daughter a pony.

I couldn't help myself. The girl really loved horses.

And horses need land.

And I was a firm believer in the value of buying good land.

So one day I took a trip to a lovely rural area of gently rolling hills just east of San Diego proper called Spring Valley, and there found a piece of property I liked very much: a one-acre lot upon which sat a small two-bedroom house.

Bingo.

Done.

And thusly did our children come to have at their disposal another weekend recreational choice: If they didn't want to take out the boat, we could instead all take the short drive out to Spring Valley, where they could take turns riding Lisa's horse.

Leaning on the fence around the riding area, watching one of the kids bounce up and down as they trotted the horse, it was easy for me to feel that, finally, it had all been worth it.

But while the property in Spring Valley was not a bad investment and certainly a boon to our everyday lives, I knew that I still needed a real estate investment that at the very least would guarantee that one day I could afford to send each of my children to a college worthy of their ambition. So I began keeping my eyes out for something upon which, in effect, my children's children could one day depend.

And then one spring day in 1967 I saw for sale a motel on Cass Street in Pacific Beach that consisted of eight separate little rental cottages homes and an office.

I looked into it a bit, and found that the asking price for the motel and property was $75,000.

So I thought about it.

It was a business, already running, that seemed to be doing pretty well. And it seemed reasonable to think it would soon start doing even better, because by any definition Pacific Beach was growing as a tourist destination: The place was just beautiful, and it was clear that every day more and more people were discovering it. Moreover, even if the hotel itself didn't pan out for me, I would still own the lot it was on, which was right in the heart of downtown Pacific Beach. Who was to say that one day it wouldn't be the site of the fabulous Walchef Towers?

On the other hand, seventy-five thousand dollars (in 1967, no less) was no small piece of change.

On still another hand, I hadn't gotten to the point where I could even *consider* such a purchase by never risking anything, by always knowing before I ever took a first step exactly where it was I'd end up.

So I bought the motel and the land it was on.

And just like that, I was a major player in the downtown Pacific Beach real estate market.

Shortly after buying that property I had a stark reminder of the way in which the acquisition of land is at the root of so much of the world's history. It was the summer of 1967, and I was in Vienna, Austria, where, through the auspices of the American Medical Society, I used to return every three years for refresher courses in surgery offered at various universities and clinics throughout the city. This particular summer, however, found Vienna suffering through unseasonably bad weather: It was cold and raining every day.

It is just possible that you recall my aversion to inclement weather; if so, you will understand my desire to just then leave behind the concerts and operas of Vienna, and instead visit somewhere I wouldn't regret leaving my new umbrella behind in my room.

I thought about it a bit, and then realized that, after all, Egypt wasn't so very far away--and it was certainly, I concluded, a place where anyone who had any chance at all of doing so should go.

Furthermore, I concluded that this was my chance.

And what were the chances of it being cold and raining in Egypt?

None, as it turned out: When the next day I stepped from my plane and onto the tarmac in Cairo, it was as warm and sunny as even a person as finicky as I could wish for.

Perfect!

I found a room in a nearby hotel, dropped my bags, and headed back out again to explore the wonders of Cairo.

By the end of that day, I felt sure that Cairo is one of the most enchanting, endlessly interesting cities in all of the world. In a word, I loved it there.

I saw the broad, shimmering Nile.

I saw the pyramids.

I saw a tribe of Bedouin tribesmen on camels moving slowly against the great, sinking sun.

Enchanting, enchanting, enchanting.

I was due to fly back to reality late that Saturday morning. So, feeling refreshed and invigorated by my time spent at the very cradle of civilization, I packed my bags, closed the door of my hotel room behind me, went to the front desk, and was there told to return to my room and wait for further instruction, because Egypt, that morning, had gone to war: The whole country was, in effect, on lockdown.

Hmmm. Being stuck in the middle of a city at war.

Wasn't anything *new* ever going to happen to me?

"What do you mean, 'war'?" I asked one of the Egyptian military police now stationed in the hotel lobby.

"War," he answered, restlessly looking about the lobby. "War. People shooting at one another." He then looked me in the eye. "War."

"Yes, I know what war is," I said. "But why? With whom? For how long?"

"Sir," he said with just a touch of impatience, "I'm afraid I can't answer your questions right now. Israel has declared war on Egypt and several of her neighbors. I do not know why. And I certainly do not know how long the war will last. If you will please just return to your room, I'm sure that everything will work out fine for you. Thank you."

The war, in fact, lasted six days: I got stuck in Cairo during The Six Day War of 1967.

Perhaps it wasn't the eternal, internal conflict of man against man that caused war. Perhaps it wasn't natural aggression, restless need, never-forgotten offenses that burn like embers in the hearts of men until finally they raise up to avenge themselves.

Perhaps it was *me!*

Maybe I was some sort of bizarre war magnet!

Either way, as I placed my suitcase back down in my room, I knew I'd be stuck in the hotel for a while. At that point, for all anyone knew the Seven Year War had just begun. War, of course, is no joke, and while of course it was a selfish concern, the fact was that this one hurt me personally because, ancient international conflict or not, I had a medical practice I needed to return to! I had a lot of patients scheduled for that Monday!

Suddenly the rain and cold in Vienna didn't seem like all that big a deal at all.

I heard some voices out in the hallway, and went to take a look. A group of American men who were staying in different rooms on my floor were all mingling together in the hall, talking about what had happened. As luck would have it, these weren't just any group of American men: They were part of a large American delegation who had come to Cairo to complete a long-term oil agreement between the American and Egyptian governments.

If anyone could get me out of Egypt, I figured it was these men.

I listened to them speaking for awhile, and then stepped up to a cluster of four or five of them, and said, "So, what shall we do?" (There were so many of them: Who's to say they wouldn't think *I* was one of them?)

"Well, we've been told to wait right here," said one of them. "This thing just started. Nobody knows what the hell is going on. All we know is they've closed all the airports and harbors: Nobody comes in or out of Cairo for a little while, at least."

"What are the boys at State saying?" asked one of his colleagues.

"They're telling us to sit. They did have one suggestion, but I don't know."

"What is it?" I asked, feeling a little bit more like an oilman every moment.

"Well, they're saying we can probably get out by going through Libya." As the men began to discuss this option I broke away from them, and returned to my room. I knew enough about international travel--and certainly about it during times of war--to know that trying to exit Egypt by going through a neighboring country could tie a person up in a knot they might never break free of. I knew that just acquiring the necessary travel visa would take so long it would probably be quicker to join the Egyptian army, get sent to the front, and just try to run away from there.

Back in my room I paced the floor a bit, and tried to think.

I was stuck in Egypt.

Egypt was at war.

I had patients coming in on Monday.

Clearly, there was only one thing for me to do. As painful as it would be, I could see I had no other choice but to turn my three-day visit to Cairo into an extended vacation in Egypt.

The trains in Egypt, after all, were probably still working!

And I'd always wanted to see the famous Egyptian city of Alexandria!

So I picked my bags back up, and headed back down to the lobby.

On my way out the lobby door the same guard with whom I'd spoken before stopped me.

"Excuse me, sir," he said, stepping in front of me. "May I help you?"

"Yes, please," I said. "Can you point me toward the nearest train station?"

"I'm afraid I must ask you where you are intending to go, sir, and what your business is there."

"Well, I was hoping to go to Alexandria. I am a tourist here, and rather than sit in my room and wait for the new war to end, I thought I would take advantage of my time here, and see more of your beautiful country. I've seen Cairo, so now I thought perhaps I would take a train to Alexandria, and see if everything I have heard about that beautiful city is true."

The man peered at me over the top of his dark shades.

"You want to go to Alexandria," he said.

I nodded.

"Now."

I nodded.

"For a vacation."

I nodded.

"Which you understand will be happening right in the middle of a war."

I nodded.

He kept his eyes on me for a few moments, and then turned and again resumed scanning the room from behind his shades. Finally he turned back at me, and, still hidden behind his shades, he said, "Alexandria is a beautiful place."

"That's what I've heard," I said.

"Okay," he said. "Go. But be careful."

"Thank you," I replied. "And I will."

"And sir?" he said as I prepared to leave.

"Yes?"

"Welcome to our country."

The guard was right: Alexandria was beautiful. As far as I know, every city on the Mediterranean coast is gorgeous--but surely none is more so than this ancient place. I had no trouble finding a room at a nice government-run hotel there; interestingly, it had up to the day before been almost filled with Russian visitors, who, according to the front desk clerk, had known the war was coming, and so had all vacated the night before.

"They knew?" I asked incredulously. "How?"

"I have no idea," said the clerk. "All I know is that they knew. It's why they left."

This fact, it seemed to me, was an excellent one to forget all about. All I knew was that I had a splendid hotel in Alexandria practically to myself, and that my vacation had just been extended indefinitely.

"What do you mean you're stuck in Egypt?" cried my secretary over the phone.

"It's a war," I said. "There's nothing anyone can do."

"But you've got a full schedule on Monday!" she said. "What should I tell them all?"

"Reschedule them," I said.

"But for when?"

"Well, I'm not sure," I said. "This thing can't last *too* long."

"But it's a *war,*" she cried.

"What do you mean you're stuck in Egypt?" cried my wife. "How? Why?" I told her what had happened.

"My God!" she cried. "Luben, that's terrible!"

"Well, actually," I said, "It's not all that bad."

"What do you mean, it's not all that bad? You're trapped in a country at *war!*"

"Well, yes," I said. "But nobody's shooting at *me*. The war isn't happening *in* Egypt. And it's certainly not happening here in Alexandria."

"You're in Alexandria? I thought you were in Cairo." So I told her what happened, there, too.

"Wait, wait," she said. "Let me get this straight. You were in Cairo; you found out a war was going on; so you decided to take a *vacation?*"

"Well, yes," I said. "Essentially ... yes."

"Oh," she said. There was a long pause, and then she said, "And you're all right." I told her I was perfectly fine: that inside the country everything was just fine.

"And I'll be able to get out soon," I said. "Don't forget, I've done this before. For a short while now everything will freeze. If the war proceeds and begins going on for some real time, normal business--certainly the kind that moves foreigners in and out of the country in a reasonable way--will resume, and I'll come home then. And if it's over quickly--then it's over quickly, and the same thing happens."

"But Luben," she said. "It's a war. Wars don't end quickly."

"Sometimes they do, my love. Sometimes they do."

And this one certainly did! Six days! That's how long it took Israel to acquire from Egypt the Sinai and Gaza Strip, from Jordan the West Bank and East Jerusalem, and from Syria the Golan Heights.

Six days!

And so that also proved as long as I had to enjoy the sea and sand at Alexandria before word of the conflict's end reached my hotel--which is when I heard also of my chance to return home via an Egyptian ship that was setting sale for Athens the very next day. This joyous news soon soured, however, as quick upon its heels came word that there were absolutely no tickets left on that ship.

So do you know what I did?

I went outside, and flagged down a taxi. I did this not because I desired to go anywhere at all; I did it because I wanted to talk to a taxi driver. Because, as everyone knows, when you need something that can't be done, or you want to find something in a city that can't be found, one must *always* go to the taxi drivers--who, as far as I know, operate at least half the world. And it's always the part one most often really *needs,* too.

"Yes, yes, of course I can get you a ticket on that ship," said my driver. "But it's going to cost you three times the price of the ticket. It's as if you had asked me for a seat on a spaceship to the moon. Nearly impossible."

"You are a taxi driver," I said. "For you, nothing is impossible."

The man threw back his head and laughed. "True!" he said. "True!"

And that is how I came, the very next day, to be seated on the deck of a cruise ship headed for Athens.

It took two days and two nights to sail from Alexandria to the port of Piraeus. On board the ship I made the acquaintance of a professor of history from Paris, with whom I began taking my meals. This charming, intelligent and perceptive fellow gave me a chance to brush up on my French, and to hear his quirky, humorous opinions on everything from social customs to literature to, well, medicine.

"Why is it," I asked him, "that you squeeze lemon juice onto virtually everything you eat?"

"To fight colds!" he said. "Vitamin C! It keeps one from ever catching a cold! I haven't had a cold in twenty years!"

And that is when I, too, began squeezing lemon juice on much of what I ate.

They say travel is the best education.

And "they," as always, are right about that.

From Athens I called my secretary to tell her I'd be home soon.

"Oh, thank God!" she cried. "I was so worried about you! I'll schedule all of your appointments starting Monday. You are going to be one very busy doctor when you come back."

I was--but first I was one very busy local celebrity. Somehow or another a journalist from one of the local television stations had heard of my adventure in Egypt, and, and on my first day back at work arrived, television crew and all, in my office to interview me.

With the bright lights very nearly blinding me, I sat behind my desk and answered his questions as best I could.

"So you decided to take a *vacation?*" he asked.

Two years after buying the property on Cass Street, I decided I could do better with it than to continue using it as a site of a motel. As a business the motel was doing all right, but it wasn't exactly going gangbusters: The whole enterprise seemed bogged down in a sluggishness I had neither the time nor temperament to shake.

It occurred to me that what would do very well on that property was a big apartment building. It wasn't long before I'd decided on just *how* big an apartment building, either: I decided a 120-unit, 12-story complex would be just the thing to set my kids and I up for life.

So I finally ended the long and distinctly uneventful life of the motel, and began a process so fraught with upset and disappointment that had I known beforehand what I was getting into, I would never have begun.

Oh, where to begin enumerating all the things that went wrong in my quest to realize The Walchef Arms? (I decided The Walchef Towers sounded too pretentious--and I'm kidding, by the way, about either name, which I never once thought of at the time, but which I mention now in order to introduce a bit of humor into something which, if I remember it too directly, will, I fear, in no time at all have me rolling around on the floor bawling like a baby.)

Okay, the first thing that alone could have pretty much doomed the development of my apartment building was that the residents of Pacific Beach, I came to learn, hated the idea of a 12-story apartment building going up downtown. There was no way I could have known about this ahead of time, of course--but no matter. When my plan for the land became known to the good citizens who lived anywhere around it, they began protesting against my would-be building with the same righteous fervor I imagine they would have mustered if I'd announced a plan to build a one hundred twenty-unit, twelve-story bordello on the same land.

The problem, it seemed, lie in the "twelve-story" part of my plan.

That, apparently, was just too tall.

People in Pacific Beach, I learned, only want *short* buildings in their town.

There actually came a time when indignant members of the Short Buildings Only coalition (I'm joking, of course: they were really called Citizens Against Neck Craning) were marching up and down the sidewalk in front of my medical office. It is a measure of just how disastrous the whole affair had turned by then that people carrying anti-me signs back and forth in front of my very business didn't even make it onto my list of Top 10 Things To Worry About.

I was in the process of losing everything I'd put into my development up until that point. Those people could have marched up and down on my *back* and I probably wouldn't have noticed. (Actually, of course, I was acutely aware of the protesters, and it pained me to be the cause of such displeasure amongst my neighbors. But, by then, I was too heavily invested in the project to even think of simply backing out. When they yelled, "Must go!", all I heard, I'm afraid, was "Must keep going!")

The second thing I did wrong was to start off without nearly enough capital. Now *that* was a mistake. (And it brings to my mind the fact that my giant, overarching, mother-of-all-mistakes on this project was undertaking a project of this magnitude without first making sure I had a deep understanding of financing real estate development in California.) The loan for one million six hundred thousand dollars that I obtained through a mortgage company was simply not enough to complete the construction of the project.

Realizing you're short on money when you've got a line of people waiting behind you at the grocery store is one thing. Realizing you're short on money when you've got three full crews of builders and an army of architects, engineers, contractors and sub-contractors waiting to get paid for the four stories of your twelve-story building that they've finished is another thing altogether.

The third big mistake I made was not hiring a real builder. Instead of a legitimate, fully-funded development firm experienced in all facets of multistoried residential rental constructions, I hired a man with a pretty nice pick-up truck and a tool belt who had just finished building a small hotel, and who assured me that he could put together a "crack team" of builders and subcontractors who could "practically pop this thing up overnight."

Even telling this story now it's embarrassing.

I may as well have strapped my every last dollar onto my body and walked around downtown Los Angeles in the middle of the night holding a huge sign that said, "I Don't Know Anything About Your Legal System. Please Rob Me."

So those were all mistakes. And taken as a whole, they don't even *begin* to measure up to the worst mistake I've ever made in my life: hiring a lawyer for this project who, all by himself, would easily be enough justification for every single lawyer joke you've ever heard.

People protesting my building, walking back in front of my office? No problem. Only having enough money to finish four floors of a twelve-story building? Piece of cake. A builder who couldn't make one log cabin from three complete sets of Lincoln Logs? Don't bother me, I'm watching a Bob Hope movie on TV.

A lawyer who makes the slithering devil in the Garden of Eden look like Santa Claus?

Kill me now, please.

So when you have a series of deep and dark problems inherent in a project as massively complex as the development of a (semi) high-rise apartment building on a major piece of downtown property, in what ways might one anticipate this conflux of concerns actually, physically manifesting?

Might people involved with the project at some point simply walk off the site?

That could happen.

Might a team of investors come and try to take advantage of the troubled owner of the project by buying him out for a bargain-basement price?

That's certainly a possibility.

Might the owner of such a worrisome endeavor simply drop dead of a heart attack?

I believe in my case that almost did happen a couple of times.

But guess what actually did happen?

Go ahead. Guess. I can wait. This'll be fun. I'll go make myself a cucumber salad, while you try to figure out One Big Thing that physically occurred in the course of my first big American real estate development project.

Mmmmmmm .... cucumber salad ... .

Okay, give up?

The answer to today's "What Happen To Dr. Walchef's Building?" quiz is: *A crane toppled over on it.*

That's right. This monstrously huge, looming construction crane, the kind that picks up sides of buildings like they're playing cards and swings them through the air like with the greatest of ease, just *fell* on my building.

There it was, looking like some giant insect sprayed by the largest can of Raid in the universe so that it just died atop my building. Like some gangly relative of Godzilla's with one too many drinks in him. Like some hulking alien from the planet Metallica who'd gotten lost and crashed right in the heart of downtown Pacific Beach.

The good news is that it created a visual I'll never forget. That's always nice. Saves money on film.

I would say that at the moment my eyes had unscrambled enough of the confusing image before it to confidently report back to my brain that the crane that was being used to build my building was indeed now lying atop it, was the moment I fully suspected that the problems that had thus far accompanied this particular foray into the world of real estate development were not likely to simply vanish anytime soon.

Not that I expected them to. But up to that point I'd at least been able to maintain the illusion that they were eminently manageable.

And then, all at once, they clearly weren't.

As I was standing at the site, looking at the crane taking a nap atop my building, the man I'd hired to *build* my building--the man with the pick-up truck, the man who so persuasively convinced me there'd be no problem at all on the site, the man in whose job description was surely found the words "Keep Crane From Falling On Building"--this man came sidling up next to me, a cup of coffee in his hands. He stood beside me for a moment, looking at what I was looking at, and then blew across the top of his cup, shook his head slightly, and said, "Boy, now *that's* a problem, isn't it?"

I myself, of course, was pretty interested in how it came to be that a crane had apparently *tripped* upon my building. But my interest in that unfortunate event was a mere fleeting thought compared to the fixated attention it inspired in the company that had loaned me the money to make the building in the first place.

They found the sight of the stumbling crane so fascinating, in fact, that on the evening of the very day it happened one of their representatives came to my house and informed me that I needed to put one hundred thousand dollars into a reserve account as collateral against the possibility that anything like that might ever happen again.

"One hundred thousand dollars!" I cried. "I don't have one hundred thousand dollars that I can just sit in a corner to make all of us feel better! I've mortgaged everything I have to get this building as far along as I have! There's no way I can now come up with another one hundred thousand dollars!"

"Then I'm afraid we're going to have to cease payment disbursements on your project, Mr. Walchef," said the man from the lending company. "We will of course issue payment for all the work that's been done so far, but I'm afraid that in light of recent events, we feel it would be irresponsible of us to continue financing construction on your building until we have that additional insurance money. I'm sorry."

He was not as sorry as I.

And my lawyer was so far from sorry he could barely contain himself from giggling. Not that he in any way let his joy show. Instead, he took pity on me, and put his caring hand upon my shoulder, and in every way displayed his loyal friendship and sincere empathy for what I was going through in this most difficult of times.

And then he sent me a bill for ten thousand dollars worth of his services. When I didn't, in effect, cut him a check the very day I received his bill, he ran behind my back and "arranged" to have the title of my building, along with all of the assets associated with its construction and development, transferred to his name.

"He *what?*" said an attorney the next day who worked for Scripps hospital. He and I had struck up a conversation over meatloaf and Jell-o in the hospital's cafeteria.

"He somehow got a legal transfer of my building into his name when I didn't right away pay him $10,000 he'd billed me for."

"Wait, wait," said my lunch mate. "This guy's *your* attorney, right?"

"Right."

"He works for you."

"Right."

"And he bills you $10,000, and when you don't pay it within--what? How long?"

"I don't know. Four days."

"Four days?!" The man was starting to yell. "You don't pay him a $10,000 fee and in a *four days* he seizes *your* assets in lieu of that payment? Am I hearing you right? Is this what you're telling me?"

"Yes."

"Your lawyer just takes your building from you."

"Right."

"A project for which you are the sole developer."

"Yes."

"And he's *your* lawyer. He's the guy you hired to protect your assets. He wasn't working for the mortgage company. He wasn't working for the building company. He was working for you."

"Yes."

"And he screwed you straight into the ground."

I looked at him.

"Luben," he said, lowering his voice and leaning across the table toward me. "Would you like me to pay your attorney a visit? What he has done isn't just unethical. It's as illegal as robbing a bank or killing someone. And he knows it, too--I guarantee it. I'd be happy to let him know that *I* know it, too. If I had five minutes with this clown, he'd be handing you back the title to your building and apologizing faster than you can say 'disbarred.'"

"Yes," I said. "Yes. See him. Of course. I'm thrilled. You would actually do this for me?"

"Yeah--and I'd be doing it for me, too. Your 'lawyer' is exactly the kind of rotten, soulless shyster who gives *all* lawyers a bad name." He looked disgusted. "He can't transfer the title of your land and your development project into his name. It's insane. He's just taking advantage of you because a lot of the stuff you're involved in might be a little new to you. Instead of doing what he's *supposed* to, which is guide you and help you *through* all that stuff, he robs you. I *hate* guys like that." My new friend took a bite of his meatloaf in a way that qualified as ferocious. "I'm looking forward to meeting this guy," he said. "When you have a chance, get me his name and address."

And sure enough, two days later I was again the legal owner of my building. And I had a new lawyer--one my savior from the hospital had recommended to me. Things were looking up! But only for a moment or two, because I could have had Clarence Darrow for a lawyer, and I still would have needed a way to come up with one hundred thousand dollars in order to continue with my building.

But no matter how I thought about it, I could see no way of securing that much money. I really had already mortgaged everything I had--including the house my family and I were living in. There was simply nothing left.

I didn't have the money the lending company was demanding.

And I wasn't going to come up with it.

And the building crew had pulled the broken crane into an upright position, and then gone home. The site lay quiet now: a ragged four floors of a twelve-story building, alone on a site.

And what began to sink in was that I was going to lose that building.

I wasn't going to finish it.

I was, I knew, in so far over my head that I was drowning. And I could see no way to the break above the water, which was everywhere pressing down upon me. It was just too dark for me to see a way out.

And then my wife, my lovely Elizabeth, began to die. She came down with pneumonia, which coupled with her chronic asthma and bronchitis to create a condition that in very short order was threatening her life.

It was absolutely unbelievable. Suddenly my wife, the mother of my children, my partner and helpmate in everything I did or thought, was fading from our lives. I called in every specialist I knew. She went into the hospital.

And finally the chief pulmonary surgeon came to find me in the hospital chapel, where he gently suggested to me that there was now really nothing left to do but bring Elizabeth back home, and wait.

Luben was 15.

Boyan was 11.

Lisa was 10.

Too young. They were all too young.

We were all too young.

"Luben," said my wife in the soft, raspy voice that had replaced her usual tones. I was sitting on the edge of her bed, cradling her hand in mine. She was so pale, now, and so weak. She'd only been home from the hospital a couple of days.

"What is it, sweetheart?"

"I want to go home." I thought I knew what she meant, but she was taking some fairly strong medications, and now spent her days rising and sinking in and out of consciousness.

"You are home, my love."

She fixed me with her sad eyes. "No," she said, smiling just a bit. "I mean to Cincinnati. I want to go home to Cincinnati."

Although she enjoyed our life in California, Elizabeth had always missed being near her family, and living in the area in which she'd been raised. That she would want to spend her final days in her hometown surrounded by all of her loving family made, of course, perfect sense.

"But you're so sick, my love. We can't travel right now. It's too long a trip; it's too strenuous. Let's wait to go until you get better, okay?"

"Luben," she whispered. The length of time for which she held me in the infinite depth of her steady gaze was long enough to contain the whole of our relationship.

"I'm not going to get better," she said.

"No, no, no, no," I said, shaking my head. "You will. Don't be silly. You'll get better."

"I won't, Luben. And I want to be with my family one last time."

So Elizabeth and I and our children drove back to Cincinnati to stay with Elizabeth's beloved sister Bernadette. We set Elizabeth up in one of Bernie's guest rooms, and for the next seven days or so whenever she opened her eyes she was sure to find one or more members of her family sitting or standing near her bed, smiling at her and ready to take her hand or wipe her brow. If she awoke to find one of her parents or siblings beside her, she might talk with them a little about the old days; if it was one of her children, they might talk a little about days yet to come.

And then there were no more days for her.

Elizabeth passed on to a better world on December 22, 1969.

I can't wait to see her again.

Chapter Eighteen

A Steal of a Deal

About four days after that, while the children and I were still at Bernie's, a telegram arrived from my sister back in Bulgaria saying that about six months earlier my father had been diagnosed with pancreatic cancer. Now, she wrote, our father was dying.

"He wants you by his side now," said the telegram. "You must come immediately."

I hadn't even known my father had cancer.

It was like him not to tell me, though.

"As much as you can," I said to Bernie that night as she and I sat alone at a little table in her kitchen, "spend time with the children while I'm gone. This is a terrible thing for them to have to go through."

She reached out and put her hand on my shoulder. "And for you, Luben."

When I looked at her again I had tears in my eyes.

"How can I leave them?" I whispered hoarsely. "Their mother just died."

Tears were in her eyes, too.

"And how can you not?" she said.

So I kissed and hugged my children good-bye at the airport, and boarded a plane to Bulgaria.

I don't remember much about the flight; I know I arrived at the hospital late at night. What I do remember is standing in the darkness outside the small light shining down upon my father's hospital bed, and barely recognizing him. He looked twice the age he had the last time I had seen him--and seemed to weigh about half as much. Now, finally, he looked like a little, old man.

I had been sitting in a chair beside his bed for maybe an hour when he suddenly groaned, stirred a bit, and opened his eyes.

"Luben," he said in a hoarse whisper. "You're here."

"I am, Father," I said. I stood and leaned over his bed railing, placing my hand upon his shoulder. "How are you feeling?"

"I've been better. I've been worse." He paused for a moment, and then said, "Wait. No I haven't."

I actually laughed.

"I'm glad you're here, son," he said. "Thank you for coming."

"Of course, Father."

"Have you talked to the doctors about my condition?"

"I spoke with the night physician in charge for a few moments. I saw your records."

"They've given me maybe a week to live."

"No," I said. I started to cry. "That can't be."

My father reached up to place his hand on my arm. "Now, now, boy. It's not as bad as all that. I'm not a young man, after all. I've had a good life. I'm ready."

And the grief and anxiety I had for so long been suppressing seemed, all in a moment, to turn my tears into something like laughter.

"Well, I'm not," I said.

"Good thing you're not dying, then."

"Oh, Papa," I said. I sat back down in the chair. "Oh, Papa."

In a serious tone, he said, "What is it, Luben?"

Through the chrome railing of his bed I looked into his eyes for a long time, but couldn't bring myself to tell him.

"What is it?" he said. "I'm dying. How bad can it be?"

"Elizabeth became very ill about a month ago. She passed away just last week." He closed his eyes, and seemed to almost push his head back against his pillow, pulling in a long breath through his tightened mouth as he did so. He held that for a while, and then opened his sad, watery eyes, and looked at me.

"My God," he whispered.

"And you can have him, too. He's no friend of mine." I smiled enough to let him know I didn't mean it.

"I'm so sorry, Luben. How are the children?"

"They're at Elizabeth's sister's house. We were actually there when I got the telegram about you. They're ... I don't know. Their mother just died."

"Sweet Jesus," my father whispered. He closed his eyes again, and kept them closed. After a long silence he opened them again.

"So," he whispered. "How were your holidays?"

Five days later I left my father back on his farm surrounded by the family and friends who meant so much to him. I didn't want to leave, but he said, "Go. Your children need you." And I knew he was right.

"I'll give your regards to Elizabeth," he said. "Life moves quickly, son. We'll all be together again soon enough."

And those were the last words I ever heard him say. He passed away five days after I left Bulgaria. He would have breathed his last just about the same time my children and I were arriving back at our home in San Diego.

Needless to say, by the time I turned my attention back to the troubled state of my Cass Street development my perspective on the whole affair had changed a bit. And I'm sad to say it hadn't changed for anything resembling the better, either. They say profound grief makes a person wiser. It may or may not, but one thing that's certain is that if it does make a person wiser, it doesn't do so right away. I was shocked with grief. When I tried to again care about the things that had previously consumed all of my attention, I found that I simply could not. I found that I didn't in the slightest care about the land, or the building, or the contractors, or the lawyers, or the loaning company, or the people who were still protesting against my development. I barely cared about my patients.

I was just ... lost.

And yet life, of course, went on. And I don't mean in any kind of larger, more general sense: I meant it continued to surprise me--from way, way back in my consciousness, which was the only place I seemed to register anything during that time--that no matter how I felt (or, more, didn't feel), I kept ... brushing my teeth twice a day, for example. I kept getting dressed before I went outside. I kept diagnosing patients, putting gas in my car, answering the phone, lying down at night in the same bed that was now so achingly empty beside me, and trying to sleep.

And if I was facing toward her side of the bed when I came out of whatever semblance of sleep I'd fallen into, I'd open my eyes, and see, again, that she was gone.

Everywhere I looked, and everything I did: She was gone. That brutal, horrible, unrelenting fact created a vast, cold emptiness into which everything, it seemed to me, rushed, never to be seen again. And that was fine with me. I didn't want any of it, anyway.

My wife had died. But I had become the ghost.

One day during this time a man came to my office, and he told me that he was the owner of a very large building company.

"I know you're having trouble with your property on Cass Street," said the man sitting in a chair on the other side of my desk. "I know you were under-funded for that project, and that the lender has shut off the spigot that was watering that thing until you pony up one hundred thousand dollars. That's a terrible mess to be in, Dr. Walchef. Just terrible."

"I'm sorry," I said, "But is there something I can do for you?"

He laughed a big, hearty, friendly laugh. "No, but I'll tell you what: There's something I can do for you. Actually, there's something we can both do for each other. Look," he said. "You've got this thing sitting like an albatross around your neck, right? It's just a big, dead liability sittin' out there for the world to see. And do you know what the problem with that development project is, Dr. Walchef? Do you?"

"If you've got a half hour or so, I could probably come up with a few things, yes."

"I'm sure you could, Dr. Walchef, I'm sure you could. But let me tell you something: It wouldn't really take all that long at all to go over everything that's wrong with that project. Because there's really only *one* thing wrong with it. And do you know what that one thing is, Dr. Walchef? Do you know what the one single thing is about that land and what you're doing on it that's killing you out there?"

I allowed as how I did not.

"It's the fact that you're building apartments on that land. *That's* the mistake you made going into this thing. You shouldn't be building apartments out there at all. What you *should* be building on that land is condominiums."

"Condominiums?"

"Condominiums. You've got to listen to this Dr. Walchef, because I wouldn't step out of my busy day, and I sure wouldn't have asked you to step out of yours to meet me like this, if what I was about to tell you isn't as true as that the sun will come up tomorrow and fish prefer swimming to walking. So let me just get right to it. Do you know why you should be building condominiums on that property instead of apartments?"

"Because it's harder for protesters to spell 'condominiums' than it is 'apartments'?

The man stared at me for a moment, as if his eyes and body were waiting to catch up to how funny his brain found my joke, and then he threw back his head and let loose a long, ringing laugh that filled my office with sound.

"Good one!" he said, banging one hand on his knee. "Outstanding! Easier to spell! Oh, Dr. Walchef, it's a wise man who can make jokes about the very thing that's troubling him. A wise man, indeed. Whoo-ee, you just about busted my gut on that one. Yessir, a laugh like that can cure a man of just about everything that ails him. You'll have to charge me for a check-up there, Dr. Walchef."

"It's on the house," I said.

"Well, let me tell you. As good an answer as that was, there's even a better one. The reason you should be building condos on that property instead of apartments, Dr. Walchef, is because lenders will fund condos in way they wouldn't dream of funding apartments." He leaned back a bit in his chair, and held his hands palms up and away from his body. "That's it. That's the mistake you made."

"It is? Are you serious?"

"As a cat staring at a mouse hole. Let me tell you something, Dr. Walchef: I don't even build apartments anymore. I haven't for years. It's just not worth it anymore. You can get so much money for building condos that the only reason *anyone* builds apartments anymore, if you'll excuse my saying so, is because they just don't know exactly what they're doing."

"Why is there such a big difference between the two?"

"Because you can sell condos as soon as they're built. *That's* the big difference! That's the *huge* difference! And it's not something lenders aren't aware of. They *know* that about condos--and they *like* that about condos! It means condos aren't a risk for them at all. They get their money back almost as soon as the job's done. For an apartment, they've got to wait until the owner realizes the value of his investment over a long period of time. Those apartments might rent, or they might not. One year the rent on them will be pretty high; the next it'll be pretty low. The money will trickle in to the owner, sure--but only over a long period of time. But with condos--they go up, they get sold, the lender gets his money back in no time at all. It's just a sweet deal for everyone involved."

"That does make sense," I said.

"You better believe it does. That's why you didn't get enough money to finish your job: Lenders get nervous putting up money for an apartment building. Come see them with a condo development, though, and they throw open their checkbooks like Vegas fat cats on a binge. And it's not too late for you to get in on some of that action yourself, Dr. Walchef. It's not too late at all. All you've got to do is back out of what you're doing, restart yourself as a developer of condos on that land, and I guarantee you that within a week you'll have all the money you'd need to build the Taj Mahal on that site, much less a twelve-story condominium project."

"Well," I said wearily, "I have to tell you that that does sound like a very good idea. And I will think about it. But I'm afraid that right now I'm not feeling particularly ... how should I say this ... ambitious. To be perfectly frank with you, I recently lost two very precious family members. And so right now I'm finding it difficult to really concentrate on anything but the most basic aspects of my life. I hope you understand."

"Dr. Walchef," said the man, "I do understand. I didn't want to say anything about your recent misfortune, but I was aware of it. And let me tell you right now how sorry I am for your loss. That's a terrible thing to bear. I lost my dear mother just last year, and it was the saddest thing that's ever happened to me in my whole life. If I had lost anyone else near to me at anywhere near the same time, I think it would have done me in. So you've got to believe me, Dr. Walchef: I wouldn't have come here today to talk about this with you if I didn't think it might actually be a way to help you unload some of the responsibilities that can be so burdensome to someone suffering what you've gone through. If you'll hear me out, Dr. Walchef, I've got a proposal I'd like to make to you."

I invited him to go ahead.

"Okay, here's my plan." He reached into his brown leather satchel and pulled out a large binder. Standing just enough to lean forward and place it in front of me on my desk, he sat back down in his chair and said, "Here are a few of the projects my company has built over the years. They're almost all condos or apartments, and at least half of them are local. If you look through this material here, you'll find that we're about as good at developing properties of this nature as anyone in the business. Our reputation is unsurpassed: We haven't yet brought in a project over budget or a single day late. Now here's what I'm proposing to do. Let us take over the headaches that have arisen from your trying to develop that land, Dr. Walchef. You're grieving right now. No man going through what you are right now should have to suffer through all the legalities and technicalities a development project like yours demands. You don't need this headache. I can point you toward the people who would fund a condo development for you, but it would still mean you contacting them, and dealing with them, and ready funds or not, I don't have to tell you the kinds of hoops you'll be made to jump through just so the money boys can see that look on your face. It's a *sound* process, but it's not exactly an easy one. Why should you have to deal with it at all? Me and my company have been doing exactly this sort of thing for years. I know a trick or two about this business, Mr. Walchef. One of the things I know, for instance, is that you don't want to fund a project like this from a single source: You want to line up a bunch of potential funding companies, and make them work for the privilege of becoming involved in such a lucrative enterprise. That keeps your rates down, see? That effects your terms in a way that's favorable for you, not for them. That's a way for you to have some power in the relationship, see?"

"That would be nice," I said.

"And there's no reason you shouldn't have it. It's your project. Anyone who lends you money will make money. But Dr. Walchef, I'm just going to be honest with you, now. You probably couldn't get that kind of power yourself. You have to know these boys. You have to know who to call, and when to call them, and what to say to them when you get 'em on the line. You have to know how to present this thing to them in just the right way to make them sit up and beg. And there's just no way you yourself can know that stuff, Dr. Walchef. How could you? You're a doctor. You save people's lives. *I* save people's buildings. And I'd like to save yours."

"How?" I said. "How exactly?"

"Well, here's what I'd like to do. Lawyers are good for something, right? And as far as I know, the *only* thing they're good for is drawing up contracts. And what I'd like to do is have them draw up a contract between you and I, Dr. Walchef, in which it's spelled out that what you want me to do is essentially save your building. And by that I mean that I will reconfigure the whole deal you've got going out there so that it becomes a condo project, and that I will get the proper funding for that project--and the proper *terms* for the funding for that project--and that I will develop that project until it is sitting on that land like a diamond on a wedding ring, and that all you have to do is sit back and wait to get paid."

"Me, getting paid. Imagine that."

"You won't have to imagine it, Dr. Walchef. It'll *happen.* You'll get paid like the king on tax day. We'll let the lawyers work out all the details in that lawyerly way they do, but the fundamental idea here is that I assume all responsibility--and accept all the legal and financial liabilities that come with that responsibility--for securing the funds for the building, and seeing that building through its entire construction. In exchange for those services, we agree that once I've sold the building, a fair percentage of the profit off the sales of the condominiums goes directly to you. So all you have to do, really, is sit back, wait, and then collect your part of the money off the sale of your condos in a market in which, by the way, condos are doing very well indeed. No matter how you look at it, Dr. Walchef, it's a sweet deal for everyone involved. Whaddaya think?"

"What percentage of the money would I get?"

"Well now, that all depends. We've got to do all the detailed calculations on all that--to be honest, we've got to figure out exactly how deep a hole I'm gonna have to dig us out of here--but it seems to me that something in the ten to forty percent range should be about right."

"And I have nothing to do with the development--with any of it. This thing is out of my hands completely. I retain rights to a percentage of the final sale of the condos once they're built, but am free from any of the concerns associated with the thing in the meantime. Right?"

"That's exactly right. And that's the beauty of it. You worry about healing people, which is what you do best, and I'll worry about that property, which is what I do best. And I guarantee you that this way we'll both end up with heftier wallets. So, whaddaya say, Dr. Walchef? Do we have ourselves a deal?"

"I don't like it," said my new lawyer when I told him about the builder's proposition. "It just doesn't sound right to me. You don't know this guy. And the arrangement he's proposing, as you've described it to me, gives him more control than any one person should have over the business of another."

"But that's kind of the idea," I said. "I don't *want* control of this building anymore. I long ago *lost* control of the whole thing. I really want to wash my hands of it. He's offering me a way to do that, and to still make money."

"Well, that's what he *says* he's offering you. But we don't know that's what he's *actually* offering you. Look, Dr. Walchef, I know … I know that this isn't the easiest time for you. I really do. But with this building, you're involved in something that's pretty complex. Guys like this, they sometimes see a situation they know they can take advantage of, and they come in, and they say something they know is exactly what you want to hear, and they get your head all turned around, and the next thing you know they've got you signing papers that you can end up regretting for the rest of your life. I've seen it happen before; I've seen it happen too many times to be comfortable with it now. I'm not saying this man is necessarily planning to take advantage of you--but I am saying I think you'd do well to proceed with caution. At the very least let me meet with his counsel, and find out what this deal's really all about."

"But I told you what he wants to do."

"I know you did, Dr. Walchef. But sometimes there can be an awfully big difference between what someone *says* they want to do, and what they instruct their lawyers to *actually* do. I want to make sure there's no difference between those two things, Dr. Walchef. I'm telling you: a deal like this involves a lot of legal paperwork, and that makes for a lot of places to bury critical details that can later jump out and bite you on the butt. I'm advising you to have me meet with the man's lawyers."

"Okay," I said. "But when? I want to get this done quickly. This entire affair has already taken entirely too much time and energy away from my medical practice. And I just … I just want it over with, is all."

"I know you do." He took a breath, held it for a moment, and then exhaled. "But here's the problem," he said. "I can't do it right away. I'm leaving tomorrow for a weeklong conference in Florida, and my wife and I have planned to get together after that and spend the rest of the month vacationing in the Keys. I'm going to be gone about six weeks altogether. I haven't had a vacation in fifteen years. It's something I've got to do."

"Six weeks? So you wouldn't be able to meet with his lawyers for at least six weeks?"

"That's right. I'm sorry. We've had this planned for about a year now."

"I don't think I can wait that long. This man is offering me a way out now."

"I understand, Dr. Walchef. I know you want to wash your hands of this building. And all I can do is advise you to wait. Six weeks just isn't that long. I can set up a meeting with his counsel before I leave, and meet with them as soon as I return. My advice to you is that you let that happen. I think anything else would be imprudent."

"Okay," I said. "Set up the meeting. I'll wait for you to come back."

That is not, however, what I did. About a week later the owner of the building company came again to my office, and before he left two hours later he had me signing papers.

I agreed, right there in my office, for ten percent of whatever profit the builder would make from selling the condos he would develop and market. He convinced me that ten percent was all he'd be able to afford, because of the costs he would incur digging himself out of a hole that was, as he put it, "deeper than a well in Death Valley."

In truth, I was barely paying attention to what he was saying, or what he was offering. All I knew was that if I signed those papers I'd make some money, and the building that had been such a plague on my life would forever disappear from my concerns.

So I signed my name on every dotted line he pointed my pen to.

And when he left my office that afternoon, the owner of the building company did so in possession of four finished floors of an apartment building located on a large lot of prime downtown Pacific Beach real estate, all of which he had purchased from me for exactly one dollar.

And then he went out and got a loan for five million dollars.

And then, picking up where I had left off, he constructed a twelve-story building of one hundred twenty condominiums.

And then, in very short order, he sold every one of those condos. At that time they would have gone for at least one hundred twenty thousand each.

Which means he grossed at least fourteen million four hundred thousand.

Take away the five million he needed to pay back the loan, and the builder, my friend and business partner, was left with about nine and a half million dollars.

And do you know how much of that he in turn paid me?

Zero.

Not one single, solitary, lonely, burnished copper Lincoln penny.

None.

It turned out, he said, that if you broke down his costs over the course of the project, and really examined all of the details of what you found, you discovered that, for the first time since he'd been involved in exactly these sort of deals, his company hadn't made one thin dime.

He did not inform me of this himself. He had one of his lawyers do it for him, through a letter.

I would like to now jump ahead and bit, and tell you this: my daughter Lisa had a son, whom she named Shawn. Shawn, now twenty-three, lives with me in my home in La Jolla, just outside Pacific Beach. He is a good, tall, strong, handsome, smart young man who in my final years has been nothing but a comfort and help to me. I love Shawn with all my heart.

Shawn is in his fifth year at the University of San Diego, one of the best law schools in the country. He is studying to be a lawyer.

Guess what kind of law he wants to practice?

Real estate law.

Wouldn't it be funny if, before I passed on, I found myself back in possession of what is, to this day, one of the two tallest buildings in all of Pacific Beach?

Now wouldn't that just be something?

Chapter Nineteen

India

They say that time heals all wounds. I myself haven't found that to
be true, but who am I to argue with the sages? In my experience, wounds
such as those I suffered during December of 1969 never "heal": What
does happen, it seems to me, is that one "simply" becomes more adept at
tiptoeing around the cavernous sites of their damage. So, of course, I got
on with my life; outside of the unthinkable, is there any choice in that
matter? Life--and I mean the steady, raw drive of the organic imperative-
-*does* continue, dragging along with it anyone who can still, technically
speaking, be counted among the living, whatever their level of participa-
tion in its events.

So one day lurched and stumbled and by the grace of God sometimes blended into the next, and then another day would come and go,
and then another, and so on until, every once in a while, I would feel as if
I had somehow brought my eyes up over a darkened ridge, beyond which
I could again make out the workings of a world I had once known, but
had long since either forgotten about, or forgotten to care about.

And not a year after Elizabeth left us I found myself in a part of the
world that I had never known at all. It's a strange and powerful experience to be traumatized by an event to such a degree that you wind up
feeling like a stranger in your own life--and then, seemingly all of a sudden, to find yourself in a place that could not, physically or in any other
way, actually *be* any more different than any life you've ever known.

I did not, of course, "suddenly" end up in India--but emotionally it
approximated something very near that, in the way that in times of stress

or grief a person will sometimes seem to all at once find themselves doing something, or being somewhere, and can only with considerable effort recall the steps or events leading up to that moment. A grieving person will at times simply find him or herself, for instance, in their garden pulling weeds, or at the grocery store holding a plastic bag of peaches they've apparently selected for purchase. The background rattle and hiss of everyday life--the dull, never-ending white noise that dominates the conscious experience of the grieving person--will momentarily cease, and then there they'll be, fully participating in a life it feels as if they were only vaguely aware of moments before.

When it happens to you, it's as if you're living on automatic--and then, suddenly, you're in manual.

And that's how it felt when one day not too long after Elizabeth's death I found myself standing before the window of a hotel room in downtown Bombay.

Bombay!

It was like I'd woken up on Mars!

Except, not really: Bombay is probably the place on earth most marked by the teeming, sweating, colorful, magical presence of what seems like infinite numbers of humans.

I had come to India as part of a contingency of perhaps twenty doctors from San Diego (many of whom were accompanied by their wives) who were traveling throughout that part of the world in an effort to learn more about how medicine is practiced there. India in particular has a rich and distinguished history in the health sciences that all of us on the trip were looking forward to learning a little something about.

From San Diego the bunch of us had flown on British Airlines to London; from there we were trundled onto a plane that took us all the way to Bombay--and the next thing I knew I found myself inside a splendid little room inside the luxurious (and British-owned) Bombay Royal Hotel.

While during my visit to India I did in fact learn a great deal about some of the innovative and exciting methods then being used by my professional brethren to heal the sick of their own country, what most profoundly impacted me were the wonders of India having more to do with culture and history than medicine.

I shall never forget, for instance, the moment when I ventured forth from the safe confines of the Bombay Royal and onto the streets of Bombay.

Inside the hotel the gently circulating air was cool--as, indeed, were the gently circulating people: All voices were held a near-whisper; all interactions were carried out in that purposefully respectful, essentially stylized way the moneyed gentry have of seeming to care about a thing only insofar as it offers them even the slightest diversion from that which perpetually preoccupies them--issues, which seem, at least, to do with only the highest orders of human concerns.

But right outside that plush and hushed hotel, in the streets of Bombay, all concerns seemed extremely focused on only the most basic of human concerns. I hadn't taken three steps along the sidewalk before I was besieged by a veritable army of painfully thin, wide-eyed children, each stretching out their hands in the hope that I would hand them a coin or two. The image of Indian waifs begging for money is one we've all seen before: but to actually have those children surround you, to experience the smell, and the dust, and the physical pushing of frenzied implorations, is (of course) an entirely different experience altogether.

Not two hours before I'd been speaking with my colleagues about all we were doing to help heal so many of the world's sick.

And here, as far as I could see, was more suffering than any of us could have even imagined, much less imagined relieving. These children, clearly, lived on the streets: Everywhere one could see the makeshift hovels and doorways in which they "lived" with the older siblings or adults who, even now, watched them from their reclining position on whatever they had found to put between themselves and the dirt at the edges of the crowded, bustling street. And yet as I walked the streets of Bombay, I noticed that while I had assumed that the kind of truly wrenching poverty I saw virtually everywhere would necessarily engender great sorrow and bitterness, instead what I found was that everywhere I went the people were astoundingly good-natured: gentle, patient, and as kind as any friend I'd ever had. And the people weren't behaving thusly in order to reap from it any kind of reward: They simply *were* kind.

It was as if all the people in India--or in Bombay, anyway, which even then I knew to in many ways be the *most* Indian of places--had by some kind of miraculous process of cultural osmosis all come to be defined by the same core belief: that this world, and all of its concerns (and most especially its material concerns) were purely and truly transitory, and that all that mattered was a person's spiritual well-being.

Anyone who's ever been to India knows of what I speak: The whole country seems steeped in some kind of deeply sincere, terribly grand, all-inclusive, ongoing, living prayer.

It was marvelous!

It was terrible: The poverty was heartbreaking!

They say India is the land of contradictions. Nothing that I've ever heard about any place is as true as that is about India. Sometimes it seemed to me like the happiest people who had ever existed in the world were the endless numbers of people then starving in India. If that isn't a contradiction, I can't imagine what is.

I also saw in India one of the most moving music and dance performances I've ever seen anywhere. Ostensibly, it wasn't much, really: After dinner one night my fellow physicians and I were "entertained" by a handful of musicians and a sole female dancer.

One never knows why or when--or even how, for that matter--one is simply going to be floored by great art. But these players, and this dancer--who performed the traditional style of Indian dance called, I believe, the *klasica*, in which the dancer arranges her hands in various exquisite geometrical shapes--created, through their exotic sounds and her breath-takingly fluid and perfectly precise movements, an aura throughout our little dining area which was nothing less than hypnotic. What began as a diversion--and one about which some of us, I could see, were even a tad uncomfortable, since none of us were in any way familiar with any of the customs relative to performing *or* watching such a show--ended up truly transporting every last one of us doctors from San Diego, California. Looking around the room after the last note had faded from the air, I saw it in the eyes of my friends: they were, as I was, essentially emotionally stunned by the sheer aesthetic beauty of what they'd just seen and heard.

I live in California, where state budget restraints have resulted in arts education being cut from public schools. Whenever I'm for whatever reason reminded of these cuts, I very often reflexively think back to those musicians and that dancer. I (of all people) know that a strong case can certainly be made for the idea that music and dance and arts generally aren't important in the way math and science is. But I also know that art can do things to and for the human soul that all the math and science in the world can't even approach.

Now art and science *combined--there's* something capable of producing wonders to stagger the human imagination.

Speaking of the Taj Mahal--I have seen it! It's absolutely mind-boggling! Following our stay in Bombay, our little medical troupe traveled to India's capital, New Delhi, where we got an outstanding tour of some palaces and government buildings. (We also, I should note, visited some hospitals, where we met and spoke with doctors who impressed us in many ways, not the least of which was with their emphasis on the prevention of diseases, rather than, as in the Western medical tradition, upon their cure. It's a method of approaching and interacting with patients that served me well throughout my medical career.) But almost from the moment we touched down in New Delhi, almost all any of us really wanted to do, it seems, was see the famous Taj Mahal, located about two hundred miles outside the capital in the city of Agra.

Finally, we were able to break away; one morning we commandeered a bus, grabbed whatever we thought we needed for a night's stay, climbed aboard, and let our imaginations go to work. And it didn't take the Taj Mahal to test the limits of our imaginations, either: On the trip along the way we stopped any number of times, and each place we marveled at snake charmers, musicians, dancers and street performers whose sole intent, it seemed, was to dazzle us. Such colors, and smells, and textures! I couldn't imagine--then or now--a place further away from anywhere I'd ever been in America than any of the little places we stopped that day on our way from New Delhi to Agra. At one point--knowing, if nothing else, that such a chance might never again come my way--I finally nodded yes to one of the countless purveyors of good times, and before I knew it was being hoisted up onto a camel.

I have performed life-saving operations. I have lived in the heart of countries at war with the world. I have sailed across oceans with nothing or no one waiting to greet me when I landed.

But I tell you that these events pale in comparison to the one *truly* nerve-wracking experience of my life: riding a camel.

You'd think it'd be just like riding a horse, wouldn't you?

Wouldn't you?

Well, take it from your uncle Luben: You'd be as wrong as wrong can be about that.

Instead it's like riding a ... . It's very similar to riding a ... .

Well. It's like riding a camel.

As our guide related the story to us, the Taj Mahal was built in the mid-1600's by an emperor who had many wives, but loved only one: she with whom he had had children. But after giving birth to their fourteenth child, the emperor's favorite wife lay dying. At her deathbed, the grief-stricken husband implored his wife to tell him anything that he could do to make her happy.

"Build me the Taj Mahal," she said--although of course she didn't put it *exactly* like that. But she did implore her husband to build from marble and fine jewels a magnificent palace in her honor. With tears in his eyes, the emperor took her hand in his, and swore to her that he would exactly that.

And so, millions of rupees and twenty or so years after bidding his beloved his final farewell, the emperor presented to the world his shrine to his wife, the incomparable Taj Mahal. Property values in the surrounding neighborhood immediately shot up. (Sorry, but you know what they say: Once a developer, always a developer.) Everyone rejoiced.

Everyone, that is, except one of the emperor's sons. Instead of celebrating his father's monumental achievement, this ultimate bad seed threw his aging father from power by having the old man thrown into a dungeon on the family grounds not far from the temple meant as a loving tribute to his mother. In that dungeon the emperor spent the last years of his life, staring tearfully at the reflection of the Taj Mahal he was able to capture in a little piece of glass he angled just so out his window.

He died with that piece of glass in his hand.

It's a story that still moves me whenever I think of it, which is more often than it's probably wise for me to admit.

There came a time in our tour of the Taj Mahal (and, frankly, it didn't come any too soon for me) when our guide had said all he had to say about the place, and we were finally left alone to simply and silently gaze upon this true wonder of the world.

And there we were, twenty doctors and any number of other visitors to the site, stunned into silence.

You've seen pictures of the Taj Mahal, no doubt. I suppose that all I can add to the impression you must already have of the place is my very firm assurance that the pictures you have seen did not, in any way whatsoever, lie to you. The Taj Mahal really *does* look like that.

Only bigger. And brighter. And a great deal more awe inspiring.

Of course, we hadn't flown three thousand miles and traveled two hundred more on a bus we could have probably beat running just to see the Taj Mahal in the normal daylight. That simple pleasure may have been enough for some, but not for us seasoned sightseers.

At least, not for some of the more intrepid among us--one of whom was yours truly. For we hearty souls, only seeing the Taj Mahal at night would do, for long had we heard the legend that when moonlight strikes the palace, it glows blue.

"A glowing *blue* Taj Mahal!" I said. "Now *that* would be something to see!"

"Yeah," mumbled one doctor in an amazed tone as he squinted through his glasses at the glittering edifice before him. "As opposed to seeing it now, which is so boring I'm surprised any of us are awake at all."

That good (if slightly sarcastic) man was not amongst the small collective I joined which later that night returned and then stood around, silently hoping against hope that the full moon would come out and turn the great palace blue. But, alas, on that night the moon got it into her mind to play coy with us, preferring to remain hidden behind clouds than to come out and do our bidding.

"It's getting late," said one of our group after some time had passed. "It's not going to happen tonight."

"It might," I said.

"I don't think so," said another. "Too many clouds."

"But that could change," I said. "I think there's a wind up there. Look at how the clouds are moving."

"Yeah--*more* of them are moving in front of the moon. Forget it, Luben: It's not going to happen tonight. Come back with us to the hotel. We'll eat. It's better than standing out here in the cold."

"You go back," I said, "But I'm going to stay out here just a little longer. I know I'll never have another chance to see the Taj Mahal glow blue in the moonlight."

"But you don't have a chance right now!" said my friend.

"I don't have *much* of a chance," I said. "Which means I have some chance. And that's good enough for me. I think the possibility is worth waiting for."

"Okay," said another of my companions, turning to go with the others. "Well, we'll leave the light on for you."

And so then I was alone, out on the grounds of the great palace, at the end of the long pool which leads up to its front.

And I waited.

And I waited.

And I got colder.

And it got later.

And I got really quite cold.

And then it happened: All in a moment, it seemed, the clouds cleared from before the moon, which turned out to be quite bright that night, and which was then free to fully beam down upon its old paramour, the mighty Taj Mahal.

Which began to glow a deep, ghostly blue that absolutely took my breath away.

So if you ever hear anyone say, "You know, rumor has it that the Taj Mahal glows blue in the moonlight," with confidence you can pipe right up and say that you know for a fact that that's more than just a rumor: you can assert that it's absolutely, one hundred percent true.

Because I am here to tell you: It is.

"Sure, Luben, sure," were the sorts of comments I had to endure the following morning. "We're sure it was just as blue as a blue jay. No problem. We believe you."

And there I had proof of another rumor I'd long suspected was true but didn't until that moment have conclusive proof either way: Doctors are not funny people.

Before leaving that evening to return to New Delhi, my friends and I stopped at a souvenir store featuring items associated with the Taj Mahal, where I purchased two items. The first was a gorgeous, brilliantly colored silk tapestry of the palace; I still have this piece of art hanging in my home, where it continues to bring me great pleasure. The other souvenir was a photograph taken of the palace at night, under a clear sky and a full moon.

"Boy, look at that," said one of my fellow physicians. "It's amazing what they can do with trick photography these days."

Doctors: No matter how hard you try, you can't read their writing--and you can't understand why, despite all evidence to the contrary, they persist in imagining that their jokes are funny.

From New Delhi we continued our tour of the Near East by next flying into Kathmandu, in Nepal. Talk about exotic! The whole country of Nepal, as far as I was able to tell, is like something out of a fairy tale--or more, perhaps, like a *dream* being had by someone in a fairy tale. It's just that ... otherworldly.

Speaking of Whole Other Worlds, while in Nepal I took a helicopter ride and flew over Mount Everest, the highest mountain peak in the world. We didn't fly all the way to its top--people (rarely) climb it, but a helicopter can't get all the way to its top!--but we did fly to and land on a clearing on the mountain that, I feel safe in saying, is higher than any place on earth I'll ever be again. From there I tried to remember to breath as I beheld the vast, white mountain peaks that seemed to stretch on forever.

I know that all of my life before I was on Mount Everest, and that all of it since then, has taken place on the same planet which holds the remarkable panorama I saw that day. But if I hadn't seen it with my own eyes, I wouldn't believe it. And even then.

Let me quickly share with you two or three other things I experienced in Kathmandu that remained with me the rest of my life. One is the sight I beheld one morning as I was walking along what seemed to me to be a fairly typical neighborhood sidewalk: a very long line of slaughtered goats, sheep and lambs.

There they were, right out on the sidewalk, as if they themselves had simply been walking along, too, going to a barn or some place, when all of a sudden they had all simply keeled over, dead.

Not at all sure what I had stumbled upon, I turned around immediately, and headed back to my hotel.

Later that afternoon my curiosity got the best of me, and I headed back over to what I now thought of as Dead Animal Alley. And there I was amazed to see not a single sign of any of the fifty or so carcasses that had been there not three hours before. That stretch of street was now as clean as everything else in the city.

How and why, I wondered, had so many slaughtered animals so readily disappeared? And why were they there in the first place?

I asked around (which took awhile, because I wasn't exactly fluent in Nepalese), and learned that, as it happened, that day was an annual day of sacrifice to God, and that the animals had been taken away to be prepared for the various feasts that were to take place throughout that evening and night. And sure enough, as the day wore on, I saw more and more places of worship teeming with more and more people, and soon the streets were alive with the joyous sounds of singing, praying, and rejoicing. It was a very heady experience--and reminded me, not a little, of similar days back in Bulgaria, when, on important occasions, we, too, would sacrifice a lamb or goat.

And at that moment Nepal didn't seem so very far away after all.

And it *really* didn't seem far away once I noticed how many of the young girls were wearing dresses marked by embroidery that was so similar to that typically found on the native dresses of my own country that for a moment I was truly disoriented: Were those *Bulgarian* dresses those young Nepalese girls were wearing?

I kid you not: They were that close.

And it all got stranger still: Later, when these same girls put on a little show of their native dances, many of the moves and gestures in their dances seemed right out of the native dances I'd so often seen performed in Bulgaria.

I've never had time to do the research, but my short visit to Nepal convinced me of one thing: Somewhere, somehow back in ancient history, the people of Nepal and the people of Bulgaria were one.

Can you imagine?

I *can*, as it turns out. I've *had* to. I've *seen* it!

The other striking thing that I've never forgotten occurred as I was, again, simply strolling about Kathmandu, and happened upon a crowd growing larger by the moment. When I looked up to see what everyone around me was looking up at, I saw a young lady, dressed in full ceremonial regalia, standing alone on a balcony of a temple.

And the people began to cheer this girl. And the crowd grew larger and larger, until before too very long at all I was in the middle of a massive throng of people cheering this single, stone-faced teenage girl.

This girl, it turned out, had been elected (through a process about which I'm completely ignorant) that year's Queen of Kathmandu, which meant that she had to leave her home and spend one full year living in the temple being the focus of fervent idolatry to the population of Kathmandu. At the end of that year, I presume she returns to her home, and another teenage girl takes her place.

I wonder what it must be like, to be the parents of a teenage girl who is back home after spending a year cooped up inside a temple being Queen of Kathmandu.

Just thinking about it gives me, a parent, the shudders, for so many reasons I can't even count them.

From Nepal we went to Afghanistan (where, at the airport, one of my two suitcases disappeared, only to be returned to the airport authorities without anything in them missing); and from there we went to Greece and Macedonia, where we beheld the glorious ruins of the ancient Greeks.

A quick swing through Iran--and then we were on our way back home, a spot that existed in a particular place on a planet which, for each of us on that trip, would forever seem at once a whole lot smaller, and a whole lot bigger.

Chapter Twenty

On Solid Ground

Back home in San Diego, I struggled to refocus on my life and priorities. My trip abroad had given me some much needed perspective, and as I attempted to reassess where I was and what I was doing, one of the things that kept making itself known to me--that kept coming back to me like some awful echo from some terrible noise I'd heard somewhere in my past--was that the builder who'd taken over my property on Cass Street had really and truly done me wrong.

He had purposely and methodically robbed me of a great fortune at a time when he knew I was grieving from the recent loss of both my wife and my father.

So I thought about what I might want do about that.

One thing I knew is that I didn't want to go after the man in any kind of personal or even legal way. It was true enough that he had hurt me. But it was also true that I had let him--that at the time I had been too consumed with grief to think clearly. The builder had known this, and taken full advantage of it.

Okay. Some people are capable of such things; they *look* to do such things. That's how they live. That's how they die.

That's not my problem. After all, a man who focuses his anger on someone who has hurt him only helps that person to hurt him more.

So I knew, right away, that I would leave the builder alone. I would not try to exact revenge. That he had to live his life being someone who would do to a stranger the sort of thing he had done to me was all the revenge I could possibly want.

What I *could* do, however, is make sure that nothing like that ever happened to me again. I was, after all, up to my neck in the quicksand of that building long before Mr. Condos had tossed me a sack of bricks. And he hadn't knocked me for such a loop that I had stopped understanding that real estate was still the surest way for me to grow the fortune I still wanted to secure for my children (and, if possible, theirs).

So what I had to do, I realized, was *really* learn about the real estate business.

And where's the best place to learn? Where else but school, of course! So I enrolled in Anthony's School of Real Estate in San Diego, where I attended classes for six months--at the end of which time I took and passed the state's examination and became a licensed real estate broker.

Now I knew a thing or two about developing real estate in California. (And so often during all of this, you know, I would be reminded of how things were back in my village in Bulgaria, where if you wanted to build a building on a piece of land you owned, you just *did* it: You shaped the mud into bricks and stacked them up and put down the pipes and laid on a roof and before too long you had yourself a house that people for generations would consider a wonderful place to live. I love America--of that there can be no doubt. But sometimes I can't help but think things are a little too *complicated* here.)

Pretty soon after I became a real estate broker (and just so there's no confusion here, I was still a physician and surgeon running a very nice private practice; developing land was just a *hobby*), I began buying connected lots in a very nice area just north of downtown San Diego called Banker's Hill.

The idea was that on the one lot I eventually made from five smaller lots I would build (of all things) condominiums: forty of them, in a six-story building.

No use getting carried away. Six stories, forty units. Small enough to do; big enough to set up my family and I for a good long time to come.

And once I had the land and the plan I went to a local bank, and secured a loan for one million eight hundred thousand dollars, which I knew would be enough to do the job.

And with that money I hired a *real* construction company, The Liberty Construction Company, to build my building.

And then the people at The Liberty Construction Company began building my building, and while they were doing so I made very sure to stay involved in every last detail of every last thing they did. I knew every nail and screw that went into that building. I knew exactly what I was paying for, and why, every time I cut a check to anybody for any reason having to do with that building.

What's that they say: Once bitten, twice shy? Well, I don't know how shy I was, but I knew that I wasn't about to get chomped on twice.

I still got stung a couple of times, though. The worst of these happened the time I was told by a building inspector that the heating and air conditioning I'd run throughout what by then was four stories of my building was all wrong. I pointed out to the building instructor that he must be mistaken, that the city had long ago poured over every last specification for my building, and had issued me a permit to build it according to the plans they okayed.

That didn't matter, he said: I was going to have to completely redo almost everything having to do with the heating and air conditioning ducts I'd run throughout the building, an undertaking involving more tearing down and reconstructing than I can possibly remember without running to the store to buy a shotgun and then going on some sort of deranged rampage.

Surely, I laughed, there's been some sort of mistake: Surely the city of San Diego wouldn't okay plans for a building, only to come in once that building was near completion and change the basis of its original permission. Surely, I said to the man, that sort of thing just doesn't happen, right?

Wrong.

It turns out San Diego is known as a place where things *exactly* like that happen to developers all the time.

Only this very deep wrinkle in my plans wasn't even *that* interesting, or official. The city proper had nothing to do with this particular injunction. This was just one building inspector, on his own, for no discernable reason, effectively issuing a decree: I could make the changes he was insisting upon, or I could announce to my construction crew that they should all pack up and go home for the foreseeable future. Those were my choices. (Later, I found out that what San Diego is *really* known for is building inspectors who do exactly what this one did to me. San Diego's a nice, big city; but no one who's lived here for any length of time--and *no one* who's ever built so much as a bird house in this town--would deny that, in many ways, it's still the small, provincial town it was not all that long ago.)

Now *that* business with the bossy little building inspector reminded me of Bulgaria. I've often wondered if that imperious little bureaucrat expected me to bribe him. I got the impression any number of times that in fact that's exactly what he mean to have occur--but I wasn't about to take that gamble. Losing my building as I had the first time around to a conniving, heartless shark was one thing; ending up in jail for trying to bribe a public official was another one altogether.

So I never did attempt to bribe the building inspector. Perhaps if he had just come right out and *asked* me to, I could have gotten away with a whole lot less money than his insane directive eventually obliged me to.

Thank God that in my original loan for the building I'd arranged to have three hundred thousand dollars set aside as an emergency fund.

Two months (and *all* my emergency money) later, we were right back where we were before Inspector Ruinurlife wandered onto our site. We had our four stories.

And then we had five.

And then we had six.

And then--*finally*--I had my condominium development.

But rather than sell them right away, I rented the condos out as apartments, because I wanted to hold onto the property as long as I could. And I refinanced the building for terms that left me with a monthly bill I easily made from my rental income.

And I hung onto that building for twenty years.

It was only in the last couple of years that I began selling the condos.

They go for about four hundred thousand each.

There's forty of them.

I'd like to do the math right here for you, but I'm feeling a tad sleepy just now, and believe that instead I will go lie down, and take a little nap.

So you see how, through the wonders of perseverance and the constant, agonizing memory of actually having traded ten million dollars for one, I finally developed into a decent enough developer. The condo building in Banker's Hill was my biggest project, but over the years following that I kept busy with others. On the plot in Spring Valley I bought so my daughter could ride her pony, for instance, I eventually built a restaurant; later, immediately behind that, I build a two-story building with twenty-six rooms that for years operated as a senior residence and is now an assisted care facility for seniors. Today, of course, that property is worth considerably more than it was thirty years ago, when it wasn't much more than an acre far away from anything with nothing on it but a two-bedroom rental property.

And I bought some properties in Big Bear Lake, and an apartment building in Pacific Beach. Things like that. Nothing that would have Donald Trump desperate to hire me as a consultant, but enough so that ... well, so that, for instance, my grandson Shawn doesn't have to worry about the cost of his college textbooks. I am happy to pay for them.

Every family, I believe, should count among its members at least one good lawyer. Shawn shall be ours.

Of all the properties I do or have owned, none is more precious to me than the one that serves as my primary residence. I bought my home in idyllic La Jolla, California in 1972. It was then a modest two-bedroom, one-bath affair, located three short blocks from the ocean and perched up on a hill that afforded it a view I take great pleasure in to this day. After thirty years of living here, it still amazes me that from almost any room in my house I'm able to see a breathtaking view of the vast blue ocean. In such a home it is difficult to remain pessimistic or depressed for too very long at all.

I bought the house from a professor in anatomy at the University of California at San Diego, who had come to feel it was simply too small for his growing young family. At that time prices for homes were reasonable in a way I fear they shall never be again--and in a way I *know* they will never be again in this part of California. I bought the home for fifty thousand dollars, which in La Jolla today wouldn't be enough to buy a shed for your lawn mower. And even then, actually, it was a considerable purchase for me: I had only just started my medical practice, and didn't have a lot of money sold. What I did have, of course, was a medical practice: In those days a very small down payment and a decent job was enough for a bank to put their trust in you. I know that young people today have a much harder time securing the kind of credit financial institutions demand for loans. Frankly, I don't know how anyone just starting out can possibly afford to buy a home anywhere in San Diego, which for years now has been one of the most expensive home markets in the country. It's a beautiful place, but one that I fear in ten years will be populated by no one except the young and very wealthy, and the retired and very wealthy.

Sure, it works for *me*. So I suppose I shouldn't complain. But it does seem a shame that so much of such a beautiful area should be unavailable to so many. But I suppose the system that creates this reality is the same system that allows anyone, from anywhere, to become among those who can, in fact, afford to live here.

After all, look where I came from! If a poor farm boy from Pordim, Bulgaria can wind up living in a three million dollar home in one of the most exclusive neighborhoods in the prettiest state in the nation, who *couldn't* wind up moving next door to me?

Back when we first bought the home, though, it hardly felt like the world was our oyster. The anatomy professor had been right: It was a small place. The difference between he and I, though, was that he really didn't grow up where I did, which meant that he hadn't ever formed mud into bricks and then just *built* whatever was needed to ensure a good living arrangement for all.

And while I certainly didn't start packing mud into wooden frames for bricks (although, let me say, I *would* have, if I hadn't already learned enough about the way things are built in San Diego to know if I so much as stacked two such bricks together I'd have a team of building inspectors and city permit people knocking on my front door faster than you can say, "Go away, I'm building something."), I did get busy figuring out how to make the home bigger.

The anatomy professor had found the house too small for he, his wife, and their one child (with another on the way). Elizabeth and I had three teenagers. If I didn't figure out *some* way to enlarge the house, I knew it wouldn't be long before Luben, Jr. would be back doing as he had not that long ago in Cincinnati: sleeping in the kitchen.

"You don't want to end up sleeping in the kitchen again, do you?" I asked him.

"I still can't believe you made me sleep in the kitchen," he said. "The kitchen. That's just wrong."

"Hey, it was warm in there," I said. "Besides, don't worry. I promise you it won't happen again."

"You're telling me it won't. I don't want people stepping all over me while they're making waffles or anything."

Teenagers. They can be so demanding, can't they?

Actually, anyone surveying our new home wouldn't have guessed the prior owners had sold it because they found it too small; they would have assumed it was the back yard that had sent them running off into the distance. Surely the jungles of Borneo are no thicker (or scarier, for that matter) than the dense brush which filled the area behind the house.

I've worked hard in my life, but I'm not sure I've ever worked as hard as I needed to in order to clear the backyard of our new home of all the bushes and undergrowth and weeds and I don't *know* what all that had, apparently, been growing back there since the time when dinosaurs ruled the earth. I thought I might actually *find* dinosaur bones back there; if it was half as thick back then as it was by the time we got to it, it was easy enough to imagine the giant creatures getting stuck back there.

Our backyard: the La Jolla Brush Pits.

Eventually, though, we discovered and then laid bare the land beneath all that growth--and then there we had it: a completely featureless expanse of backyard. And then the question became what to do with it.

"Put in a pool," said Luben.

"Yeah, a pool," said Boyan.

"Do, Daddy, do!" said Lisa.

"Whaddaya' think?" I asked Elizabeth.

"A pool would be nice," she said--which made it unanimous.

And one week later we had in our backyard the nicest built-in pool you've ever seen anywhere!

About this, I am kidding. In reality, it was extremely difficult to build a pool in our backyard; at least that's what the city building people told me.

"It's too steep," they said. "It'll never work. You can't build a pool on land that steep. Even if you wanted to, you couldn't find anyone to build such a pool."

They turned out to be correct about that: I had people from three different pool companies come over to assess the viability of building a pool in my backyard, and all three of them said it couldn't be done.

See--now that right there is just about the one thing in life you never want to tell a Bulgarian.

So I decided to build the pool myself.

"Let me tell you something about that pool you want to build," said the man behind the corner at the city permit office when I told him of my plan. "It's called a free-standing pool. There are only three such pools in the entire county. And there's only one engineer in San Diego--or just about anywhere else I know of--who can *maybe* design that pool for you. I'm going to give you the name and address of that engineer, Dr. Walchef, and I highly recommend that you consult with him before you even start on this thing. Okay?"

"Thank you very much," I said--and sure enough, I did contact that engineer, and he came over to my house, looked at my backyard, said, "I think it can be done." And then drew up the design that proved it could be.

When the neighbors caught wind of what I was doing--it was the tractors and the big hole developing in my backyard that probably tipped them off--they let me know in no uncertain terms that they were vehemently opposed to it.

"You can't put a pool on such steep land," they said. "When that pool gives way, all that water is going to come pouring down onto *our* homes!"

"But it won't give way," I said. "I have an outstanding structural engineer who made up foolproof plans for the pool. It won't give way. I promise."

"You can promise it won't rain for two months, too," said one of them. "But that sure doesn't mean it won't."

"You are welcome to see the plans," I said. "Please come see them."

"I don't care about the plans," said one man. "Plans can show anything. The fact is you're trying to build a pool on land that's too steep to hold one!"

Thirty years later, that pool is still the jewel of my backyard--and in all that time it hasn't developed so much as a hairline fracture. It's nine feet in the deep end, and four feet in the shallow. Over the years it provided my family with countless hours of healthy fun; I still swim in it first thing every day.

Coffee is good for waking up in the morning. But for starting a day right, nothing I know of compares to a nice swim in a heated pool.

Well, one thing *might* compare: and, for me, that thing is waking up in my bed at a place I love so much I call it my Alpine Castle. It's not in Germany, of course--but the high desert mountains of northeast San Diego has so much of the same rustic charm I adored in Germany that I loved the area the moment I stepped out of my car and first smelled its fresh mountain air some twenty years ago. I had been driving throughout the area around Mount Palomar--simply exploring, in the way that is my wont, keeping an eye out for everything from a beautiful bird to a wonderful piece of land that might be for sale--when I saw a sign that said something about there being mineral pools at Hot Springs Mountain.

Mineral pools!

At a place called Hot Springs Mountain!

Now we were talking Germany--and all the rest of Europe, for that matter. Throughout Europe, visiting hot mineral baths is as common as … I don't know … perhaps going bowling is here in America. The Europeans have long known about and believed in the restorative powers of such baths; soaking in warm natural mineral water is a traditional curative with a long and distinguished history everywhere from Spain to Russia (and *especially* Russia). Whole economies are based along the baths; as people in America might during the winter go to Arizona or Florida for a vacation, so people in Europe flock to any of the great number of hot water springs located across the continent.

I used to love frequenting such places, no matter where I was in Europe. There is nothing that rejuvenates one's mind and body like a good long soaking in a hot mineral bath. It's really that simple.

Or it *had* been that simple, anyway, until I came to America. For some reason, people in America never really embraced taking mineral baths. I've never understood why; as far as I know, there are as many naturally occurring hot springs in America as there are anywhere else in the world. Perhaps it's the communal nature of the baths that puts Americans off: For all of their much-touted sexual liberation and open-ended mores, Americans are known throughout the world as being, in actual practice, quite modest, if not downright prudish (if not, now that we're on the subject, downright *repressed*--but let's not go there). So it may be something along those lines that renders an indoor pool at the neighborhood Y more attractive to an American than might be a hot mineral springs on the outskirts of town. Perhaps the reason Americans never took to hot springs is found in the intrinsically organic nature of the natural bath experience: It is natural, which means the entire experience has about it a certain earthiness that, to my experience at least, isn't something particularly appealing to Americans. Americans tend to like things neat, and clean, and ... separated. Private. Orderly. They like to keep different foods on their plate apart, so to speak.

In Europe, things--and especially, I think, things having to do with the human body--are more ... well, natural.

Absolutely none of these thought were in my mind, by the way, when I saw the sign about the mineral baths at the foot of Hot Springs Mountain. All I thought at that moment was, "Oh, boy! Mineral hot springs!"--and then I got back in my car, and drove the direction in which the sign was pointing.

When I arrived at what I later learned was, indeed, the foot of a mountain called Hot Springs, I was delighted to find there not only hot mineral baths just waiting to rejuvenate and invigorate me, but an entire resort community built around them.

"What is this place?" I asked the man behind the counter in a bungalow with a sign on its door saying "Office."

"This is Warner Springs Ranch!" said the man.

"Ah!" I said. "I'm sorry: What exactly does that mean?"

"It means you're standing in the middle of one of the best places in all the world to get away from it all--to just relax, and have a wonderful time!"

"That sounds very good!" I said. "Please keep explaining!"

The man happily did just that. And what I learned from him was that Warner Springs Ranch was a twenty five hundred acre (oh, be still, my developer's heart!) resort facility nestled at the base of, yes, Hot Springs Mountain.

"We've got everything here!" said the man. "We've got golfing--we've got a PGA golf course, one of the finest 18-holes you'll ever play! You play golf? No? Well, it doesn't matter, because there's so much to do here even people who *do* play golf sometimes forget to get around to it!"

"So people come here to play golf? And to soak in the springs?"

"Well, no. I mean, yes. I mean, they don't come here *just* to do those things--but a lot of them *do* do those things. But there's *lots* of stuff to do up here. This is a resort ... *town*, almost."

"A resort town? Is it really?"

"It is! Why, we've got over two hundred little bungalows spread all over this land, see? Some of them were built one hundred years ago, or even earlier than that: Some of them, in fact, were built by the Cupa Indians who used to live all around here--they used to call this place Aqua Caliente, or 'hot water.' All those bungalows--and a lot of them a lot more modern than those--are still right here. And on top of those, we've got two Olympic-sized swimming pools (one of which is filled with mineral spring mineral water that's naturally heated to about one hundred fifteen degrees); we've got the golf course and driving range; fifteen tennis courts; an equestrian center; all kinds of hiking and riding trails .... we've even got a hang-gliding school up here! Everything! It's a full resort! It's quite famous, too! Back in the heyday of Hollywood, all the big stars used to come up here! Mary Pickford and Douglas Fairbanks used to come up here to get away from it all. So did Charlie Chaplin, Gary Cooper and Jean Harlow. Clark Gable used to come here; so did John Wayne, and Bing Crosby! They all did! They'd fly in, or drive in, and just take the whole place over!"

"Is it anyone free to enjoy this place?"

"Well, I don't know about *free*," said the man, "but yeah, that's the idea. What it is, see, is that we sell what are called 'shares of ownership' to the whole Warner Springs Ranch. There are two thousand of these shares available, see? People either buy a full share, or a half-share. If they buy a full share, then they can come up here anytime they want, no restrictions, and have full use of anything on the entire place. They can go horseback riding, play tennis, hike, golf, sit in the hot springs, whatever they want. The whole place is basically theirs. If they buy a half-share, they get the same deal, but for only half the year: They can come anytime they want, too, but only every other month." The man folded his hands upon the counter between us, looking quite pleased. "And that's all there is to it," he said. "It's a pretty darned good deal, if you ask me."

"It does sound good," I said. "Is it all right if I have a look around the place?"

"By all means!" said the man. "I'll be glad to show you around myself if you'd like."

"No, but thank you very much. I'll just take a little look around myself if you don't mind. Oh, one more thing," I said. "Is there any way that just plain old visitors can use the hot mineral baths? It's something I would very much like to try."

"Well," said the man, "they're not supposed to. It's for members only. But it's pretty slow in there today--so it's just possible we could work something out."

"Very good," I said. "Well, I'll go have myself a look about this recreational wonderland, and then come back here, and we'll see about how we might be able to work something out."

So I left the office and began walking about Warner Springs Ranch, to see what I could see.

And what I saw impressed me very much.

The land around and upon which now sits the Warner Springs Ranch is marked by a truly fascinating history. I'm hardly an expert on that history, but my understanding is that since ancient times it was inhabited by a tribe of Indians known as Cupa, who revered the mountain now called Hot Springs, and who held its heated water sacred. Eventually the land fell into the hands of the Mexican government; and then into the American.

The Indians fared poorly in the exchanges, and were eventually marched off their traditional homeland; they were "relocated" to the Pala reservation, some seventy miles away. (Their march from Aqua Caliente to Pala is sometimes referred to as the "Mini-Trail of Tears.")

The Warner Ranch (so-named for Juan Jose Warner, a naturalized Mexican citizen who received the land via a grant from the Mexican Government in 1844, two years before America's war with Mexico) eventually became very well known across the country for being a way-station along the southern route typically used by settlers coming West in search of gold and/or land. Being halfway between the Colorado River and the Pacific Ocean made Warner's ranch an ideal place to found a trading post, which quickly became a welcomed sight in the eyes of many weary travelers in the years after the Mormon Battalion first blazed a trail through the area. So popular did the outpost become that by 1858 John Butterfield's Overland Mail was carrying passengers and mail by way of the ranch on its route from St. Louis to San Francisco. It's been estimated that over the next three decades, more than two hundred thousand people entered or left California through Warner's Ranch. It was, literally, the gateway to the West.

Many years later an Italian immigrant from San Francisco named Carl Rossi came to the ranch and purchased a hotel there; very soon thereafter he also purchased a nearby hot mineral spring, swimming pool, and golf course. It was his idea to use those properties as the core around which he would develop all the land now known as Warner Springs Resort--and to then sell two thousand single shares of ownership of the entire "spa facility."

Not a bad idea!

Then again, I'm a sucker for just about any immigrant who comes to America with bold ideas about real estate development.

Anyway, Mr. Rossi took his plans for his new resort community to the bank, and received from them a loan for enough money to turn his vision into a reality. The interest on that loan was high, but Rossi was confident he would be able to sell enough shares of his ranch community to pay off the loan--and then some.

Sadly, Mr. Rossi was terribly wrong about that.

At first he started selling individual shares of the Warner Springs Resort for seventeen thousand dollars. That was going pretty well for him; but he soon found that it was not going to bring him the money he needed to pay back his bank loan. So he began charging more and more for the shares, until they finally reached the price of thirty five thousand dollars for one.

And that's about when Mr. Rossi found out that while people certainly do enjoy riding horses and sitting in hot water, nobody likes it *that* much. Even if it is mineral spring water.

I myself bought one of Mr. Rossi's shares; I believed in his development, and was convinced Warner Springs could once again become the Mecca to the jet-set it had once been. I paid twenty five thousand five hundred dollars for my first share; three weeks later, I bought another for their new price of twenty-seven thousand five hundred dollars. (You see the rate at which Mr. Rossi was trying to dig himself out.)

Alas, Americans never did catch on to the allure of hot springs, and before long poor Mr. Rossi was, truly, poor: Despite having sold his house in San Francisco in order to pay his debt, he was still unable to catch up all the way, and eventually he had to sell the land altogether.

The new owners did a wonderful job of keeping alive the dream begun by Mr. Rossi. They seemed, if nothing else, to have a better understanding of financial matters than did the former owner of Warner

Springs; they re-priced ownership shares of the ranch to something along the lines of two to three thousand dollars each. This did not make me, of course, feel much like Howard Hughes or Andrew Carnegie, but in truth it was never my intention to make money reselling my shares; I simply wanted to avail myself of all there was to do at such a wonderful, beautiful place. (The shares are now selling, I believe, for about three thousand dollars. So it's just possible that, generations of Walchefs from now, someone in my family will be able to break even on my original purchase.)

I so much wanted to partake in the offerings of Warner Springs, in fact, that quite soon after buying my shares of it I determined that I needed to *live* near it, too. I couldn't reside there permanently, of course--with all that hot mineral water to soak in, who in that area would ever need a doctor?--but I did start looking about the area around the resort for a plot of land upon which to build my future Alpine Castle.

"There's one last lot I can show you," said a realtor showing me about Los Tulles, a rural community adjacent to the Warner Springs resort area. "But I guarantee you wont like it."

"Why not?"

"Because you can't build anything on it--and you *sure* can't build a house on it."

"Why not?" I asked, growing more interested by the moment.

And that's when the realtor said the magic words: "Because it's too steep."

Well, and she was right: It was a *very* steep lot. But what a view! I could see right away that any house which was built upon such a peak would have, literally, a bird's eye view of the surrounding mountains. And there was certainly no doubt about it being the highest point in the whole surrounding area.

"How much is this lot?" I asked.

She laughed. "Who cares? But it's thirty-five thousand dollars."

"I'll take it," I said.

"Excuse me?"

"I said I'll take it."

"But Dr. Walchef," said the realtor, "I thought you said you wanted a lot you could build a house on."

"I do."

"But this lot is much too steep. That's why it's been on the market for so long. And look at all these trees! You can barely walk around the lot at all!"

"It's a funny thing," I said, "But if I didn't know better, I would guess that you were actually trying to talk me out of buying this lot."

She stared at me for a moment, and saw something in my eyes that made her sigh, look about, smile, and then look at me again and say, "When you're right, you're right. If you want this lot, it's yours. Of course it's yours."

"Then you have yourself a deal," I said.

"And you have yourself a nice place to come up and sit," she said.

It wasn't too long after that I began to fear that the realtor might have been right after all: I might *not* be able to do much on my new acquisition beyond sitting. And even *then* I could go tumbling off a place so steep.

Still, I kept calm, and paced about my new land--or at least paced as far as I could without hitting another tree, which was never more than two steps in any direction--and thought about what to do.

Well, the first thing I'd have to do, I knew, was to clear the land. So I phoned some landscape and development people, and got that done.

And once the trees and the brush were cleared from it, I was able to really *look* at the land, and see exactly what I had.

And what I saw was that I had was a lot that was really, *really* steep.

And that's when I knew: It was so steep that I should just lop the top of the thing right off.

And I could use that dirt to build the driveway up to the house!

Driving home that night, I knew I'd done it: I'd figured out a way to build a house upon the tallest peak in all of Los Tulles.

"You want me to what?" said the man at the backhoe company as he stood at the bottom of Mt. Luben.

"I want you to knock off the top of this little mountain," I said.

He looked at me. "Why?" he asked.

"Because I want to build a house on top of it."

"On top of *that?* Don't you think that's a little *steep* for a house?"

"I do," I said. "And that's where you come in."

So the man shrugged, took my check, and got to work bulldozing off the top of my mountain.

"Don't forget we're going to use that dirt to make a driveway up to the house!" I yelled.

From the jittering driver's seat of his rumbling little monster the backhoe owner smiled down at me like I was crazy. But I didn't care, as long as he kept bulldozing.

You will recall, perhaps, the time when, while developing my land in Pacific Beach, the crane we were using for that job broke? Remember that? Wasn't that extraordinary? Wouldn't you think that something like that could really only happen once in a person's life?

Well, I hope you wouldn't think that, because you'd be wrong.

The man clearing the top off my mountain broke his backhoe.

"I told you it was too steep up here!" he cried in the ringing silence of his machine's demise. "Now look at my backhoe!"

"Wow," I said. "It's really broken. I can see that."

"You're goddamn right it's really broken! *Now* what in the hell am I supposed to do?"

"Buy a new one?"

The man looked at me like I really *was* crazy--only this time there was no smile at all.

What was I supposed to do? The man had a defective backhoe. He hadn't oiled it enough, or fed it properly, or something. I could not for the life of me see how it was supposed to be my fault. You hire a man; you hire his equipment.

And so, disgruntled and mumbling at, I am sure, me and every single relative I might ever have, the man with the defective backhoe went away. And then there I was, alone, looking at the work he'd left behind.

And if you'd been there with me at that moment, you would have seen a big smile slowly grow across my face.

Because what the man had left behind was, I could see, entirely good enough.

It was good enough!

I would build my country chateau upon that flattened piece of heaven or my name wasn't Dr. Luben Walchef, from Pordim, Bulgaria.

Next, working with a very good architect I hired, I drew up plans for the house.

I then got a permit from the city to build the place.

And then we dug; we stopped; we dug some more; we cursed to the high heavens at all the infernal rock up there--huge, monstrous, record-breakingly large slabs of rock no mortal using any means could ever hope to cut through or dislodge at all. We despaired about that rock--until we figured out how to work *with* it instead of against it, and so turned it into what amounted to almost all of the building's foundation.

And then we had that foundation.

And then we laid the pipes.

And then we built the skeleton of a house.

And then, finally, I knew that my Alpine Castle was going to move from the wondrous, shimmering arena of my imagination to a real place.

Chapter Twenty-One

Expanding Interests

That was 20 years ago--and the house everyone said couldn't be built hasn't suffered from so much as a foundation crack in all that time. Rain, flood, earthquake, fire--none of it seems to have in the slightest damaged my mountain fortress. Over the years the place has grown in that organic way all good homes should: It now boasts three bedrooms; a two-bedroom quest quarter I sometimes rent to the good men who over the years have helped me maintain the place; and a wide, spacious deck that serves as a platform from which one can marvel at the vast view of the mountains and valleys that seem to stretch on below forever. In the yard I have cultivated a garden rich with fruit: I have cherry trees, apple, pear, apricot. I even have vines upon which grow heavy bunches of the same grapes we used to make wine back in Bulgaria.

There is no palace on earth I would trade for my hilltop home in Los Tulles. I love it in a way I've never cared for any other place on earth. It's perfect for me. Over the years--and, indeed, to this very day--whenever the cares and woes of life press too hard down upon me, I simply get in my car and take the pleasant ride to my precious mountain getaway, where I know I can always rest peacefully among all the books and souvenirs I've collected over my many years of study and travel. Always ready to greet me upon my arrival is my good and faithful dog, Metchka (which means "bear" in Bulgarian), who is, in reality, the lord and master of my manor. I come and go, but Metchka lives at my mountain retreat full time.

(I must tell you that for years Metchka had a canine companion, Heidi. What a splendid and loyal dog Heidi was! Too loyal, perhaps: Recently, a bobcat came onto our property, and Heidi decided to do something about this most outrageous of transgressions. She and the big cat fought, and Heidi was killed. I know that dear Metchka misses her-- as much, I am sure, as I do myself.)

And when I am done relaxing and am ready for something a little more physical, I have all of Warner Springs Resort to take advantage of: A mere walk away is all the tennis, horse riding, hiking and other forms of exercise this old body of mine could possibly require.

And when *that* is all done, I can do the one thing that brought me up here in the first place: I can sit and soak in a natural, hot mineral spring bath.

Of course, my life is not all petting dogs, eating fruit, and soaking in hot water--nor would I want it to be. A life without work is not, after all, any life at all: Work keeps us focused, primed for whatever life is pre- paring for us next. And so it was that round about in the mid-90's (hav- ing some time before that retired from my medical practice), I began in earnest my second career as a restaurateur. Why not? I have always loved food: the growing of it, the care of it, the preparation of it into fine, deli- cious meals. Why shouldn't I run a restaurant?

The decision to run a restaurant was made easier by the fact that I was already the *owner* of a successful restaurant. Remember the prop- erty in Spring Valley I had long ago purchased as a place upon which my daughter Lisa could enjoy riding ponies? Do you recall how when I bought that land there was already a small home built upon it? Well, around 1980, long after my children were all full grown, I decided to rebuild that little house into a restaurant. Why not? When my family and I used to regularly visit the area, the one thing that always drove us crazy was that there were no restaurant nearby where we could pull in to eat after a long day playing with the horses.

If we felt that way, it only stood to reason other must, too. Besides, I could see that Spring Valley was growing. And what does more people mean, if not more *hungry* people?

So I invested in the building of a good, solid eatery. It was quite a process, of course: Building a restaurant isn't like building ... well, it's not like building anything else I know of. There are vents to worry about, and ovens, and all sorts of plumbing concerns I'd not had to deal with before--and, of course, there were the ubiquitous city inspectors, *and* their fastidious brethren, the health inspectors.

If anyone had told me, before I began to build a restaurant, that the number of city inspectors who would become involved in that process would double over any number of them with whom I'd had to deal in the past, I don't believe I would have even begun.

Be that as it may, before too long our humble little house had turned into a formidable little restaurant. At that time I had no interest in running a restaurant; I only wanted to lease one, and was happy to finally meet a woman named Jennifer who had, it seemed, a deep desire to run a restaurant. So I leased mine to her; she named the place Country Comfort, and just like that, I was in the restaurant business.

Jennifer, it turned out, was exceptionally good at restaurant managing, and for the next fifteen years or so, Country Comfort made me a comfortable income. There came a time, however, when I turned my eye to the very large plot of land immediately behind the restaurant, which I also owned.

It was just …sitting there.

And empty land is land that's not growing anything. Which means it's not doing what land is *supposed* to do. Which is wrong: Land is supposed to grow things. Could be fruit, could be trees, could be grass--as long as it's something. And I, for one, think that one of the very best things that can be grown on land is money for its owners.

So I decided to build upon that land something capable of doing just that.

But since only a fool makes the acquiring of money his primary goal, I wanted to think of something good I could build on that land. Something useful. Something that helped people.

I am a doctor, after all. Helping people is what I *do*.

And so I started to think about my life. And I didn't have to think about it very long before I was thinking what a good life it was. And I thought how fortunate that was, how lucky I was to be able to grow old in comfort: to see my children, and their children, going out into the world without having to worry about where their next meal might come from, or where their clothes.

I looked back on my life, and I liked what I saw.

And I looked ahead from where I was then, and found that view at least as pleasant.

But then I began to think about others who might not be as fortunate as I. What about them? What did their lives look like at my age? What if, for whatever reason, I had not been able to acquire the modest fortune I'd been blessed with? What if, at the age I was then (not to mention the age I am now), I had to look ahead to the rest of my life, and instead of seeing a nice home in La Jolla and a splendid cabin in the mountains next to a world-class resort, I instead saw doubt, and concern, and all the world of fear that comes from not only not knowing exactly what or even where you're going to be eating, but knowing that you lack the physical or even mental powers to much effect it one way or the other?

And that's when I thought that what I would build upon my land was a place for low-income seniors to live.

And thus was born Villa Troy. ("Villa" because, well, because I like the word, and "Troy" because it is located on Troy Street. See? And people think developing property is hard ... .)

Villa Troy is a modest place, to be sure: the building is but two stories high, and holds twenty-six rooms.

Nobody driving by the place would ever mistake it for, say, the Taj Mahal.

To the old folks who live there, it's better than that. It's home.

For me and the seniors who would one day live there, that I was building Villa Troy was very good news indeed. It was news less exciting, however, for Jennifer and her Country Comfort restaurant. It's a difficult thing to be running a business directly in front of a large building being built: Construction of Villa Troy created noise, dust and parking problems that eventually caused Jennifer to give up the lease on the restaurant she'd been so lovingly running for fifteen years. I felt bad that building Villa Troy essentially forced her out of her business, but by the time either of us realized the extent to which the construction would inconvenience her, it was too late for me to undo what I'd begun.

So Jennifer and I shook hands, and parted ways.

Which left me with an unoccupied restaurant.

Yes, I could have turned over the lease to someone else seeking to make a living serving breakfast, lunch and dinner to the good folks living in or passing through Spring Valley. It was a good restaurant, doing good business; it wouldn't have been hard to find another restaurateur to take it over.

But the more I thought about it, the more I came to see that operating a restaurant was exactly the sort of challenge I wanted in my own life. There are very few things in this world I dislike more than too long remaining idle; it was time, I thought, to get back into the game.

And the restaurant game seemed as good as any out there. Better, in fact: There are very few things in this world I like more than being around food.

So I rolled up my sleeves, tied on an apron, and went to work.

Well, what *really* happened is that I rolled up my sleeves, tied on an apron, and then called my family together and told them of my idea that they should all *help* me run the restaurant. That was, in fact, one of the main reasons I chose to become involved with the actual day-to-day operation of the place: I felt that it would bring together and focus my family the same way similar endeavors so often did, and do (and probably always will) strengthen families back in the old country.

They say the family that plays together, stays together. True enough--but I think a case can be made that the primary reason the saying runs that way is because it's so difficult to come up with a word that rhymes with "works."

My first recruit into the restaurant business was a woman who practically was a member of my family, someone with whom by then I'd already been friends for some ten years. I had met Ann when she came into my medical office; we had immediately struck up a friendship. I was impressed by her knowledge and very really love of opera and classical music, both of which I am a tremendous fan. We began accompanying one another to the San Diego Opera--which, surprisingly enough, is one of the finest opera companies in the nation.

We went to hear the San Diego Symphony.

To a person who loves the musical arts as I do, finding another person who shares that passion is a wonderful thing indeed.

Ann readily responded to the idea of helping me run the restaurant; in fact, she took to it with a good deal more enthusiasm than I--and I was *quite* enthusiastic about it. But she was positively avaricious in her desire to know everything there was to know about the kitchen, the staff, the ordering of food, the running of the dining room--everything. She gobbled up knowledge in the way we could only hope our customers would gobble up the food.

"I like this!" she beamed, a giant pot in her hand. "I can do this!"

And so the Country Comfort restaurant was reborn (except it was now called Country Choice, so that the restaurant's loyal customers might get the idea that the business was under new management, but hadn't really changed at all.)

Ann proved to be as helpful running my family restaurant as over the years she had proved to be helping me run my family. In a very real sense she was a member of our family: She moved into our La Jolla home when my daughter Lisa was there with me, struggling to raise her son Shawn by herself. It was very often Ann who got Shawn up in the morning; who fed him; who made sure that when he left for school he was wearing clean clothes, and had a lunch--and at night, it was often Ann who saw to it that Shawn ate a decent dinner, and finished his homework, and got to bed on time. Her help proved invaluable to my daughter, my grandson, and to me.

And when he got older, Shawn helped her to run the family restaurant. It was not, perhaps, his first choice: Like any high school boy would, Shawn naturally resented being so often asked to forgo playing with his friends to instead bus dishes at our Spring Valley restaurant.

"There's always time for your friends, young man," Ann would say, "But for now, there is work to be done."

And Shawn would grumble, and grouse--but he would always climb into the car for the drive out to the restaurant, and when there he would always work as hard as any of my regular employees.

I can't tell you how proud it used to make me to sit and watch that boy conscientiously busing tables, or making change, or jovially interacting with the customers or staff. Like any fluid, bustling enterprise, the restaurant business can be a very hectic one in which nerves become frayed and patience worn thin, but Shawn's easy-going, unflappable manner never failed to have a calming effect on the place. And I think in some ways working so hard in the restaurant all those years had a similar effect on him--and one that I believe he has come to truly value. At the end of his junior year, when he was studying abroad at a university in Spain, I was thinking of selling the restaurant, as the sheer work involved with keeping it operating had by then become too daunting an everyday challenge. I thought that if anything the news of my selling the restaurant would please Shawn--at the very least it would mean he'd never again have to show up there early on a Sunday morning to bus tables and wash dishes. Instead, though, he wrote me a long letter in which he eloquently pleaded with me to keep the restaurant. In that same letter he further surprised me by expressing his intent to return home and finish his college education in San Diego--he very much wanted, he said, to pitch in and do what he could to relieve me of the work involved with the restaurant!

Now *that's* a good kid--if I do say so myself. Which I do. Because he is.

And, indeed, the whole family--all my children, and any number of their children, and even a couple of my relatives from Bulgaria who now live in America--proved of absolutely invaluable assistance in the day-to-day running of my Country Choice restaurant. (I am particularly grateful to my nephew Simeon, the son of my youngest sister Veska. This kind, hardworking man immigrated to America in December 1992--he came straight to my home, basically, and has been a comfort and help to me ever since. Before we took over the restaurant, Simeon drove me to Warner Springs, and worked very hard on my property doing the infinite number of chores that always need doing to keep such places up. Once the restaurant opened, he blossomed into as fine a soup chef as you're likely to come across.) All of them sacrificed in order to keep that little restaurant alive. I am inordinately proud of every single one of them.

Because in the end, all you ever have--or certainly the *best* of all you ever have--is family.

Chapter Twenty-Two

Coming Full Circle

An immigrant is always haunted by the fact that in a very real way he will never be able to fully bring his family together: Too much history has gone by; there is too much distance between the family who came before him and the family who comes after. In some real and fundamental ways people raised in different cultures really *are* different people: They see the world and their place in it in different ways; they process information differently; the body of assumptions and believes which inform their every moment can be as different as night and day.

I was raised in a time and place my grandchildren simply cannot imagine. What do they know about living in a small farm out in Nowheresville, Bulgaria? What do they know about what it is like to cower in the night while all around you bombs dropped from low-flying planes are leveling a city that is revered throughout Europe--and that you call home? What *should* they know about such things? Nothing, I suppose. (Well, not *nothing*: For as long as people walk on this earth, everyone should know a considerable bit about World War II. That cataclysmic chapter in world history didn't take place too very long ago at all--and anyone who believes such a thing could never happen again has already assumed the *only* mindset that is necessary to ensure that it can. It's less easy for history to repeat itself if everyone can recognize it when it comes around the corner and is, again, heading toward them.)

And yet, of course, one always yearns to communicate something of his past to his progeny--especially when that past is so long ago, and so far away.

I live in America, and am extremely proud to call myself an American. Yet in many ways I am, and will always be, a European.

My children are American.

Their children are American. I have no idea what my grandchildren might or might not know about Europe. Probably about as much as I knew about America when I was their age--if that: America, then as now, was always in the middle of the world's attention. For all I know, my grandchildren think nothing more about Europe than that it is the place across a great body of water where short doctors who talk with funny accents come from.

Which is why, in the summer of 2003, I was so thrilled to spend some time in Europe with my grandson Shawn. Since he was planning to return to San Diego following his junior year spent studying at university in Alicante, Spain, I jumped at the chance to meet him at his school the moment the final bell rang, and to Shanghai him and drag him about Europe with me for a while before we returned to our regular lives back in San Diego.

"Yes!" he answered on the phone when I called to tell him of my idea. "Yes! Do! Come over! Let's go!"

Ah--the impassioned exuberance of the young! Always ready to stop what they're doing at a moment's notice in order to reach out and embrace the world with all the vigorous optimism of their age!

And Shawn seemed pretty interested in going, too.

And for the first five days of our five-week jaunt across Europe, he played tourmeister, showing me about the ancient city of Alicante on the eastern coast of Spain (and I do mean ancient: The place was founded 300 years before Christ). I (and he, and everyone else who comes through that magnificent city) was particularly impressed with the Castillo de Santa Barbara, one of the largest medieval fortresses in the world.

As I say, we were in Alicante for five days. I won't even try to relate all the things we did and saw there--but let us say, for the record, that in the course of our time there each of the following figured significantly in one way or another: the broad white beach of Playa de San Juan; the breathtakingly ornate Gavina Palace; the Iglesia de Santa Maria (one of any number of magnificent old cathedrals in the city); some terrific museums; the wonderful "old quarter" of the city; the harbor (once the port of Madrid); bullfighting; and puppets.

Why aren't there more puppet shows in America? It's not the first time I've wondered that (but will be, I promise, the last time I wonder about it in these pages).

After Alicante, we flew to the Canary Islands (southwest of Spain; northwest of Africa: right by Morocco), renowned for having the cutest name of any island group in the world. Did you know that there is very good reason, dating back to the days of the Greeks and Romans, for guessing that if the magical kingdom of Atlantis ever really existed, it existed on the Canary Islands? No? Well, did you know that the original inhabitants of the islands, called *Guanches,* were very tall, very *white* people? No?

Well, see? You should travel more. I'm not sure I'd recommend the Canary Islands as the first place one should see in Europe (it's become a bit, well, touristy), but it's not a bad place to start. The beaches there are, as they have always been and will probably always remain, simply gorgeous.

Still, that was enough lollygagging; it was time, I thought, to go to Paris and see the French Open, which was just then happening!

Some of you may, perhaps, remember what a tennis buff I became over the years.

What's that? You missed the part of the book where I played tennis with my old girlfriend Irmgard?

Well, I refuse to tell you exactly where in the book you'll find that lovely passage. You'll just have to read the whole book over again.

Which, it goes without saying, you were planning to do anyway.

And when you do, you'll be reminded of what you may have inferred--but which I am now stating explicitly: I am a Major Tennis Fan.

As is Shawn.

And the French Open was right over there in Paris!

We were sitting in the grandstand at Roland Garros stadium watching the Women's Finals before you could cry "Out!"

And hence did a long-standing dream of mine--to see any of the playing at the French Open--come true.

That night, we bought tickets at the Paris Opera House to see a performance of Mozart's great opera, *Cosi Fan Tutti.* During my time in Paris I had seen many shows at the Opera House; I very much wanted to experience being there with Shawn.

Ostensibly, our trip around Europe was supposed to be for Shawn:
The idea was that I would take him to all the places I'd been before, and
perhaps impart a little to him of what I knew about them. But sitting in
the grand old Paris Opera House as the lights went down for the show, it
hit me that it was I, not Shawn, who was probably getting the most out
of our trip.

Except after the show I know we both rejoiced in what we experienced: The incomparable French cuisine--enjoyed at the ultimate French
restaurant, 95, located in the Eiffel Tower.

And after that, we continued our glorious decent into self-indulgent
excess by taking a boat trip down the Seine River to the Moulin Rouge,
where we took in a show. (Before the show I was careful to make sure that
Shawn promised to keep his eyes shut during the more risqué parts of the
show. He promised me that he would, and I am sure that he did, because
Shawn is a good boy who would never disobey his grandfather.)

The next morning we did the only thing we could: We attended
mass at Notre Dame Cathedral. Right with God again, we then hustled
over to Roland Garros, and caught the Men's Final of the French Open.

That night we stayed in Paris.

"What next, Grandpa?" Shawn asked the next morning.

"The *piece de resistance!*" I declared. "Bulgaria! We shall drive to Bulgaria! We'll start today!"

"Drive?" said Shawn, his eyes opening wide. "We're going to *drive* all
the way to Bulgaria?"

"Not we. You. You will drive all the way to Bulgaria. I will sit in the
passenger seat, and watch Europe pass by out the window."

"But Grandpa," said Shawn. "I don't know if I can drive all that way.
I haven't really driven in Europe all that much."

"Then this is your chance to practice!" I said. "Come! Bulgaria
awaits!"

And so we rented a blue Opal minivan, and Shawn climbed behind
the driver's wheel ("I hate this already," he said. "The wheel's *on the
wrong side.*")

And we were off.

For our first stop, for lunch, we ate at a place in Luxemburg where
I used to meet my good, old friend Marcel, who would regale me with
stories about whatever fantastic thing was then capturing his ardor. It was
good, so many years later, to sit and remember Marcel's wonderful en-

ergy and boundless enthusiasm. He was a good man, and as fine a friend as anyone could hope for.

Next, Shawn drove us to Heidelberg. I was so excited about showing him the city that had figured so prominently in my life! I hadn't been back to the city in 50 years, and while much of it seemed (or clearly was) different from the days when I first walked its quaint, vibrant streets, the heart of the place--the soul of it, really--remained as it had for hundreds of years before I was ever there. Heidelberg is, after all, timelessness itself.

This comforting truth was made abundantly clear to us both when we stood looking out over the Neckar River valley from the grounds of Heidelberg Castle.

"It's phenomenal," whispered Shawn.

And right he was, of course.

From there we spent two nights in Koignsse ("king's lake"), a small village on the edge of Germany near Austria. We took a boat ride on the lake that we felt safe in assuming must have one time belonged to one German king or another; and then we took a gondola ride to the top of the Alps.

From there we went to Salzburg, and were no less dazzled to stand in the place where Mozart drew his first breath than we were by the breathtaking Salzburg Cathedral.

Next stop: Vienna! And there we did the two things any visitor to that splendid city must: We took a boat ride on the Danube, and we went to see a presentation of the magnificent opera, "La Boehm." (The boat ride went considerably smoother than did our trip to get into the opera, which, it turned out, was sold out. Fearing not, though, I turned to that ever-reliable resource, the taxi drivers, and before long was buying two scalped tickets at a price which was fair enough, considering how much it costs to put gas in one's taxi and feed one's family and dress presentably, and so forth.)

The next day we waved good-bye to Austria--and, via Shawn's newfound proclivity for driving at the speed of Europeans everywhere--arrived for our night's rest in Belgrade, Serbia.

And the next morning we were headed for Sofia, the capital of Bulgaria.

I don't know if up to this point in the book I've been clear about this, but I was born in Bulgaria.

So of course it was nice to be home.

And our first welcome home came via fairly unlikely means: the border guards.

"You are Bulgarian!" one of them cried to me.

"I am, yes!" I said.

"Welcome back to your mother country! I see now that you are living in America! Incredible! What is it like in America?"

"It's everything you've always heard it is--and more," I said. "It's a wonderful country. A man can make of his life whatever he wants to there."

"Ah," said the guard, looking wistful. "I wish to go there myself one day."

"Do," I said. "And, once you're there, be absolutely sure to do what I did."

"What's that?"

"Wait a while--and then come home again."

The guard laughed, and patted me on the back.

"What are you guys saying?" asked Shawn.

"You don't speak Bulgarian?" I said. Shawn gave me that look young people give you when they're instantly exasperated with your efforts to be cute.

"He said that I was welcome back home," I said, "but that you, unfortunately, having never before been inside Bulgaria, must first prove you are worthy of a visit to the country by spending four days picking potatoes in the field behind the station. Don't worry: It's pleasant work, and you're sure to meet lots of interesting people. My advice to you is to keep the bag you're filling on your shoulder; time goes by faster when you're concentrating on physical pain. I'll be back to pick you up in three days. Oh: Be careful of the water. Try to boil it before you drink it. Better yet, just try to go without it. 'Bye!'"

And there was that look again.

Why is it that today's young people just cannot seem to properly respect their elders?

We spent that night in Sofia with my niece, Tinka, and her son, Ellian. Tinka is the daughter of my youngest sister, Veska. Needless to say, Tinka was as eager to hear about America as I was to hear about Bulgaria. We all stayed up late into the night, swapping stories, catching up. It was good to be with members of my family back in the old country.

The next day we drove with Tinka to Pleven, where I attended my last two years of high school. But that's not why the town meant so much to me; it was because Pleven is where Tinka's mother--my sister Veska--lived.

Veska and I cried when we saw each other, and hugged so long I thought we might never let go of one another. And that would have been just fine with me.

It was a good, good night for me: one of the best of my life. And I hold it especially precious, because that visit was the last I'd ever share with my sister Veska, who passed away only a few months after we left her in order to go and visit Pordim.

Although it should have surprised me, for some reason it didn't to see how little Pordim had changed in all the years since I'd been away. Tiny cobbled stone roads; grape vines in the yard of almost every little home; fathers driving their children in horse buggies filled with produce … everything was more or less exactly how I remembered it.

"Grandpa," said Shawn. "It's exactly how I always pictured it."

"It's exactly how I've always remembered it!" I said. "Nothing has changed!"

That impression did not, alas, remain long: The first place I took Shawn in Pordim was Dr. Haskell's American College, which I was saddened to see had fallen into a fairly miserable state of disrepair. It was still operating (thank God), but its glory days were definitely behind it: the once finely kept grounds were now bedraggled and coarse; the playground equipment was rusted and in need of repair; the school building itself had in every way deteriorated.

I met with the director of the school. I told her who I was, and how much the school had meant to me.

I wrote her a check for enough money to return the school to something much closer to the inspiring place I remembered.

What good is money, if not to do some good in the world?

That place had defined, fed and launched my dreams for a better future.

I want it to do the same for as many other young dreamers as it possibly can.

The next place we went was to the home in which I grew up. Amazingly (after all, as you might recall this was a home my grandfather and father had built out of mud bricks formed by the then-tiny feet of yours truly), the place was still standing. It was *more* than standing: It looked as sturdy as ... well, as sturdy as a home built by two farmers out of Bulgarian brick.

"That's your house?" said Shawn. "That's the place you grew up in?"

"It is."

"It's looks *exactly* like I thought it would!"

"It is amazing," I said. "It hasn't changed much, if at all."

"And look!" Shawn said. "People still live there! It's amazing."

"It really is," I said. "Why are we whispering?"

Shawn shrugged.

"Come on," I said. "Let's go meet the people who are living in the house built by my father and grandfather." I stepped forward to the little gate leading from the sidewalk up to the front door.

"You're just going to go in there?" asked Shawn.

"Sure," I said. "Why not?"

"Because you don't *know* these people?"

"What's to know? They're Bulgarian. I'm Bulgarian. That's enough."

"Wow," said Shawn, following as I made my way to the front door of my childhood home. "I can't imagine thinking that in, like, Los Angeles."

"This is a long way from Los Angeles."

Shawn looked around the yard.

"No argument there," he said.

The man who answered our knock upon the door turned out to have purchased the home from my father; he, his wife and their two children had been enjoying the place ever since.

"I bought the house from your father?" he cried. "Come in! Come in! This is a rare and wonderful thing! We love this house! Are you telling me you grew up here? Fantastic!"

He called his wife out, and we all had a marvelous time touring what had once been my home, and was now theirs. The couple was very generous in their time and spirit: You'd have thought Shawn and I were visiting dignitaries of state.

So much was the same. Everywhere I looked, I saw a tree I planted; a fence I built; a door I hung.

I found the whole affair deeply moving. I don't know why, exactly. Something about returning, at the end of one's life, to the place one began that life--especially, perhaps, if there is such a very great distance between the two.

I lived in such a different world than the one in which I'd begun.

And now here I was, back home.

To a place that would never be mine again.

I managed to maintain my emotions quite well--up until the point where the woman of the house kindly offered me a fig from the tree in our front yard I'd planted so many years before.

I bit into it, and the sweet juice hit my tongue the tears sprung from my eyes.

From Bulgaria we drove over the Balkan Mountains, stopping along the way to see some of the famous rose fields from which the world-famous Bulgarian rose oil is produced. Roses, as far as the eyes (and the nose!) could see! It was a marvelous thing: I had wanted, all of my life, to see these renowned fields, but while living in the country had never had the time or means to do so. Now, seventy years later, I was standing in the Bulgarian rose fields!

I tell you: I swooned.

From there, we drove to a little town on the Black Sea called Pomorie, where Shawn and I spent two days relaxing and swimming in the Black Sea.

And then on to Munich!

Munich is, truly, one of the great cities of the world. Shawn and I spent two days sightseeing there--and I don't think we saw one-one hundredth of all the glories that city has to offer. Shawn said he wanted to return to the city, as do I.

I could see where he would make it back. I could see where I would not.

"If you make it back here and I don't," I said, "You must promise to eat a bratwurst in my memory."

He promised.

He's a good boy.

From Germany we flew to London, where we spent six days doing and seeing as much as we possibly could.

I said that I thought Munich was one of the great cities of the world--and it is. But the *greatest* city in the world, I am convinced, is London.

No--wait. It's Munich.

No--it's *Heidelberg.*

No--excuse me; I am an idiot. The greatest city in the world is, hands down, Paris.

Oh, I have no idea which is best.

All I know is that we live in a big, beautiful world, full of big, beautiful places, and that a man could spend his whole life trying to see it all, and barely get started.

But if you've not traveled at all, and *are* going to start, start with Europe.

And then hang onto your hat, because you're in for the time of your life.

Chapter Twenty-Three

Adieu

Come to think of it, just being *alive* means being in for the time of your ... well, life. (And now you see why I became a scientist, and not a philosopher.) Who can understand life? Not I. In fact, at 85-years old, about the only thing I do feel entirely confident asserting about life is that it definitely looks different toward the end of it than it does toward its beginning.

Then again, it doesn't. All along the way, what's beautiful remains beautiful. What's ugly and wrong remains ugly and wrong. The basic, purer truths endure.

Okay, here's a truth about life that no two people who have ever walked the earth could possibly disagree about: What does *not* endure is the physical body.

Inside of our hearts and minds, we remain the same.

Outside, of course, our bodies, taking routes of their own, succumb to time.

About twenty years ago, mine in particular succumbed to diabetes. During that time I used to take two or three-day mini-vacations to my properties at Big Bear Lake (located in the mountains about one hundred fifty miles away from San Diego), where I would ski, fish, and relax.

One morning I grabbed my little dog Suzie, a bottle of my favorite brand of pop, and took off for Big Bear. But on the ride I noticed that I had to make a restroom stop much more often than I was used to: about every twenty or thirty minutes.

Something, I knew, was wrong.

As a doctor, I knew that I had to make an appointment to see myself immediately.

After we'd run a urine analysis, my nurse gave me the news.

"Dr. Walchef," she said, "You have diabetes."

Imagine my surprise.

Diabetes is an incurable disease that comes in two forms: juvenile, and adult onset. While the cause of juvenile diabetes remains unknown, it seems to be primarily a function of genetics; the pancreas of a child born with the disease simply does not produce enough insulin. Such a child must keep to a restricted diet, exercise regularly, and take insulin for the rest of their lives.

The other form of diabetes--the kind I have--is called adult-onset diabetes, because it usually comes over people in their forties or fifties. While again genetics seems to play a role in one's propensity for develop-ing this form of diabetes, some behavioral or environmental factors also seem to play a role. Obesity and high levels of stress are two of the more prominent of these factors.

I'm a little heavy, but I'm not obese, and never have been.

Stress, however, is not exactly a stranger to my life.

I have now been living with diabetes for twenty years. For the first ten I successfully controlled it through a fairly rigorous routine of exercise and diet; after that I had to start daily insulin injections, which I now do three or four times a day.

Other than that, I am pleased to say that I live a normal, vigorous life. I still play tennis, though I am beginning to realize that I may have to give up my dream of winning a Grand Slam tournament. I swim in my haven't-yet-flooded-the-neighbors pool every morning. I take walks as time permits.

And, of course, I eat plenty of yogurt.

We Bulgarians, you might recall, are known for eating yogurt and living a very long time.

Yogurt, exercise and a healthy diet are good for you.

Stress, alcohol, nicotine, drugs and air pollution are bad for you.

Get as much of the first as you can, and as little of the second.

After that, try not to fall off any cliffs, or get hit by a bus.

And if everything goes well, who's to say that you, too, won't live to be eighty-five years old--or older! I personally have my eyes dead set on quite a bit older.

Either way, I am approaching the end of my journey. It's certainly been a long one; as you've read, it saw me starting off on a humble farm in Bulgaria, living and working in several countries (and so learning several languages), and finally realizing my wildest dream of coming to the greatest and richest country of them all, America.

I hope you come away from my story believing that with ambition, vision, hard work and persistence, anyone can make their dreams come true.

I wish you as much good luck and success in your life as I've had in mine.